EVERYDAY
French
COOKING

Brimming with creative inspiration, how-to projects, and useful information to enrich your everyday life, quarto.com is a favorite destination for those pursuing their interests and passions.

First Published in 2022 by The Harvard Common Press, an imprint of The Quarto Group,
100 Cummings Center, Suite 265-D, Beverly, MA 01915, USA.
T (978) 282-9590 F (978) 283-2742 Quarto.com

The Harvard Common Press titles are also available at discount for retail, wholesale, promotional, and bulk purchase. For details, contact the Special Sales Manager by email at specialsales@quarto.com or by mail at The Quarto Group, Attn: Special Sales Manager, 100 Cummings Center, Suite 265-D, Beverly, MA 01915, USA.

26 25 24 23 22   1 2 3 4 5

ISBN: 978-0-7603-7357-6
Content in this book was previously published in *The Bonne Femme Cookbook* (Harvard Common Press, 2011) by Wini Moranville.

Digital edition published in 2022
eISBN: 978-0-7603-7358-3

Library of Congress Control Number: 2021950017

Cover Design and Page Layout: Ashley Prine, Tandem Books
Cover Image (Roasted Asparagus and Cheese Tartlets, page 204): Richard Swearinger
Interior Photographs: Richard Swearinger

Printed in China

Always follow the most up-to-date food safety guidelines when cooking, handling, serving, and storing food, and use common sense when working with kitchen utensils and appliances. Food safety guidelines can be found at www.fsis.usda.gov.

EVERYDAY
French
COOKING

Modern French Cuisine
Made Simple

Wini Moranville

HARVARD
COMMON
PRESS

Dedicated to the French cooks who opened my eyes to the wonder and warmth of the everyday French table

OPPOSITE: Any-Day Chicken Sauté, page 76

CONTENTS

OPPOSITE: One *Bonne* Starter Salad, page 30

Introduction

It happened again, on the very day that I was to sit down and write this introduction. I mentioned to someone that I was writing a cookbook on easy, everyday French cooking.

"Really?" she asked. "Is there such a thing as easy, everyday French cooking?"

Yes, there is. And I've spent over 25 summers in France discovering beautiful, life-enhancing—yet simple—recipes that prove it.

Here's what I've found:

Everyday French cooking favors frugality over splurges—the French home cook understands how to make a beautiful meal from less-expensive cuts of meat; ease of preparation trumps fussy techniques any day. French cooking also marches to the beat of the seasons—whatever looks at its freshest, in-season best is likely to end up on the table. Intuition and improvisation are also key—French home cooks know how to substitute an ingredient they have on hand for something they don't, and how to make a pan sauce for just about anything (and you will, too, once you've cooked a few recipes in the "Sauté, Deglaze, and Serve" chapter).

Few Americans are familiar with this casual side of French cooking. When we think of French food, we envision splurge-worthy, anything-but-everyday restaurants with a small army of chefs hovering over sauces for hours at a stretch, crafting elegant dishes that require obscure utensils, expensive ingredients, and architectural precision.

When we consider bringing French cooking to our own home tables, we picture toiling for three days over a cassoulet, hunting all over town for veal bones for a reduction, ordering a lobe of foie gras or specialty cuts of wild boar online, and stirring way too much butter and cream into every dish.

But, in fact, most French cooks don't spend all day at the market or in their kitchens, any more than most of us do. Often, both men and women work outside the home, juggling their families and professions and the overall speeding-up of life, just like us. And yet they still manage to bring fresh, life-enhancing food to the table night after night.

I know this because I have had the good luck to spend long stretches of time in France, where I have dined at the tables of quite a few French hosts. And for years, I have cooked over French stoves myself.

I first got a taste of true everyday French cooking at the home of the Lavigne family, who hosted me on a high school exchange stay in Burgundy. Monsieur and Madame Lavigne and their teenage daughters, Annie and Françoise, lived in a snug, charming two-bedroom apartment in the industrial town of Montceau-les-Mines, where Monsieur Lavigne worked in a crane factory.

Evening after evening, we sat around their table, which was set up each night in the small living room, kicking off with perhaps a pâté one meal, a quick omelet the next, or an appetite-rousing soup. Next would come lovely main dishes: a succulent beef stew, perhaps, or pan-grilled steaks brought to the table with fascinating, intense pan sauces Madame made as effortlessly as my midwestern grandmother made gravy.

Madame would then make us a salad with a vinaigrette she prepared fresh at the table. Next would come some cheese to place on the plate on which our salads had been served. Dessert was often something she had picked up from the bakery—a cake layered with mousse, or a glistening fruit tart.

All throughout dinner, Madame and Monsieur would fill their daughters' glasses—and mine—with wine, cut with a little water in consideration of our youth.

My first night at the Lavignes' table, I remember thinking that surely this was a celebratory feast for me. I felt touched that although their guest of honor was just a 16-year-old from the American Midwest, they had obviously put out their best for our first evening together.

But the next amazing meal came, and then the next, and I realized that the Lavignes ate this way pretty much every night. And each dinner *was* a celebration, a simple yet splendid daily gathering put on so that we could enjoy each other's company. I loved the way conversations stretched into the evening, filled with plenty of laughter and affection, and how the Lavignes never tired of trying to understand my badly pronounced high-school French, even if it sometimes took us 10 minutes to negotiate the simplest exchange.

Like many a young person who discovers France at an early age, I fell in love with the country—the food, the people, their way of life. It was only natural that I became a French major in college. Afterward, I moved to New York, where I worked for a time in a French bank and traveled to France as often as I could.

While my career took a few twists and turns, my love for France was constant. Once I got into my 30s, I carved out a life that would allow me lengthy visits to France in summer, while living the rest of the year close to my family in the Midwest. And partly because a love for France *is* a love for food, I became a food writer and editor, working on a great variety of cookbooks, magazines, and websites in the past 25-plus years.

When my husband and I travel to France, we spend extended periods of time in one place. On most stays we rent a little apartment, so for weeks at a time we get to *faire le ménage* (keep house) like French people. This, of course, means cooking at home—and that entails its own daily rituals: heading to the markets in the morning, sniffing melons at the produce stands, chatting with the butcher, choosing the day's cheeses at the cheese shop, picking up a baguette at the *boulangerie*. And then we head home, and I cook something beautiful but never difficult. After all, there are beaches to visit, coffees to sip in cafés, *Herald Tribunes* (later the *International New York Times*) to read, outdoor markets to haunt. I have no interest in spending all day in the kitchen—but I do want to eat well. And when I follow the French home cook's lead, we do.

Our extended stays have also allowed us to befriend French families, giving us the chance to experience today's everyday French cooking in French homes, ranging from a five-course Easter dinner *chez* the Briffeille family in the Gers (a remote *department* in southwestern France) to a more casual weeknight supper at the home of Martine, our landlady in the Mediterranean resort town of Collioure. Each meal reveals again and again what Madame Lavigne shared with me all those years ago: There is nothing exclusive or snobbish or difficult about a good French meal. All it takes is a certain generosity of spirit and a little know-how.

Day after day, summer after summer, I have acquired that know-how. Taking inspiration from French cooks I've met and from the homestyle fare I've found at the tables of the unassuming *maman-et-papa* inns and bistros I've dined in, I've discovered how doable it is to cook and eat like a French person, without spending a lot of time in the kitchen or a lot of money on obscure or expensive ingredients. Over the years, I've collected, developed, and perfected a variety of recipes that tap into the everyday side of French cooking that I first experienced at the Lavignes and then on my later trips to France. I prepare these dishes in France; when home, I cook these same easygoing French meals for family and friends at my own table in Iowa.

My favorites fill the pages of this book.

Some recipes are straight-up classics—dishes such as Beef *Bourguignon*, *Coq au Vin Assez Rapide*, and *Crème Caramel Chez Vous*—that the French have been making for decades if not centuries and continue to bring to their tables. In many of these recipes, I've found a modern way to simplify the method, while staying true to what made the dish a classic in the first place. Forget boiling and peeling pearl onions for *coq au vin*; use frozen pearl onions (no one will know the difference). *Crème caramel* can be made easier and more luscious with a high-quality purchased caramel sauce—and you can skip caramelizing the sugar yourself (a tricky step French cooks sometimes skip, too). Go ahead and use purchased puff pastry (and even, in a pinch, purchased pie pastry)—French home cooks do it all the time. I'll also show you how you can savor the warmth of a streamlined cassoulet that you can make in a few hours rather than a few days.

And while the traditional style of everyday French cooking often signals rustic and hearty home fare, I've included many recipes that combine ingredients in light, quick, and fresh ways that are more in line with the way the French cook today. Some of these recipes, such as the Salmon with Wine, Leeks, and Garlic and the Roast Chicken Breasts Stuffed with Ricotta, Shallots, and *Fines Herbes*, were inspired by dishes I found in French magazines, cookbooks, and websites. Others are home cook-friendly renditions of recipes I enjoyed while dining out at casual bistros, inns, and cafés—places where you're likely to encounter a more everyday style of cooking. The goat cheese salad with honey and pine nuts at a casual bistro near Bordeaux, the wondrous Tartine with Brie and Salami at a café near the Swiss border, a lovely fish with saffron cream at a *maman-et-papa* inn somewhere in the Auvergne, Lemon Curd *Crème Brûlée* in Menton—these are just a few of the dishes that provided inspiration for my recipes.

I've also included recipes that simply came about when I took good ingredients home from the market and prepared them using French techniques and flavor combinations. Curry and Comté cheese—a flavor duo I discovered while traveling in eastern France's Franche-Comté region—adds unmistakable French-ness to a chicken and spinach salad. Apricot and sage, a combination I once spotted in a recipe for rabbit fillets, make a lovely flavoring for pork. Other recipes combine readily available foods you'll find at your market with staples of the everyday French kitchen—*herbes de Provence*, vermouth, *fines herbes*, olives, shallots, wine, Dijon mustard, olive oil, capers, lemon, and some of the more commonly found French cheeses—for dishes that would taste right at home on a French table.

Speaking of ingredients, when it comes to casual cooking, the French generally don't drive all over town for specialty ingredients, so why should you? And, as I mentioned earlier, frugality and flexibility are hallmarks of this kind of cuisine. In some recipes I've replaced an obscure or expensive ingredient with an easily found, less-expensive one (whenever I could do so and still remain true to France). For example, although vermouth-braised rabbit with black olives is a classic French recipe, chicken thighs are much easier to find and make an appropriate substitute for the rabbit. Italian sausage links make a surprisingly good stand-in for hard-to-find Toulouse sausages in my Pork and White Bean Cassoulet *Ce Soir*. I've never been able to snag the exact Mediterranean fish of choice for bouillabaisse in a U.S. market, but for my 30-minute version of the great French stew, red snapper or striped bass will work just fine, and in a pinch, I've even used a good wild-caught Alaskan cod. I'll also tell you which domestic cheeses you can use when it's not possible or practical to get your hands on the exact cheeses a French cook would use.

Throughout the process of writing this book, I have had one goal in mind: to interpret today's everyday French home cooking in ways that will translate fluently to the American table. I included recipes that tap into the styles of light, fresh fare that both French and American cooks prefer today. I have tried to avoid an overabundance of cream and butter, though both do appear, in moderation, in many recipes. I avoided recipes with difficult to find (or terribly expensive) ingredients or tricky preparations when I couldn't come up with a substitution or a streamlined technique that was worthy of the dish.

To make it easy to choose which recipe to make tonight—or this weekend—I've placed the bulk of the main-dish recipes into two chapters. For busy weeknights, start chopping a shallot and flipping through the recipes in the chapter "Sauté, Deglaze, and Serve." Many of these recipes, such as Chicken Tarragon, Pork Chops with Mustard Sauce, and Fish with Buttery Parsley and Garlic, can be made in less than half an hour.

When you have a little more time to cook, look in the "Braise, Stew, or Roast" chapter. These recipes may take longer, but none are difficult; after some initial prep, most of the kitchen time is hands-off cooking in the oven or on the stovetop. They include dishes that can be ready in an hour, such as Basque-Style Chicken and Gascony Pork Chops, as well as selections that take longer to stew or braise, such as Pomegranate *Pot-au-Feu* and Beef *Bourguignon*.

You'll find other chapters that offer ways to anchor a meal. While pot pie and tagliatelle might not come to the top of your mind when you think about French food, the "Casseroles and Pasta" chapter shows you how these and similar recipes are part of the French home cook's main-dish repertoire. Likewise, "Sandwiches, Pizzas, and Savory Tarts" shows you how the French turn bread, pizza dough, and puff pastry into casual-yet-stylish weekend lunches and weeknight dinners. And who knows how to transform eggs into a gratifying lunch or dinner better than a French cook? Find quiche, omelets, and baked eggs in the "Eggs and Cheese" chapter.

In my sides chapter, you'll learn how French cooks round out a main course with satisfying starches, such as Any-Night Baked Rice or Celery Root and Potato Purée, as well as colorful vegetables, including Peas with Pearl Onions and Thyme, French Green Beans *Classique*, and Glazed Carrots the French Way.

The remaining chapters offer recipes that span the scope of the French meal, from appetizers to dessert.

The "Appetizers and Cocktails" chapter shows you how to start the evening, French-style, with everything from tapenades to keep on hand to quick bites made with puff pastry. "*Les Salades*" helps you decide which green-, legume-, or vegetable-based salads to serve when—such as Belgian Endive Salad with Blue Cheese and Walnuts to start a meal, Green-on-Green Salad to go alongside a main dish, or Roasted Shrimp and Green Lentil Salad to serve as a main course. (For a salad to serve after the main course, with cheese, look for A Bright Mini-Salad for the Cheese Course in the "Eggs and Cheese" chapter.)

Soups also rank among the French cook's favorite recipes, as either an appetite-rousing starter or a satisfying meal-in-a-bowl. In "*Les Bonnes Soupes*," I've included a variety of recipes, both classic—such as *Soupe au Pistou*—and modern—such as Roasted Butternut Squash Bisque with Sweet Curry.

And then there are "*Les Desserts.*" I've focused mostly on everyday-simple recipes that French cooks truly make at home, including clafoutis, crème caramel, Alsatian apple tart, and crêpes. However, I couldn't resist adding a few pastry shop favorites, such the Classic French Fruit Tart and French Lemon Tartlets. Truth be told many French cooks would buy such delights at a nearby *pâtisserie*. But since the majority of Americans don't live near a French pastry shop, I've included them here to make when you have a little extra time.

And while the French often eat in courses, even on weeknights (to find out more about how the French structure their meals, see page 40), flexibility and freedom are touchstones of everyday French cooking. You'll soon see that you can adapt these recipes to the way you and your family and friends enjoy eating.

For those readers who already enjoy French cooking, I think you will find many new ideas, and new twists on classic recipes, in this book. For others who have been intimidated by the thought of French cuisine, I hope my book teases out the French home cook in you. You will soon learn, as I did at an early age, that the joys of the French table are open to everyone. You can live modestly and cook simply, yet dine splendidly, night after night. ■

APPETIZERS AND COCKTAILS

When the French invite friends over for apéritifs, the foods served alongside the drinks can be quite simple: hard sausages and cured meats, olives or tapenade, some crackers or cheese puffs, and maybe a surprise or two, such as savory pastries made from purchased puff pastry kept in the freezer. Here's how to bring it all together, with a few *cocktails maison* that prove that the French know what to do with a shaker.

OPPOSITE: Flaky Green Olive and Cheese Spirals and Flaky Tapenade *Noire* and Chèvre Spirals, page 22

Tapenade *Noire*

What sheer delight it is to go to French markets and pick up a batch of black olives to chop into a tapenade; with different olives in nearly every market I go to, I rarely end up with exactly the same tapenade twice. Yet no matter what mix of black olives I use, the results are always delightful.

I keep a batch of this spread on hand both when I'm in France and when I'm at home. Yes, it's a great party food, but it's also a perfect any-day treat to slather on a cracker during *l'heure du pastis* (roughly, the Provençal equivalent of the cocktail hour). At home, I enjoy the same nibble with that after-a-long-day glass of wine.

You can also use tapenade as a finishing touch to other dishes; for example, tuck some into omelets, spoon onto deviled eggs (or *Oeufs Durs Mayonnaise*, page 192), spread into a cheese, turkey, or roast chicken sandwich, or dollop a little atop potato soup as a garnish. **Makes about 1 cup**

1½ cups (8 ounces) pitted kalamata olives or mixed black olives

2 tablespoons capers, drained

1 teaspoon dried *herbes de Provence*

1 teaspoon anchovy paste

1 garlic clove, minced

1 tablespoon extra-virgin olive oil, plus more if needed

2 to 3 teaspoons fresh lemon juice (optional)

Place the olives, capers, *herbes de Provence*, anchovy paste, garlic, and oil in a food processor. Process until the mixture becomes a coarse paste, scraping down the sides of the bowl occasionally. Taste the tapenade. If you like it tangier, add some lemon juice. If it seems dry, add a little more olive oil. Transfer the tapenade to a bowl and serve at room temperature. Store leftovers in the refrigerator in a tightly covered, nonmetal container for up to 1 week.

Vous Désirez un Apéritif?

One of my favorite moments in life comes immediately after I'm seated in a restaurant, well before I even crack open the menu. It's when the waiter (or, in more formal restaurants, the maître d') comes over, pulls out his pen and pad from his suitcoat pocket, and asks, *"Est-ce que vous désirez un apéritif, monsieur-dame?"* (Sir, madam—would you care for an apéritif?)

My answer is always an unequivocal *"Oui."*

Whether at home or in a restaurant, the apéritif has a way of making everything that came before it (whether a day's work or a day's drive on the *autoroute*) slip away. The French believe that this little pre-dinner drink helps stimulate the appetite, and while this may be true, I think more than anything it simply readies the spirit for the joys to come. To me, the apéritif is in some small way like arriving somewhere remarkable after a tiresome journey—the first few sips of an apéritif resemble those moments of giddy joy at starting a new adventure. I always serve one to dinner guests the minute they walk through my door.

Yes, there's also a little lift from the alcohol, but the apéritif is usually not a high-proof drink; even when it is, it is not served in head-spinning portions.

One choice that's easy to find stateside is Lillet. Made in the Bordeaux region from wine, fruit brandy, citrus peels, and other flavorings, it's traditionally served chilled, on ice, with an orange slice.

French apéritifs vary from region to region. If you're ever in Gascony, try Floc de Gascogne, made with unfermented grape juice and Armagnac; in the Charentes region, ask for Pineau des Charentes, made with unfermented grape juice and Cognac. The south of France is known for drinks based on anise-flavored pastis, while *vin de pêche* and *vin de noix*—peach- and walnut-flavored wines—often kick off dinner in the southwest.

And in Champagne, the question *"Est-ce que vous désirez un apéritif?"* may well be replaced by the simple query, *"Une coupe de Champagne, monsieur-dame?"* (Sir, madam—a glass of Champagne?)

If you do travel to France, rather than trying to remember all of the kinds of apéritifs available, simply ask the server to recommend an apéritif of the region. I always do, and I'm always delighted.

I've also found in France that ordering an apéritif is a secret code for telling the waiter, "Hey, I might speak French with an American accent, but I know what's supposed to happen in a French restaurant!" More than once, a server has approached our table asking if we were ready to order, without suggesting an apéritif (likely thinking that, being Americans, we might not be clued in to the ritual). When I've said, politely (and in French), "Would it be possible for us to begin with an apéritif?" I've seen the waiter do a double take, kick into gear, and, with a relief in knowing that we'd duly appreciate everything to come, say, *"Mais oui! Bien sûr, madame! Qu'est-ce-que vous désirez comme apéritif?"* (Yes, of course, madam. What would you like for your apéritif?) The meal generally proceeds wonderfully and congenially from that moment on.

Tapenade *Verte*

You can use this spread as a finishing touch to other recipes, as you would the Tapenade *Noire* (see headnote, page 16). While I enjoy it solo on a cracker, it tastes even better on a hummus-topped cracker, as in the photo, opposite.

If you're making this for a party, set aside a couple of tablespoons for yourself and tuck it away in the refrigerator. That way, you can have some to slip into a Rolled French Omelet with Tapenade *Verte* and Sheep's Milk Cheese (page 196) the day after *la soirée*. Enjoy it at breakfast while you go over the post-party gossip.   **Makes about 1 cup**

---

1 teaspoon fennel seeds

1½ cups (8 ounces) pitted large green olives, with or without pimientos

2 tablespoons extra-virgin olive oil, plus more if needed

1 garlic clove, minced

¼ teaspoon dried red pepper flakes

¼ teaspoon dried tarragon

¼ teaspoon curry powder

1. In a small skillet, toast the fennel seeds over medium heat until warm and fragrant. Pour into a small bowl. Using kitchen shears, snip away at the seeds to break some of them apart (or sprinkle the seeds with a few drops of water and crush them with a mortar and pestle).

2. Place the olives, oil, garlic, red pepper flakes, tarragon, and curry powder in a food processor along with the toasted fennel seeds. Process until the mixture becomes a coarse paste, scraping down the sides of the bowl occasionally. If the tapenade seems dry, add a little more olive oil. Transfer the tapenade to a bowl and serve at room temperature. Store leftovers in the refrigerator in a tightly covered, nonmetal container for up to 1 week.

Olives with Fennel and Pernod

In the south of France, when you order a Pernod or other pastis, the server will more often than not bring your drink with a small saucer of tiny black Niçoise olives. They make a great match—a good little quaff and snack before you head home, slightly lifted by the drink, yes, but also by the changing light and beauty that surrounds you and the anticipation of a fine dinner at the end of a day.

Even if you don't love Pernod as a drink, you can still enjoy a little splash in your olives for a similarly irresistible south-of-France effect. Enjoy these with a cool glass of dry rosé for another true-to-France apéritif.   **Makes about 1½ cups**

1 tablespoon extra-virgin olive oil

½ cup chopped fennel

2 garlic cloves, crushed

¼ cup Pernod, Ricard, or Pastis 51

1½ cups (8 ounces) Niçoise or other pitted imported black olives

1 tablespoon chopped fresh chervil or ½ teaspoon dried *fines herbes*, crushed

⅛ teaspoon cayenne pepper

Heat the olive oil in a skillet over medium heat. Add the fennel and sauté until just softened, about 5 minutes. Add the garlic and cook until fragrant, about 30 seconds. Remove the skillet from the heat. Off the heat, slowly pour in the Pernod, taking care not to let it spatter. Return the skillet to the heat and cook the mixture briefly, until reduced by half. Add the olives and heat through, stirring. Remove the skillet from the heat and stir in the chervil and cayenne. Transfer the mixture to a serving bowl, cool to room temperature, and serve. Alternatively, refrigerate the mixture overnight and bring it to room temperature to serve. Store leftovers in the refrigerator in a tightly covered, nonmetal container for up to 1 week.

Gougères

These savory little cheese puffs make excellent party bites—just line them up on a platter and watch them disappear. Serve them solo, or slice them open and tuck in a savory filling, such as cream cheese mixed with tapenade or a slice of salami.   **Makes 20 to 24 cheese puffs**

½ **cup all-purpose flour**

½ **teaspoon salt**

½ **teaspoon dry mustard powder**

⅛ **teaspoon cayenne pepper**

½ **cup 2 percent or whole milk**

4 **tablespoons (½ stick) unsalted butter, cut into pieces**

2 **large eggs**

½ **cup finely shredded Comté, Gruyère, Emmental, or cheddar cheese (about 2 ounces)**

1. Preheat the oven to 400°F. Line a baking sheet with parchment.

2. In a small bowl, stir together the flour, salt, dry mustard, and cayenne; set aside.

3. In a medium-size saucepan, heat the milk and butter over medium heat until the butter is melted and the milk comes to a boil. Add the flour mixture all at once to the milk mixture. Beat with a wooden spoon until the mixture pulls away from the sides of the pan. Cook and stir for 1 minute more. Remove the pan from the heat and let the mixture cool for 10 minutes.

4. Add the eggs, one at a time, beating the first until it is completely incorporated and the dough is smooth before adding the second. Beat in the cheese.

5. Use a pastry bag to pipe 20 to 24 mounds of the dough onto the baking sheet. (Alternatively, the dough may be dropped by tablespoons.)

6. Bake the *gougères* for 15 minutes. Reduce the oven temperature to 350°F. Continue to bake until golden brown on the outside, 8 to 10 minutes more. The insides should be dry but soft—pull one open to test it. Transfer to a wire rack to cool. Serve warm or at room temperature.

7. Leftovers may be sealed in an airtight container and frozen. Reheat from a thawed or frozen state in a 350°F oven for 6 to 10 minutes.

Flaky Green Olive and Cheese Spirals

French home cooks rarely make puff pastry from scratch. Good-quality commercial pastry is as widely available throughout France as it is here, and it's exceedingly simple to work with. When purchasing puff pastry, look for a brand with butter in the ingredient listing—it will taste the best.

These roll-ups balance the nutty snap of Pyrénées sheep's milk cheese with the tang of olives. It's a great combination. You can use just about any similarly firm cheese you have, such as Comté, Gruyère, Manchego, or even a good white cheddar.   **Makes 15 spirals**

½ **package frozen puff pastry (1 sheet)**

1 large egg

1 tablespoon water

½ **cup chopped pitted green olives, with or without pimientos**

¾ **cup shredded Pyrénées sheep's milk cheese (such as Ossau-Iraty or P'tit Basque), or Manchego (about 3 ounces)**

1 small garlic clove, minced

1. Thaw the puff pastry according to the package directions. Whisk together the egg and water in a small bowl.

2. Unfold the pastry on a lightly floured surface. Brush with some of the egg wash; cover and refrigerate the remaining egg wash for later use. Top the pastry with the olives, cheese, and garlic. Roll up the pastry starting with a short side. Refrigerate the pastry roll for at least 15 minutes or up to 2 hours.

3. Preheat the oven to 400°F. Line a baking sheet with parchment.

4. Slice the pastry roll crosswise into 15 slices that are a little thicker than ½ inch. Place the slices flat on the parchment-lined baking sheet, and brush the tops with some of the reserved egg wash.

5. Bake until golden, 15 to 20 minutes. Transfer to a serving platter and serve warm or at room temperature.

Variation

Flaky Tapenade *Noire* and Chèvre Spirals. Replace the green olives with ⅓ cup Tapenade *Noire* (page 16, or purchased) and replace the sheep's milk cheese with ¼ cup crumbled or diced soft-ripened goat cheese. You won't cover the entire pastry, but try to spread it as evenly as you can.

Chutney-Ham *Amuse-Bouches*

Yes, French cooks use chutney, often when they want to add global inspiration to their recipes. Here, a little goes a long way to enliven the sweet fruits and salty ham in these irresistible little bites.

An *amuse-bouche* ("amuse the mouth") is a delightful little morsel often served before dinner to placate hungry mouths and stomachs as the evening begins. **Makes about 25 bites**

½ **package frozen puff pastry (1 sheet)**

¼ **cup finely chopped dried apricots**

2 **tablespoons raisins, preferably golden**

1 **tablespoon rice wine vinegar**

1 **tablespoon mango chutney or apricot preserves**

½ **cup diced ham**

1 **scallion (white portion and some tender green tops), finely chopped (about 2 tablespoons)**

2 **garlic cloves, minced**

⅛ **teaspoon cayenne pepper**

Salt and freshly ground black pepper to taste

1. Thaw the puff pastry according to the package directions.

2. While the puff pastry thaws, place the dried apricots and raisins in a bowl; stir in the rice wine vinegar and let the mixture stand for at least 15 minutes. Snip any large pieces of fruit in the chutney and add it all to the dried apricots and raisins. Stir in the ham, scallion, garlic, and cayenne; season with salt and pepper.

3. Preheat the oven to 400°F. Line a baking sheet with parchment.

4. Unfold the pastry on a lightly floured surface and cut it into three rectangles, about 9¼ x 3 inches each. Spread one-third of the filling down the center of each pastry rectangle, parallel to the long edges. Fold each pastry in half lengthwise over the filling, pinching the long sides together to seal. Cut the pastries crosswise into 1-inch pieces.

5. Place the pieces on the baking sheet. Bake until light brown, about 15 minutes. Transfer to a serving platter and serve warm or at room temperature.

Cognac Julep

A few years ago, I traveled through the Cognac region in west-central France to learn about the time-honored French spirit. I was somewhat surprised to hear producers extolling Cognac's virtues in cocktails, as I had thought that they might raise an eyebrow at the idea of serving the hallowed sip any way but in its purest form. Turns out, Cognac has long been a favorite ingredient of mixologists in France and the United States—it adds depth and finesse to cocktails.

I was also surprised to learn that mint juleps were originally made with Cognac or brandy instead of bourbon. What a difference a switch in spirit makes! This is one smooth Julep.

FOR EACH COCKTAIL:

6 fresh mint leaves

1 teaspoon simple syrup, or more to taste

Crushed ice

2 ounces Cognac

Place the mint leaves in a short tumbler; press with a muddler or the back of a spoon to break up the leaves and release the mint's fragrance. Stir in the simple syrup. Fill the glass halfway with crushed ice; add the Cognac and stir well, until the glass is frosty.

Kir with a Kick

Cognac adds virility to the classic kir royale, which is made with Champagne and black currant liqueur. It's a dashing way to kick off the evening.

FOR EACH COCKTAIL:

3/4 ounce Cognac

1/4 ounce *crème de cassis* or Chambord

Chilled Champagne or sparkling wine

1 raspberry (optional)

Pour the Cognac and the *crème de cassis* into a flute; fill the flute with Champagne. Garnish with a raspberry, if you like.

Le Coucher de Soleil

It's funny. Sometimes when the French want to show off, they use a phrase or two in English; we do the same, of course, using French. I saw this drink—titled "Sunset," in English—on a French menu. I enjoyed the way the pinkish-red grenadine and the slice of lemon or orange resemble the streaks of color in a sunset. Yet when it comes to the name, I like the ring of the French translation better. Meant for enjoying at the end of a hot day, it's a drink I once enjoyed at a seaside resort.

FOR EACH COCKTAIL:

1½ ounces gin

¾ ounce Cointreau or triple sec

¾ ounce fresh lemon juice

4 or 5 ice cubes, plus more for serving

3 to 4 ounces chilled tonic water

Drizzle of grenadine syrup

1 lemon or orange slice, for garnish

Combine the gin, Cointreau, lemon juice, and ice in a cocktail shaker. Shake well and strain into an ice-filled old-fashioned or similar-size glass. Top with chilled tonic water and stir gently. Drizzle with just a little grenadine and garnish with a lemon or orange slice.

Come for a Cocktail

On one of my recent stays in France, my landlady, Martine—who has also become a good friend over the years—invited me to her house for a cocktail. When I arrived, Martine—who had just come home from work—brought out a bottle of well-chilled white wine from her region (the Roussillon), some olives, a few salted almonds, and a long, slender cured Spanish sausage (she lives a stone's throw from Spain). She presented the sausage quite unceremoniously, on a cutting board with a knife, in "serve yourself" fashion.

We drank the wine and nibbled on the food while sitting in her garden. I enjoyed the well-chosen bites as much as if she had spent all afternoon in the kitchen. I thought to myself, why do I make such a huge fuss when I have friends over in the United States? Why do I always feel I have to cook something? Why can't I just put out some local charcuterie (such as La Quercia prosciutto, made just down the road from me), a few olives, and a bowl of nuts?

I know it seems strange for a cookbook author to tell you not to cook, but even the food-loving French don't always do so when inviting friends over. I've offered the appetizer recipes in this book for those times when you want to bring something special to the table. However, if the task of cooking up something for a simple drink with friends is going to keep you from inviting someone over, then don't cook—but pick up the phone anyway. Sometimes, not cooking can be in the spirit of everyday French life, too.

LES SALADES

Salads are a mainstay of French home cooking. It's rare to sit down to a lunch or dinner without enjoying greens or other fresh, uncooked vegetables thoughtfully dressed and presented in one delightful way or another. Here, you'll find some favorites in the French cook's repertoire, along with fresh new ways to serve salads, whether before, with, or after your main course—or as the main course itself.

OPPOSITE: Clockwise from top center salad: Tarragon–White Bean Salad, page 45; *Carottes Râpées*, page 43; *Pois Chiches* Salad, page 46; Tomato Salad with *Fines Herbes*, page 43; Avocado and Radish Tabbouleh, page 47

One *Bonne* Starter Salad

The French rarely start a meal with a simple lettuce salad, as we so often do. When they do kick off with a green salad, it's usually an interesting one—a palate-rousing combination that gets everyone excited for what's to come. That's what this spicy-tangy-nutty recipe does.   **Makes 4 servings**

1 fennel bulb

1 recipe Lemony Tarragon Vinaigrette

1 large head butterhead lettuce, such as Boston or Bibb

½ cup crumbled soft-ripened goat cheese

1 recipe Spiced Toasted Almonds

Fresh tarragon sprigs, optional

1. Discard the stalks, core, and outer layer of the fennel; slice the fennel as thinly as possible. Toss the fennel slices with a small amount of the dressing.

2. Tear the butterhead lettuce into bite-size pieces. Toss with enough of the remaining dressing to make the leaves slick. Divide the leaves among four salad plates. Scatter the fennel over the lettuce.

3. Divide the goat cheese and almonds atop each serving. Drizzle a little more dressing atop each serving and top with a tarragon sprig if you like. Serve.

Lemony Tarragon Vinaigrette

In a small bowl, whisk together 2 tablespoons fresh lemon juice, 1 teaspoon Dijon mustard, a few drops hot pepper sauce, and salt and freshly ground black pepper to taste. Slowly add 5 tablespoons extra-virgin olive oil, whisking to emulsify. Stir in 2 tablespoons snipped fresh tarragon.

Spiced Toasted Almonds

In a small heatproof bowl, combine 2 teaspoons sugar, ½ teaspoon snipped fresh rosemary, ¼ teaspoon ground cumin, and ¼ teaspoon ground coriander. In a small skillet, toast ⅓ cup slivered almonds over medium heat, watching carefully and stirring until golden brown. Sprinkle the sugar-spice mixture over the almonds; cook briefly, stirring, until the rosemary and spices release their fragrance and the sugar melts onto the nuts. Remove the skillet from the heat and pour the almonds back into the heatproof bowl to cool.

Belgian Endive Salad
with Blue Cheese and Walnuts

Here's a classic salad that deserves a revival. As is often the case with French salads, the leaves are not meant to be the bulk of the salad (as the lettuce in American salads often is). Rather, the endive provides a pleasantly bitter, nicely crisp backdrop to the cheese and nuts, which are the true stars.   **Makes 4 servings**

3 tablespoons walnut oil or extra-virgin olive oil

1 tablespoon fresh lemon juice or white wine vinegar

Salt and freshly ground black pepper to taste

5 to 6 Belgian endives (1 pound)

¾ cup walnut pieces, toasted

¾ cup crumbled blue cheese

1. In a large bowl, whisk together the walnut oil, lemon juice, and salt and pepper.

2. Trim the endive ends so that the leaves can separate; cut each endive in half lengthwise and remove the tough core. Separate the leaves, rinse under cold water, and drain well. Thinly slice the leaves crosswise and add to the bowl of dressing, tossing to coat.

3. Add the walnuts and blue cheese and toss gently. Arrange the salad on four salad plates and serve.

Poaching Eggs

You can purchase all kinds of egg poachers, from simple gadgets to electric appliances. My favorite is the perforated bowl attached to a long handle. You simply break the egg into the greased bowl and, using the handle, submerge the egg into a pot of boiling water.

I find eggs cook best at water that is just boiling—that is, boiling at an active simmer, not a full, rolling boil.

Cook the eggs until the whites are completely set and the yolks are cooked as desired (4 to 5 minutes for yolks that are thickened but not hard).

Drain the eggs well; if water has settled on top of the eggs, blot it away with a paper towel.

Poached Egg Salad with Bacon

In France, this would generally be served as the first course of a hearty meal; however, I often serve it as a main dish, made with the best farmers' market greens, alongside plenty of crusty bread and cheeses.   **Makes 4 servings**

---

4 slices bacon, cut into 1-inch pieces

4 cups torn mixed greens, such as baby spinach, radicchio, Belgian endive, frisée, and arugula

½ cup sliced red onion

4 large eggs

1 recipe Sherry-Mustard Vinaigrette

Salt and freshly ground black pepper to taste

1. Cook the bacon in a skillet over medium heat until crisp; remove the skillet from the heat and set it aside.

2. Toss the greens and red onion in a medium-size salad bowl.

3. Using an egg poacher, poach the eggs to the desired doneness according to the manufacturer's directions (see page 32). Drain the eggs and set them aside.

4. When the eggs are almost done, reheat the bacon in the skillet over medium heat; remove the bacon pieces with a slotted spoon and add them to the greens mixture in the bowl. Toss in enough vinaigrette to coat the leaves nicely; you may not need the entire recipe.

5. Arrange the salad among four serving plates and top each with a poached egg. Season each egg with salt and pepper and serve immediately.

Sherry-Mustard Vinaigrette

In a small bowl, combine 1 to 2 cloves minced garlic with salt and freshly ground black pepper to taste. Mash them together with the back of a spoon to make a rough paste. Add 1 tablespoon sherry vinegar; whisk with a fork or small whisk until the salt is dissolved. Whisk in 2 teaspoons Dijon mustard. Slowly add 3 tablespoons extra-virgin olive oil, whisking until incorporated. Whisk in a drop or two of hot pepper sauce, if desired.

Green-on-Green Salad

This pretty salad—with its monochromatic play of various green ingredients—provides an irresistibly perky and peppery contrast to dishes with rich flavors and a deep dark hue, such as those cooked with red wine, sweet sherry, or Madeira. It's also a pleasant sit-down first-course salad.   **Makes 4 servings**

1 garlic clove, minced

Salt and freshly ground black pepper to taste

2 tablespoons fresh lime juice

4 tablespoons extra-virgin olive oil

2 teaspoons honey

1 or 2 drops hot pepper sauce

4 cups baby arugula or chopped full-size arugula

½ cup halved, thinly sliced cucumber

¼ cup thinly sliced scallions (white portion and some tender green tops)

1 avocado, peeled and sliced

1. In a small bowl, use the back of a spoon to mash the garlic with the salt and pepper. Add the lime juice and whisk until the salt is dissolved. Add the olive oil, whisking until incorporated. Whisk in the honey and hot pepper sauce.

2. In a large bowl, toss the arugula with enough dressing to make the leaves appetizingly slick. Arrange the arugula on a platter. Toss the cucumber and scallions with a bit of the dressing; arrange them on top of the greens. Arrange the avocado slices atop the salad. Drizzle just a little more of the dressing atop the avocado and serve.

When to Serve Salad—*Mythe et Réalité*

It's often said that the French *always* eat salads after the main course. However, I've seen salads served before the main course and with the main course (especially at lunch alongside the classic *steak frites*), as well as after the main course. It truly depends on the salad. For example, the French generally wouldn't serve complicated salads—those with poached eggs, beets, or a variety of ingredients beyond greens—after the main course; such a complex salad would likely be a starter. In fact, salads served after the main course are usually quite simple—greens tossed with a tart vinaigrette—served as a palate refresher as you move to the cheese course or dessert. Sometimes such a salad is even served *with* the cheese course (see page 207 for an example).

The French probably wouldn't serve a multi-ingredient salad, such as my Green-on-Green Salad, alongside a main course or a soup; however, in my experience, the salad is a fine choice for such a presentation.

Green Bean Salad with Tomatoes

Green beans tossed with vinaigrette are a popular summertime salad in France, when beans (and tomatoes) are at their freshest. In general, the French cook their green beans a little longer than we do, preferring them more tender than crisp. If you like your green beans more crisp, start checking them at 5 minutes. The cooking time will partly depend on how thick your beans are.   **Makes 4 to 6 servings**

1 large shallot, finely chopped (about ¼ cup)

3 tablespoons extra-virgin olive oil

2 tablespoons white wine vinegar

Salt and freshly ground black pepper to taste

1 tablespoon kosher salt

1 pound thin green beans, trimmed (see Note)

2 medium-size tomatoes, seeded and coarsely chopped

2 to 3 tablespoons snipped fresh parsley

1. In a small bowl, whisk together the shallot, olive oil, vinegar, and salt and pepper. Set the dressing aside for 30 minutes to mellow the flavor of the raw shallot.

2. Bring a large pot of water to a boil. Add 1 tablespoon kosher salt. Add the beans and boil until done to your liking, 5 to 10 minutes. Drain the beans and rinse under cold running water until cool. Drain the beans well and wrap them in paper towels to remove excess water.

3. Place the beans in a large bowl; add the tomatoes and parsley. Add the dressing and toss to combine. Serve.

Note: If you can find thin French haricots verts, use these instead and reduce the cooking time to 3 to 4 minutes.

Roasted Beet Salad with Blue Cheese

No need to seek out an imported French cheese to crumble over this quintessentially French salad—American cheesemakers craft beautiful blues. Two of my favorites are Point Reyes Blue from California and Bayley Hazen Blue from Vermont's Jasper Hill Farm. Of course, you can also use a great blue you've found from your own part of the country. **Makes 4 servings**

4 to 5 medium-size beets
 (1½ pounds)

1 tablespoon extra-virgin olive oil

Salt and freshly ground black
 pepper to taste

1 garlic clove, minced

1 teaspoon Dijon mustard

1 tablespoon red wine vinegar

2 tablespoons walnut oil or extra-
 virgin olive oil

½ red onion, thinly sliced
 (optional)

1 cup arugula, baby greens, or
 small, tender lettuces

½ cup crumbled blue cheese

Snipped fresh chives (optional)

1. Preheat the oven to 375°F.

2. Trim the stems and roots from the beets and peel them. Cut the beets into 1-inch pieces and place in a 9 x 13-inch baking pan. Toss the beets with the olive oil and spread them out in the pan. Season the beets with salt and pepper. Cover the pan with foil and roast for 20 minutes. Remove the foil and roast until the beets are tender, 10 to 15 minutes more. Set aside to cool slightly.

3. In a serving bowl, whisk together the garlic, mustard, vinegar, walnut oil, and salt and pepper. Add the warm beets and, if you like, the onion; toss to coat. Allow to cool to room temperature (about 20 minutes). Add the arugula and toss again. Sprinkle the salad with the blue cheese and the chives, if you're using them, and serve.

Note: Running out of time? Do as a French home cook might do in the same situation: Buy pre-cooked beets, often available at gourmet grocers, and skip the peeling and roasting step.

Melty Goat Cheese Salad
with Honey and Pine Nuts

This lovely warm goat cheese salad is similar to one I came across while dining at a simple sidewalk café in Cadillac, near Bordeaux. I love the way the honey contrasts with the tangy goat cheese; the buttery pine nuts also add richness.

    A great warm goat cheese salad calls for not only warmed goat cheese, but warmed *ripened* goat cheese. Fresh, chalky, bright-white, rindless goat cheese—the kind sold in plastic tubes in the supermarket—just doesn't melt nicely. If you can find a soft-ripened Crottin or Chabichou goat cheese, the presentation will be especially enticing—the interior of the cheese rounds will melt a bit, leaving the rind standing like a little wall around a pool of semi-liquidy lusciousness—*ça, c'est classique.*   **Makes 4 servings**

---

1 tablespoon rice wine vinegar

1 garlic clove, minced

Salt and freshly ground black pepper to taste

3 tablespoons extra-virgin olive oil, plus more for brushing

4 (½-inch-thick) baguette slices

4 (½-inch-thick) slices soft-ripened goat cheese, such as Crottin or Chabichou (about ⅓ pound total; see Note)

5 cups mixed tender greens, preferably including arugula

2 tablespoons toasted pine nuts

4 teaspoons honey

1. Preheat the broiler.

2. In a large bowl, whisk together the rice wine vinegar, garlic, and salt and pepper. Whisk in the olive oil.

3. Toast both sides of the baguette slices in a toaster oven or under the broiler, then brush one side with a little olive oil. Place the baguette slices, oiled sides up, on a small baking sheet and top each with a round of goat cheese. Watching carefully, broil 3 to 4 inches from the heat until the goat cheese is softened and melted in places, about 3 minutes. Remove the pan from the broiler.

4. Add the greens to the large bowl and toss to coat well with the dressing. Divide the greens among four salad plates. Top each with a cheese toast. Sprinkle the pine nuts over each salad. Drizzle the honey over the toasts. Serve.

Note: Other soft-ripened goat cheeses can be used; however, they come in a variety of shapes and sizes. If necessary, cut the goat cheese to fit on top of the baguette slice without any cheese hanging over.

Dining in Courses—or Not

Whenever I've been the guest of a French family, every time we sat down to dinner we enjoyed at least three courses—more often four, and sometimes even more. At first, I wondered if French families always ate this way, or if my hosts were pulling out extra stops just because I was their guest.

I don't believe that the French eat more than we do—it's just that they stretch the meal out over a few courses, which allows them to enjoy more time at the table with family and friends. After dining with and talking to French people over the years, I've learned that a traditional French dinner at home follows this basic formula:

Entrée. Confusingly, the first course of a French meal is called an entrée (the same word we use for our main course). But the French usage makes linguistic sense, as this is how you "enter" the meal. At its most basic, the entrée is a soup in winter or a *salade composée* (a mixed-ingredient salad) in summer. Other classic entrées include pâté, a platter of air-cured meats, *Oeufs Durs Mayonnaise* (page 192), leeks vinaigrette, and an *assiette de crudités* (a platter of raw-vegetable salads). If guests are invited, the first course may become more elaborate; for example, seafood, a savory tart (such as quiche or a cheese tart), an omelet, a soufflé, or a puff-pastry-based dish might kick off the meal. I've been served everything from creamed kidneys to smoked duck on a bed of lentils to grilled anchovies as a first course.

Plat Principal. This is the main course. As with our main courses, the fish, chicken, or meat is nearly always served with a side dish or two—either a vegetable or a starch, and sometimes both—though rarely in the abundance we've come to expect in the United States.

Salad. A simple green salad may appear as a separate course, before the cheese or dessert course, but if fresh salad greens have already been served earlier in the meal, they would not likely make another appearance here or with the cheese.

Fromage. The optional cheese course is very often a local cheese (or perhaps two or three), served with bread. Sometimes the cheese comes with *sa petite salade verte* (its little green salad). The vinaigrette-tossed greens offer a great contrast to a plate of creamy cheeses.

Dessert. This can range from ice cream or a simple fruit salad to custards, cakes, tarts, and the like. Keep in mind that the lucky French have high-quality pastry shops in nearly every village and city neighborhood; I'm also absolutely astounded by how good the supermarket desserts can be. In fact, I rarely ever make desserts in France— the pastry shop delights as well as some store-bought versions of tiramisu, chocolate mousse, *crème caramel*, and *crème brûlée* are so good, I needn't bother. But to get French-quality desserts to my table at home, I usually have to make them myself.

For special occasions, and when hosting *les invités* (guests), the French may add a course or two to the formula. Perhaps some *amuse-bouches*—playful little nibbles such as *gougères* or canapés—will be served with the apéritifs or cocktails before everyone is seated. Sometimes a second entrée—such as a soufflé or fish dish—will be inserted after the entrée but before the *plat principal*. For *very* special occasions, I've even enjoyed meals that included two entrées and two main courses, followed by salad, cheese, and dessert. Coffee, by the way, is served after (not with) dessert.

It's worth noting that whenever I've asked French people to elaborate on how they eat, most say they do eat in courses at home, but they're always quick to add, "But there are plenty of people in France today who do not eat in the traditional way." I, however, have not met any of these people.

So, if you cook like the French, do you have to eat like the French—which is to say, in courses? Of course not! As my friend Muriel told me, *"En fait, il n'y a pas de règles strictes, tout dépend des invités et du milieu dans lequel tu vis"* ("There are no strict rules, in fact; it all depends on whom you are inviting and the milieu in which you live"). So do as you wish.

Butterhead Lettuce Salad
with Walnuts and Comté

This recipe is a classic way to serve Comté; thanks to the fabulously complex flavor of this French mountain cheese, this salad is interesting enough to serve as an enticing first course. However, you could also serve it alongside a good, hearty soup, such as French Green Lentil Soup (page 68). While it's true that the French do not traditionally serve soups and salads together, I've found that doing so is a great way to bring a windfall of French pleasures to the table quickly and easily.   **Makes 4 to 6 servings**

¼ cup sunflower oil

1 tablespoon sherry vinegar

1 teaspoon Dijon mustard

¼ teaspoon ground coriander (optional)

Salt and freshly ground black pepper to taste

2 heads butterhead lettuce, such as Boston or Bibb, washed, dried, and torn into bite-size pieces

4 ounces Comté, Gruyère, or Emmental cheese, cut into very thin matchsticks

½ cup walnut pieces, toasted

In a salad bowl, whisk together the oil, vinegar, mustard, coriander, if you like, and salt and pepper. Add the lettuce, cheese, and walnuts and toss gently to coat with the dressing. Arrange among salad plates and serve.

Vinegar and Oil for Salads

With every recipe, I've specified the kinds of oil and vinegar to use, choices I made based on how I find them to complement the other ingredients in the salad.

When it comes to vinegar, you can always experiment with ones you like best, or substitute whatever you have on the shelf. If you're going to stock just two vinegars, I'd recommend keeping white wine and red wine vinegar on hand—they're used often in French cooking.

As for the oil, grapeseed oil is a very mild-flavored oil, while walnut oil adds a distinctive nutty flavor. Olive oil, however, is much more commonly used in French salads.

A real epiphany for me in recent years, however, has been sunflower oil, *huile de tournesol,* which French cooks also use in salads and vinaigrettes. It's a mild oil that lets the flavors of other ingredients shine through. I substitute it often in the Vinaigrette *Maison* (page 242) when I'm not looking for the added flavor dimension of olive oil.

Carottes Râpées

In delis throughout France, *carottes râpées* (grated carrot salad) is an option you'll see again and again alongside other favorites, like tabbouleh, beet salad, and celery root salad. I enjoy serving this as an accompaniment to a sandwich—it's an especially perky contrast to an egg salad sandwich.

Makes 4 to 6 servings

---

8 ounces carrots

2 tablespoons fresh lemon juice

2 tablespoons extra-virgin olive oil

2 teaspoons sugar

1/4 teaspoon Dijon mustard

1 tablespoon chopped fresh parsley or chives, or a combination

Salt and freshly ground black pepper to taste

Peel the carrots and grate them into long, thin strips (you'll have about 3 cups; see Note). Place the carrots in a medium-size glass serving bowl. In a small bowl, whisk the lemon juice, olive oil, sugar, and mustard until combined. Pour the dressing over the carrots. Add the parsley and season with salt and pepper; toss to coat. Taste, and add more lemon juice or olive oil (or, for that matter, sugar, mustard, salt, or pepper) if you like. Chill the salad for at least 30 minutes to blend the flavors; toss again before serving.

Note: To achieve long, thin strips of carrots, as pictured on page 28, use a julienne vegetable peeler.

Tomato Salad with *Fines Herbes*

As a teenager on my first trip to France, I stayed with the Lavigne family in Burgundy. One day, Madame Lavigne made lunch for her husband when he came home for his midday break from his job. Alongside homemade *steak frites*, she brought out a simple tomato salad topped with chopped shallots and fresh tarragon. I had never in my life tasted anything quite like it; it was surely the first time I ever tasted fresh tarragon.

Ever since I started to cook, this has been one of my favorite salads to serve in summer. I especially like it alongside a grilled steak (recalling the steak that Madame Lavigne served me all those years ago).

Makes 4 servings

---

4 medium-size ripe tomatoes, sliced

1 small red onion, chopped (about 1/2 cup) or 1 large shallot, finely chopped (about 1/4 cup)

3 tablespoons fresh *fines herbes* (see page 164)

Salt and freshly ground black pepper to taste

1 tablespoon extra-virgin olive oil

1 teaspoon white wine vinegar

Arrange the tomatoes on a serving platter. Scatter the onions and *fines herbes* over the tomatoes and season with salt and pepper. Sprinkle the olive oil and white wine vinegar over all. Serve.

Tarragon–White Bean Salad

In this recipe, the softness of the beans combined with the crunch of the greens is simply wonderful. Tarragon provides its hallmark spring-fresh, anise-like flavor, and the olives add spark. It's the tarragon that makes this salad particularly French, but if you find yourself bereft of tarragon, you can substitute another herb, or a combination of herbs. Sage and parsley work especially well together here. Just remember that the stronger the herb, the less you'll need. A little like a salad and side dish all in one, this dish, plus some crusty bread, would be all you need to make a meal out of grilled or broiled tuna or wild salmon.

Makes 4 servings

1 (19-ounce) can cannellini beans, rinsed and drained

¼ cup halved pitted Niçoise or kalamata olives

1 large shallot, slivered (about ¼ cup), or ½ red onion, slivered (about ½ cup)

2 tablespoons snipped fresh tarragon or other fresh herbs (see headnote)

3 tablespoons extra-virgin olive oil

1 tablespoon red wine vinegar

1 garlic clove, minced

¼ teaspoon paprika

Salt and freshly ground black pepper to taste

3 cups torn mixed greens

1. In a medium-size bowl, stir together the beans, olives, shallot, and tarragon.

2. In a small bowl, whisk together the olive oil, vinegar, garlic, paprika, and salt and pepper. Add the dressing to the beans, stirring to coat.

3. Arrange the greens on a platter or in a shallow bowl; top evenly with the bean mixture and serve.

La Grande Assiette de Crudités

One much-loved first course in casual French bistros is the *assiette de crudités*, a collection of three or four small servings of raw vegetable salads, all attractively presented on one plate per diner. The salad selections vary according to region and season; classics include *céleri rémoulade*, dressed cucumbers, tomato salad, beet salad, and *carottes râpées*. Sometimes a mayonnaise-dressed hard-cooked egg and an olive or two also garnish the plate.

In summer I like to create my own *grande assiette de crudités*. On a large platter, I arrange some of these vegetable classics as well as one or two legume- or grain-based salads, such as Tabbouleh *Chez Vous* (page 47), *Pois Chiches* Salad (page 46), and Tarragon–White Bean Salad (above). I set it out with a tray of cheeses, a platter of air-cured meats, some baguettes (or, better yet, *Pissaladière*, page 186), and a few bottles of dry French rosé, for summer dining at its patio-perfect best.

Pois Chiches Salad

Chickpeas—*pois chiches*—often make their way into French salads, especially in the south. Here, inspiration comes from a classic Sicilian salad, but the *fines herbes* and shallot contribute decidedly French effects. As with many legume-based salads, this could anchor a meal with cheeses served alongside—if doing so, omit the cheese in the salad.   **Makes 6 servings**

¼ **cup extra-virgin olive oil**

1 **medium-size onion, halved and thinly sliced**

1 **shallot, sliced (about ¼ cup)**

2 **garlic cloves, minced**

1 **cup snipped fresh *fines herbes* (see page 164)**

2 **(15-ounce) cans chickpeas (also called garbanzo beans), rinsed and drained**

½ **cup freshly grated Pyrénées sheep's milk cheese (such as Ossau-Iraty or P'tit Basque) or Manchego (about 2 ounces; optional)**

Heat the olive oil in a large skillet over medium heat. Add the onion and shallot and cook, stirring, until soft and brown in places, about 5 minutes. Add the garlic and *fines herbes*; cook and stir for about 30 seconds, just long enough to release their fragrance. Stir in the chickpeas; cook and stir until heated through. Transfer the mixture to a large bowl and top with cheese if you like; serve warm or at room temperature.

Tabbouleh *Chez Vous*

Like *Carottes Râpées* (page 43), tabbouleh is another one of those salads that most every deli in France sells, though usually it's made with couscous instead of bulgur.

This is a basic recipe, but by choosing whatever strikes your fancy at the market or trying the combinations I suggest below, you can make this salad a specialty of your house. Just keep in mind that the more items you add, the more you may need to adjust the amount of dressing—simply increase the lemon juice and olive oil in equal parts as you add ingredients to the bowl.

In summer, when farmers' markets are in full swing, have the bulgur softened, drained, and waiting in the fridge. Then, go to the market, pick up whatever looks great, and toss it into this salad. You can have a colorful, in-season salad ready in minutes once you return home.   **Makes 4 servings**

---

1 cup uncooked bulgur

2 medium-size ripe tomatoes, seeded and chopped

¾ cup snipped fresh parsley

¼ cup thinly sliced scallions (white portion and some tender green tops)

3 tablespoons fresh lemon juice

3 tablespoons extra-virgin olive oil

Salt and freshly ground black pepper to taste

1. Cook the bulgur according to the package directions. Drain the bulgur in a fine-mesh sieve and place in a large bowl.

2. Stir in the tomatoes, parsley, and scallions. In a small bowl, whisk together the lemon juice, olive oil, and salt and pepper. Add the dressing to the bulgur mixture and toss to combine. Cover and chill the tabbouleh for at least 1 hour to meld the flavors. Stir and taste before serving, adding more lemon juice, salt, and/or pepper if necessary.

Variations

Avocado and Radish Tabbouleh. Instead of ¾ cup fresh parsley and ¼ cup scallions, use ½ cup fresh parsley, ¼ cup fresh chives, and ¼ cup fresh mint. Omit the tomatoes. Just before serving, stir in 1 peeled, chopped avocado, ½ cup sliced radishes, and 2 cups torn salad greens, preferably with some frisée in the mix.

***Mâche* Tabbouleh.** Substitute mint for the parsley, omit the scallion, and add ½ cup thinly sliced onion. Just before serving, stir in 1½ cups shredded *mâche* (a delicately tangy salad green).

Chicken, Comté, and Spinach Salad
with Apples

While traveling in the Franche-Comté region of France—a lush, mountainous region that borders Switzerland—I've enjoyed a few main-dish salads that had been emboldened with a delicate sprinkling of Comté cheese, the region's mighty take on Gruyère. The salads reminded me a little of the way that Americans sometimes shower chef's salads with much larger planks of Swiss or cheddar. The difference, of course, is that a little Comté (in thin, delicate strips) goes a lot farther to add deep, rich flavor than three times as much domestic "Swiss" cheese.

Once home, I recalled how chefs had expertly paired Comté with curry, and it wasn't long before I came up with this French take on the chicken-and-greens salad. Comté cheese is worth seeking out at a specialty or gourmet market; alternatively, try an imported cave-aged Gruyère or Emmental.

Makes 4 main-course servings

1¼ **pounds boneless, skinless chicken breast halves**

Salt and freshly ground black pepper to taste

3 **tablespoons extra-virgin olive oil, plus extra for brushing the chicken**

1 **tablespoon white wine vinegar**

1 **tablespoon mayonnaise**

½ **teaspoon sweet curry powder**

3 **ounces baby spinach**

2 **ounces Comté, Gruyère, or Emmental cheese, cut into matchsticks**

1 **tart red apple, such as a Washington Braeburn, cored and thinly sliced**

¼ **cup walnut halves, toasted and chopped**

1. Preheat the oven to 350°F.

2. Brush lightly with olive oil and season the chicken breasts with salt and pepper. Place the chicken breasts in a shallow baking dish and bake until the internal temperature registers 170°F on an instant-read thermometer, about 20 minutes. Transfer the chicken to a cutting board to rest until cool enough to handle.

3. Meanwhile, in a small bowl combine the vinegar with salt and pepper; stir until the salt dissolves. Whisk in the olive oil, mayonnaise, and curry powder.

4. Slice the chicken crosswise. Place the spinach, Comté, apple, and chicken in a large bowl. Toss the salad with the desired amount of dressing (you might not use it all). Divide the salad among four plates, top with the chopped toasted walnuts, and serve.

Swiss Chard with Roasted Chicken,
Apples, Pistachios, and Blue Cheese

The French cook with Swiss chard, but they certainly don't call it that; rather, it goes by the name of *blettes*. *Tarte aux blettes*—a savory tart—is a well-known way to showcase this crinkly-leafed green.

The emerald-green leaves also work nicely in salads, but are best shredded and added as a flavor accent rather than the greater part of the salad. I generally don't use much balsamic vinegar in salads, as its big flavors can overwhelm the more subtle and tender greens. But for Swiss chard, it's perfect—the sturdy greens stand up to the heft of the vinegar just fine. **Makes 4 main-course servings**

1¼ **pounds boneless, skinless chicken breast halves**

Salt and freshly ground black pepper to taste

2 **tablespoons extra-virgin olive oil, plus extra for brushing the chicken**

4 **ounces Swiss chard leaves, coarsely shredded**

1 **large tart red apple, such as a Washington Braeburn, peeled, cored, and diced**

¼ **cup crumbled blue cheese**

3 **tablespoons coarsely chopped pistachio nuts**

1½ **tablespoons balsamic vinegar**

1. Preheat the oven to 350°F.

2. Season the chicken breasts with salt and pepper and brush them lightly with olive oil. Place the chicken breasts in a shallow baking dish and bake until the internal temperature registers 170°F on an instant-read thermometer, about 20 minutes. Transfer the chicken to a cutting board to rest for 5 minutes or so.

3. Meanwhile, combine the Swiss chard, apple, blue cheese, and pistachio nuts in a large bowl. Whisk together the olive oil, balsamic vinegar, and salt and pepper in a small bowl.

4. Cut the chicken into bite-size pieces. Add the chicken to the chard mixture and toss to combine; the chard leaves will soften somewhat from the heat of the chicken. Add the vinaigrette and toss again to combine. Divide the salad among four shallow bowls and serve.

Wilted Escarole Salad
with Provençal Fish Fillets

This salad sets warm fish over wilted escarole, a green that gets plenty of play in France but not nearly enough here. Its pretty leaves—ranging from medium green to almost white—offer a refreshing crunch and pleasant bitterness. Find the sweetest tomatoes available—such as drippingly ripe farmers' market cherry tomatoes. Their near-fruity sweetness will marry all of the other bits of this salad beautifully.

Out of season, consider making the oven-fried fish on its own—it's a simple and tasty way to serve a good, fresh piece of fish.   **Makes 4 main-course servings**

½ cup fine cracker crumbs

1 tablespoon dried *herbes de Provence*, crushed

1 garlic clove, minced

½ teaspoon salt

¼ teaspoon cayenne pepper

4 (6-ounce) skinless snapper or flounder fillets (about ½ inch thick)

1 tablespoon walnut oil or extra-virgin olive oil

2 tablespoons grapeseed oil or extra-virgin olive oil

12 ounces escarole, or a mixture of escarole and frisée, torn into bite-size pieces

1 recipe Vinaigrette *Maison* (page 242)

10 sweet cherry tomatoes, halved if large or left whole if small, or 2 medium-size tomatoes, chopped

1. Preheat the oven to 450°F. Grease a shallow baking pan.

2. In a shallow bowl, stir together the cracker crumbs, *herbes de Provence*, garlic, salt, and cayenne. In a large bowl, gently toss the fish with the walnut oil until coated. Dredge the fish well in the crumb mixture, pressing the crumbs into the flesh to coat it thoroughly.

3. Arrange the fish in the baking pan. Bake until the fish flakes easily with a fork, 4 to 6 minutes.

4. While the fish cooks, heat the grapeseed oil in a large skillet over medium-high heat until shimmering. Add the escarole; cook and stir until it is just barely wilted, about 1 minute (you want the greens softened a bit but not cooked through).

5. Toss the escarole with just enough vinaigrette to slicken the leaves. Divide the greens among four dinner plates or place on one large serving platter. Arrange the baked fish pieces atop the greens. Arrange the tomatoes around the fish. Drizzle with more vinaigrette, if you like, and serve.

Roasted Shrimp
and Green Lentil Salad

In the winter, French home cooks use French green lentils for hearty dishes like soups or a salad with sausages. But in the summer, these nutty little gems can take a walk on the lighter side with seafood, such as the shrimp in this recipe. **Makes 4 main-course servings**

1 cup French green lentils (preferably *lentilles du Puy*)

Salt and freshly ground black pepper to taste

1 pound large shrimp, shelled and deveined

4 tablespoons extra-virgin olive oil

2 large garlic cloves, minced

2 tablespoons minced fresh tarragon

5 scallions (white portion and some tender green tops), 1 thinly sliced and 4 cut into matchsticks

1 tablespoon white wine vinegar

1 teaspoon Dijon mustard

Dash of hot pepper sauce

1 large Belgian endive, root end trimmed, tough core removed, and leaves cut crosswise into ½-inch slices

1 cup watercress or arugula, rinsed, tough stems removed

Butterhead lettuce leaves

1. Rinse, drain, and sort through the lentils to discard any pebbles or other debris. Place the lentils and 3 cups water in a medium-size saucepan; add salt as desired. Bring to a boil, then reduce the heat and simmer, partially covered, until the lentils are tender but still firm, about 15 minutes. Drain and rinse the lentils; cool to room temperature.

2. Preheat the oven to 400°F.

3. Pat shrimp dry. Place the shrimp in an 8-inch square baking dish. Season the shrimp with salt and pepper, then toss with 1 tablespoon of the olive oil, the garlic, tarragon, and the sliced scallion. Bake until the shrimp are opaque throughout, 8 to 10 minutes.

4. Meanwhile, in a small bowl, combine the vinegar, mustard, and hot pepper sauce with salt and pepper; whisk in the remaining 3 tablespoons olive oil until emulsified.

5. In a large bowl, toss the lentils, endive, watercress, and scallion matchsticks until combined. Drizzle the salad with the dressing and toss again.

6. To serve, arrange the butterhead lettuce leaves on a large platter. Add the lentil salad and top with the shrimp.

LES BONNES SOUPES

For centuries, French home cooks have relied on soups to transform whatever they could find in their gardens or at the market into nourishing first courses or main dishes to warm and satisfy their families. Find some beloved classics here, along with contemporary-styled recipes that bring new flavors and combinations to the French-inspired soup bowl.

OPPOSITE: Roasted Tomato and Garlic Soup, page 67

Silky and Light Potato Soup

If it's been a long time since you've enjoyed puréed potato soup (*sans* the extra thickeners that more hearty soups often bring), then please give this a go. Here, the soup's true nature comes through. Earthy potatoes pulled from under the soil get a fresh jolt of green herbs plucked from above the ground. It tastes of the miracle that is a garden itself.

Fresh and light, this soup is classically served as an appetite-rousing first course; however, you can also serve it as a light supper with a tray full of fun bites, such as mini prosciutto sandwiches, a few wedges of cheese, and some tapenade and crackers. **Makes 6 first-course or side-dish servings**

---

2 tablespoons unsalted butter

2 medium-size leeks (white and pale green parts only), halved lengthwise, rinsed, and sliced crosswise (about 1 cup)

6 cups low-sodium chicken broth, plus more if needed

1½ pounds yellow or white potatoes, peeled and roughly chopped

Salt and freshly ground black pepper to taste

1 tablespoon heavy cream

¼ cup snipped fresh parsley, chervil, or chives, or a combination

1. Melt the butter in a 4-quart saucepan over medium heat. Add the leeks and cook, stirring, until tender but not brown, 4 to 5 minutes. Pour in the broth slowly so that it does not spatter. Add the potatoes and salt and pepper. Bring to a boil. Reduce the heat, cover the pan, and cook at an active simmer until the potatoes are very tender, about 30 minutes.

2. Allow the soup to cool slightly. Working in batches, purée the soup in a blender until smooth (see below). Return the soup to the pan and reheat gently. If the soup is too thick, stir in additional chicken broth until it reaches the desired consistency. Stir in the cream. Season with additional salt and pepper, if needed. To serve, ladle the soup into bowls and garnish with the fresh herbs.

Puréeing Soups

I find that a blender works better for puréeing soups than a food processor. However, when puréeing hot mixtures in a blender, you need to take care to avoid the explosion that can occur when steam builds. First, cool the soup slightly. Fill the blender no more than halfway. Secure the lid, but remove the round plastic cap in the center of the lid. Hold a kitchen towel over this opening to allow steam to escape. Start blending on slow speed, then increase the speed as needed to purée. You can also use an immersion blender to purée soups right in the pot.

Roasted Butternut Squash Bisque
with Sweet Curry

Here, a little curry and white wine vinegar—one contemporary and one a classic staple of the French cook's pantry—both deepen and enliven the flavors of a classic bistro soup. Serve this French style, as a sit-down first course, or American style, as a side dish with sandwiches or savory tarts.

Makes 6 first-course servings

1 large butternut squash (about 3 pounds), halved, seeds removed

Salt and freshly ground black pepper to taste

1 tablespoon sunflower or canola oil

1 large onion, chopped

2 large carrots, peeled and chopped

1 teaspoon curry powder, preferably sweet

5 cups low-sodium chicken broth, plus more if needed

1 tablespoon white wine vinegar

Crème fraîche or light sour cream

Ground nutmeg

1. Preheat the oven to 375°F.

2. Season the squash halves with salt and pepper and place them, cut sides up, on a large rimmed baking sheet. Bake the squash until tender, about 40 minutes. Cool slightly.

3. Meanwhile, heat the oil in a Dutch oven over medium heat. Add the onion, carrots, and curry powder and cook, stirring, until the onion is tender but not brown, 4 to 5 minutes.

4. Scoop the flesh from the cooled squash and add it to the carrots and onions. Add the chicken broth and bring to a boil. Reduce the heat, cover the pot, and simmer until the carrots are completely tender, 10 to 15 minutes.

5. Allow the soup to cool slightly. Working in batches, purée the soup in a blender until smooth (see opposite).

6. Return the soup to the Dutch oven and reheat gently. At this point, check the consistency of the soup. If it's too thick (like baby food), stir in additional chicken broth, about ¼ cup at a time, until it reaches the desired consistency. Stir in the vinegar; taste and add additional salt and pepper if needed. Serve in soup bowls topped with *crème fraîche* and a few sprinkles of ground nutmeg.

Roasted Carrot Soup
with Curry and Coconut Milk

Here, *Potage Crécy*, the classic French carrot soup, gets an update with southeast Asian ingredients that often make their way into the French cook's repertoire. About the rice: Once puréed, it's undetectable—it's simply there to help thicken the soup. **Makes 6 first-course or side-dish servings**

1½ pounds carrots, peeled and sliced into 1-inch pieces

1 large leek (white and pale green part only), halved lengthwise, rinsed, and sliced crosswise into 1-inch pieces

2 tablespoons sesame oil

Salt and freshly ground black pepper to taste

1 tablespoon minced ginger

1 garlic clove, minced

4 cups low-sodium chicken broth

¼ cup white rice

1 teaspoon curry powder, preferably sweet

½ cup unsweetened coconut milk

1 cup water

1. Preheat the oven to 375°F.

2. On a large, shallow rimmed baking sheet, combine the carrots, leeks, and sesame oil. Mix the carrots and leeks until coated with the sesame oil. Spread them out evenly in a single layer. Season with salt and pepper. Roast the carrots and leeks for 15 minutes. Remove the pan from the oven, sprinkle the carrots and leeks with the ginger and garlic; stir well, then spread them again into a single layer. Continue roasting until the carrots are nearly tender and the leeks are lightly caramelized, 10 to 15 minutes more. Remove the pan from the oven.

3. Meanwhile, in a large saucepan, bring the chicken broth to a boil over medium-high heat; add the rice. Reduce the heat, cover the pan, and simmer for 10 minutes.

4. Add the roasted vegetables to the broth and rice. Stir in the curry powder. Reduce the heat and simmer, partially covered, until the carrots are very tender, 10 to 12 minutes. Remove the pan from the heat. Add the coconut milk and water.

5. Allow the soup to cool slightly. Working in batches, purée the soup in a blender until smooth (see page 58). Return the soup to the pan; add more water if it seems too thick. Reheat the soup and add more salt and pepper if needed. Ladle the soup into bowls to serve.

French Onion Soup

Just about everyone who's ever been to Paris in winter likely has a story of enjoying *soupe à l'oignon gratinée*. Here's mine:

On New Year's Eve in 1988, my husband and I dined well, but it was one of those good-but-overpriced meals that we really couldn't afford at the time. The next day, looking for a meal that might help us get back on budget, we drifted into a little café near our hotel on the Left Bank and ordered *soupe à l'oignon gratinée*, the classic French onion soup, for our meal. While I cannot remember what was on the menu of the fancy dinner we ate the night before, I'll always remember how fortifying, satisfying, and warming this soup tasted, and how comforting it was to know that you could get so much joy out of something so humble. I now make it almost every New Year's Day to celebrate the life-affirming truth that dining well doesn't have to mean dining expensively.

I've come to learn that French onion soup is all about the broth and the cheese. Of course, the best choice is homemade beef broth, but a top-quality canned broth will do. You can also use a reduced veal stock product available at gourmet stores (just reconstitute it according to the directions). The cheese options are a little narrower. Only Comté, Gruyère, or Emmental will do. They're the classic choices for good reason: They melt wonderfully and add an irresistibly complex flavor.

I always serve this soup in wide, shallow bowls. That makes it easier to cut up the cheese-topped toasts with your spoon as you eat. **Makes 4 hearty first-course servings or 4 light main-dish servings**

---

2 tablespoons unsalted butter

2 tablespoons extra-virgin olive oil, plus more for the bread

1½ pounds onions, sliced into thin half-moons

Salt and freshly ground black pepper to taste

1 tablespoon all-purpose flour

4 cups beef broth

½ cup dry white wine

4 slices French bread, toasted

1 garlic clove, halved

1 cup shredded Comté, Gruyère, or Emmental cheese (about 4 ounces)

1. In a large Dutch oven, melt the butter in the olive oil over medium heat. Add the onions and cook, stirring, until softened but not brown, 4 to 5 minutes. Season with salt and pepper. Reduce the heat to medium-low and cook the onions, stirring occasionally, until they are slithery, tender, and just starting to take on a lightly golden-brown hue in places, about 40 minutes.

2. Stir in the flour with a wire whisk; cook and stir for 1 minute. Slowly stir in the broth, then the wine. Bring to a boil. Reduce the heat, cover the pan, and simmer the soup for 15 minutes. Taste and add more salt and pepper if needed.

3. Preheat the broiler.

4. Rub one side of each slice of toasted French bread with the garlic halves (then discard the garlic); brush that side of the bread with some olive oil. Place the bread slices, oiled sides up, on a baking sheet. Divide the cheese among the slices. Watching carefully, broil 3 to 4 inches from the heat until the cheese is bubbly and light brown in spots, about 1 minute.

5. Divide the soup among four shallow bowls; top each with a cheese-topped bread slice and serve.

A Case for the First-Course Soup

Somewhere along the line, many Americans abandoned the sit-down first-course soup; perhaps it's because our soups are so often heavy and filling: beef noodle soup, steak vegetable soup, chunky baked-potato soup with cheese, and the like. Rarely—except at better bistros—are they vivid and striking, appetite-rousing soups.

Yet first-course soups are alive and well in France, in both homes and restaurants. They're never overly weighty; rather, they're usually purées or light creamed soups made with good stock and market-fresh vegetables. More often than not, they're as freshly and painstakingly made as everything else that comes to the table.

The French have a saying: *L'appétit vient en mangeant*—"The appetite comes with eating." They rely on the first course to ease them into the meal. I can't count the number of times in France I've sat down to a table thinking I wasn't hungry, but when I put a spoonful of a freshly made soup to my lips, suddenly I'm eager for the next two or three courses.

Remember this especially when you entertain. Even if you have quite an elaborate spread for the main course, your guests will better enjoy all that is to come if you start gracefully, and a thoughtful soup is a pleasurable and rather simple way to do this.

Roasted Vegetable Soup *Classique*

Potage purée de légumes—puréed vegetable soup— is one of those first-course soups you often spot at mom-and-pop country inns and corner bistros in France. I like to serve this miraculous root garden in a bowl with a *Pissaladière* (page 186) for a light but satisfying supper.   **Makes 8 hearty first-course or side-dish servings or 4 to 6 main-dish servings**

8 cups vegetables cut into 1-inch chunks (use a selection of carrots, parsnips, sweet potatoes, butternut squash, red bell peppers, celery, turnips, and/or yellow potatoes, including at least 2 root vegetables; peel if needed)

1 large onion, coarsely chopped (about 1 cup)

2 garlic cloves, peeled

3 tablespoons extra-virgin olive oil

Salt and freshly ground black pepper to taste

¼ cup snipped fresh parsley

6 cups low-sodium chicken broth

½ to 1 tablespoon white wine vinegar (optional)

Snipped fresh chives (optional)

1. Preheat the oven to 425°F.

2. Spread the vegetables, onion, and garlic in a single layer on a large rimmed baking sheet (if they don't fit in a single layer on one sheet, use two). Drizzle with the olive oil and toss to coat. Season generously with salt and pepper. Roast until the vegetables are tender and lightly browned, 25 to 30 minutes. If using two baking sheets, rotate their oven positions after about 15 minutes. Cool the vegetables slightly.

3. Working in batches, purée the roasted vegetables in a blender or food processor, adding the parsley to the first batch. Blend or process until smooth (see page 58); if needed, you can add ½ cup of the chicken broth to each batch to help the mixture purée more easily.

4. Transfer the puréed vegetables to a 4-quart pot. Stir in the remaining chicken broth. Heat the soup over medium heat, stirring occasionally. Taste the soup; if it seems sweeter than you like, add a little white wine vinegar.

5. To serve, ladle the soup into bowls and garnish each serving with snipped fresh chives, if you like.

Soupe au Pistou

Italy gets most of the credit for pesto, but the French have their own *pistou*—a heady paste flavored with garlic, basil, and olive oil. And like the Italians, the French toss *pistou* with pasta; they also use it *pour tartiner*—to spread on bread. But perhaps the most famous way to use *pistou* is in *soupe au pistou*, a minestrone-like soup topped with *pistou*—a finishing touch that makes all the difference and adds an irresistible spark of brightness. **Makes 6 to 8 first-course servings**

1 tablespoon extra-virgin olive oil

½ cup finely chopped onion

2 garlic cloves, minced

6 cups low-sodium chicken broth

2 medium-size carrots, peeled and sliced (1 cup)

⅓ pound red-skinned or yellow potatoes, peeled and diced (1 cup)

1 (15-ounce) can white beans, such as cannellini, Great Northern, or navy, rinsed and drained

4 ounces green beans, cut into 1-inch pieces (1 cup)

4 ounces zucchini or yellow squash, diced (1 cup)

¼ cup snipped fresh parsley

1 large tomato, seeded and chopped (1 cup)

Salt and freshly ground black pepper to taste

½ recipe *Pistou* (page 251), or ½ cup purchased pesto

1. Heat the olive oil in a Dutch oven over medium heat. Add the onion and cook, stirring, until tender but not brown, 4 to 5 minutes. Add the garlic and cook, stirring, until fragrant, about 30 seconds more. Carefully add the broth. Add the carrots and potatoes and bring to a boil. Reduce the heat and simmer for 5 minutes. Add the white beans and the green beans, simmer for 5 minutes more.

2. Add the zucchini and parsley; simmer until all of the vegetables are just tender but not drained of color, about 5 minutes more. Stir in the tomato and heat through. Season with salt and pepper. To serve, ladle into bowls, and top each with a spoonful of *pistou*.

Roasted Tomato and Garlic Soup

On a September visit to France, I relished a startlingly fresh tomato soup—sparked with garlic and sunshine—similar to this one. That's exactly when I suggest you enjoy this recipe: in September, when you still have more tomatoes than you know what to do with, but there's a chill in the air that makes you sense, once again, how fleeting and precious the bumper crop—and summer—really are.   **Makes 4 to 6 first-course or side-dish servings**

---

2 pounds ripe red tomatoes, cored, halved, and seeded

6 garlic cloves, peeled

2 tablespoons extra-virgin olive oil

Salt and freshly ground black pepper to taste

2 cups low-sodium chicken broth

1 to 2 tablespoons sugar

1 teaspoon snipped fresh thyme

Fresh thyme sprigs, optional

1. Preheat the oven to 400°F.

2. Toss the tomatoes and garlic with the olive oil on a large rimmed baking sheet; season with salt and pepper. Roast until the tomatoes are soft and starting to brown, about 20 minutes.

3. Transfer the tomatoes and garlic to a large saucepan. Add the chicken broth, 1 tablespoon sugar, and the snipped thyme. Bring to a boil, reduce the heat, and simmer, stirring occasionally, for 10 minutes to meld the flavors.

4. Allow the soup to cool slightly. Working in batches, purée the soup in a blender until smooth (see page 58). Return the soup to the saucepan; taste and add another tablespoon of sugar if more sweetness is needed. Reheat the soup gently. To serve, ladle into bowls and garnish each bowl with a fresh thyme sprig, if you like.

Variations

Though this soup is magical on its own, you can add a few stir-ins for extra layers of flavor, if you wish:

- While the tomatoes are roasting, sauté 2 canned anchovy fillets in a little olive oil, stirring until they break apart and dissolve into the oil. Cool and add to the tomatoes before puréeing.

- Drizzle the finished soup with any complementary-flavored oil you might have around, such as avocado oil or lemon-garlic olive oil.

- Season the finished soup with a specialty sea salt, such as smoked alderwood.

French Green Lentil Soup

Like most home cooks the world over, French home cooks sometimes need to substitute a good ingredient (such as certain dried herbs) for a great one (such as fresh herbs) when practicality demands. But in the case of French green lentils, there is no substitute. Don't make this soup with regular brown lentils—it will be drab and boring. And while domestic green lentils are indeed better than brown lentils, they are still not nearly as good as true French green lentils from around the south-central French city of Le-Puy-en-Velay. Fans of *les lentilles du Puy* say it's the volcanic soil in this region that give the lentils their distinction. Olive green in hue, with a little steel blue dappling, these beady gems hold their nutty-firm texture even after cooking. Once a product Francophiles had to order by mail from France (or stuff in a suitcase when heading home), they're becoming readily available at serious markets, such as Whole Foods Market or health food stores.

Serve this soup with a nice, garlicky green salad, a good baguette, and a hunk of your favorite French cheese (Morbier makes a great choice) for an easygoing light supper.   **Makes 4 main-dish servings**

---

1 cup French green lentils (preferably *lentilles du Puy*)

2 tablespoons extra-virgin olive oil

1 large green bell pepper, seeded and chopped (about 1 cup)

1 medium-size onion, chopped (about 1 cup)

2 garlic cloves, minced

5 cups low-sodium chicken broth

2 tablespoons snipped fresh parsley

1/2 teaspoon dried marjoram, crushed

1/8 teaspoon cayenne pepper

Salt to taste

8 ounces fully cooked smoked sausage, such as kielbasa, cut into bite-size pieces

1. Rinse, drain, and sort through the lentils to discard any pebbles or other debris.

2. Heat the oil in a large saucepan or Dutch oven over medium heat. Add the green pepper and onion and cook, stirring, until the vegetables are tender but not brown, 4 to 5 minutes. Add the garlic and cook, stirring, until fragrant, about 30 seconds more.

3. Slowly add the chicken broth so that it does not spatter. Stir in the lentils, parsley, marjoram, cayenne, and salt. Bring to a boil. Reduce the heat, cover the pan, and simmer until the lentils are tender but still firm, about 20 minutes. Add the sausage and cook until heated through. To serve, ladle the soup into bowls.

Bouillabaisse Ce Soir

When I've visited Marseilles, I've found quite a few takes on *bouillabaisse*. Most versions of this classic south-of-France fish stew fall into one of two camps: the white-tablecloth, fine-china take (which includes high-end shellfish like langoustine and shrimp) and what I've come to call the backpacker's version, made mostly with fish and, if it has any shellfish at all, less-expensive varieties such as mussels. Either version, however, is sheer delight, because the stars are the rich, heady broth, redolent of herbs and spices, and, frequently, the accompanying toasts with *rouille*—a rust-colored garlic mayonnaise.

In the spirit of this book, I've based this *bouillabaisse* on the easier-on-the-schedule, easier-on-the-budget (yet equally heady) version. It's ready in just over half an hour, making it great for spontaneous any-night dining. Use the freshest fish possible, and do not by any means skip the toasts with *rouille* (my version is a bit *faux* because we're not using a from-scratch mayonnaise). You slather the *rouille* atop the toasts and let it float around the stew, which thickens, enriches, and flavor-charges the broth tenfold.   **Makes 4 servings**

---

2 tablespoons extra-virgin olive oil

1 small fennel bulb, chopped

1 small carrot, peeled and sliced

4 to 6 garlic cloves, minced

½ cup dry white wine

4 cups low-sodium chicken broth

½ cup bottled clam juice

1 *bouquet garni* (see Note)

1 bay leaf

Pinch of saffron threads, or
    ½ teaspoon turmeric

1½ pounds striped bass, red
    snapper, or cod fillets, cut into
    1½-inch pieces

2 ripe red tomatoes, seeded and
    chopped

1 tablespoon tomato paste

Salt and freshly ground black
    pepper to taste

½ cup finely snipped fresh parsley

Toasted baguette slices (8 if the
    baguette is large and wide; 12 if
    it's a thin baguette)

1 recipe *Faux Rouille*

1. In a 6-quart Dutch oven, heat the olive oil over medium heat. Add the fennel and carrot and cook, stirring, until the vegetables are slightly softened but not brown, 4 to 5 minutes. Add the garlic and cook, stirring, until fragrant, about 30 seconds more. Slowly add the wine; cook and stir until reduced by half. Carefully stir in the broth, clam juice, *bouquet garni*, bay leaf, and saffron. Bring to a boil. Reduce the heat and simmer for 15 minutes. Add the fish fillets and tomatoes and simmer for 5 minutes. Stir in the tomato paste and simmer until the

fish fillets are opaque and separate easily but are still intact, about 5 minutes. Remove and discard the *bouquet garni* and bay leaf.

2. To serve, spoon the stew into shallow bowls; sprinkle each serving with parsley. Pass a basket of the toasted baguette slices and the bowl of the *faux rouille*. Encourage diners to slather the *rouille* onto the bread slices and float them atop the stew.

Note: For this *bouquet garni*, use kitchen string to tie together 3 sprigs fresh thyme, 2 sprigs fresh marjoram or oregano, 1 sprig fresh sage, and 3 sprigs fresh parsley. Or tie the herbs in a piece of cheesecloth. If fresh herbs aren't available substitute, ½ teaspoon oregano, ½ teaspoon thyme, ½ teaspoon sage, but use 1 tablespoon fresh parsley if possible.

Faux Rouille

In a small bowl, stir together ½ cup olive oil mayonnaise, ⅓ cup fine seasoned bread crumbs, 1 to 2 finely minced large garlic cloves, ¼ to ½ teaspoon cayenne pepper, and sea salt to taste. Cover and chill before serving.

Sausage, Red Pepper, and White Bean Soup

Sausage, garlic, and red bell peppers are popular ingredients in Basque cooking, and with white beans, they make a hearty one-dish meal. *Piment d'Espelette*, made from ground sweet-smoky red peppers, adds an extra *basquais* touch. For a casual soup supper, serve this soup with a baguette and a few slices of that other southwestern France treat, Pyrénées sheep's milk cheese. Incidentally, the predominant red, green, and white colors of this soup are also the colors of the Basque flag.   **Makes 4 servings**

1 tablespoon extra-virgin olive oil

1 medium-size onion, chopped

1 red bell pepper, cored, seeded, and chopped (about 3/4 cup)

2 garlic cloves, minced

1/2 cup dry white wine

5 cups low-sodium chicken broth

1 (15-ounce) can white beans, such as cannellini or Great Northern, rinsed and drained

2 bay leaves

1/2 teaspoon *piment d'Espelette* or Aleppo pepper, or 1/2 teaspoon Spanish paprika and 1/8 teaspoon cayenne pepper

1/2 teaspoon dried thyme, crushed

12 ounces sweet Italian sausage (see Note)

1/2 cup water

8 ounces fresh spinach, washed and drained, tough stems removed

Freshly ground black pepper (optional)

1. In a large saucepan, heat the olive oil over medium heat. Add the onion and bell pepper and cook, stirring, until tender but not brown, 4 to 5 minutes. Add the garlic and cook, stirring, until fragrant, about 30 seconds more. Slowly add the wine; simmer until the wine is reduced by half, about 1 minute. Slowly add the chicken broth. Add the beans, bay leaves, *piment d'Espelette*, and thyme and bring to a boil. Reduce the heat, cover the pan, and simmer to allow flavors to meld, about 15 minutes.

2. Meanwhile, prick the sausage all over with a fork. In a medium-size saucepan, bring the sausage and water to a boil. Reduce the heat, cover the pan, and simmer until the sausage is no longer pink, about 15 minutes. Uncover the pan and continue to cook the sausage in the simmering water, allowing the water to evaporate and the sausage to cook through and brown in its own fat, turning as needed. Remove the sausage and cut into bite-size pieces.

3. Remove the bay leaves from the soup and discard.

4. If you like a thick soup, remove 1 cup of the cooked beans and a small amount of the liquid, cool slightly, and purée in a food processor or blender (see page 58). Return the purée to the soup.

5. Add the sausage to the soup; simmer to allow the flavors to meld, about 5 minutes more. Add the spinach and cook just until slightly wilted, about 1 minute. Taste the stew and add more *piment d'Espelette* or some freshly ground black pepper if needed (depending on how spicy your sausage is, you may not need more seasoning). Ladle into soup bowls and serve.

Note: If you happen to live near a market that sells fresh Toulouse- or Provence-style sausages, you can substitute either of these if you like. You'll need to adjust the cooking time, as these sausages are often thinner than Italian sausages.

Chaudière **of Scallops** with *Fines Herbes*

In French cooking, hearty doesn't necessarily mean rustic, and this main-dish soup is a case in point. The potatoes make the soup satisfyingly filling, but the *fines herbes* and scallops add finesse. Incidentally, if you think this resembles a chowder, you're right. Our word for chowder may well have derived from *chaudière*, the French word for cauldron.   **Makes 4 main-dish servings**

1 tablespoon unsalted butter

2 medium-size leeks (white and pale green parts only), halved lengthwise, rinsed, and sliced crosswise (about 1 cup)

1 large shallot, finely chopped (about 1/4 cup)

1 garlic clove, minced

1/2 cup dry white wine

1 cup low-sodium chicken broth

1 cup fish stock or bottled clam juice

1 pound red-skinned potatoes, scrubbed and cut in half if 1 inch in diameter or smaller, in quarters if larger than 1 inch

1 bay leaf

1 tablespoon snipped fresh *fines herbes* (see page 164), or 1 teaspoon dried *fines herbes*

Salt and freshly ground black pepper to taste

1/2 cup heavy cream

1 pound sea scallops, quartered, or bay scallops

2 tablespoons snipped fresh parsley

1. Melt the butter in a large saucepan over medium heat. Add the leeks and shallot and cook, stirring, until the leeks are tender but not brown, 4 to 5 minutes. Add the garlic and cook until fragrant, about 30 seconds. Add the wine and cook until reduced by half, 1 to 2 minutes. Add the broth and the clam juice, taking care not to let them spatter. Add the potatoes, bay leaf, *fines herbes*, and salt and pepper. Bring to a boil. Reduce the heat, cover the pan, and simmer until the potatoes are tender, 15 to 20 minutes. Remove and discard the bay leaf.

2. Add the cream to the pot and bring to a simmer. Add the scallops, return to a gentle simmer, and cook the scallops until they are opaque throughout, 2 to 4 minutes. Take care not to overcook them.

3. Remove the pan from the heat; season the soup with additional salt and pepper if needed. To serve, ladle the soup into shallow bowls and sprinkle each serving with snipped fresh parsley.

SAUTÉ, DEGLAZE, AND SERVE

Every recipe in this chapter is a variation on a theme: You sauté tonight's choice of meat in a skillet; then, you deglaze the pan by pouring wine and broth into the drippings. As it boils and reduces, you stir up the tasty browned bits left in the skillet. Add a few defining touches—apples, cherries, or olives here, tomatoes or mushrooms there, and fresh herbs almost everywhere. And there you have it: dinner quick enough for any night of the week, served with a rich and intense, true-to-France pan sauce.

OPPOSITE: Chicken Tarragon, page 81

Any-Day Chicken Sauté

This is the sauté-deglaze-serve recipe at its most basic. Try it, and you'll see how just a handful of ingredients and a few minutes in the kitchen can add up to so much pleasure at the table. I can't count the times I've made this dish—both in France and at home—after I've come back from the market carrying a basket brimming with pick-of-the-season vegetables for a knock-out salad or side but no particular idea about what to serve as the main course. At such times, this simple sauté always comes through. Note that the touch of cream is optional—use it if you want a little extra richness in your sauce.   **Makes 4 servings**

4 boneless, skinless chicken breast halves (about 1¼ pounds total)

Salt and freshly ground black pepper to taste

3 tablespoons unsalted butter

2 tablespoons snipped fresh parsley, chives, or chervil, or a combination, plus more for serving

1 large shallot, finely chopped (about ¼ cup)

¾ cup low-sodium chicken broth

¾ cup dry white wine

1 tablespoon heavy cream (optional)

1. Place the chicken breasts, one at a time, between two sheets of plastic wrap and pound to ¼-inch thickness. (Alternatively, you can halve each breast horizontally, or butterfly them, as described on page 78.) Season both sides with salt and pepper.

2. In a large skillet, melt 1 tablespoon of the butter over medium-high heat. Add the chicken (in batches, if necessary) and cook, turning once, until cooked through (internal temperature 165°F), 6 to 8 minutes (reduce the heat to medium if the meat browns too quickly). Transfer the chicken to a platter, sprinkle with the parsley, and cover with foil to keep warm.

3. Add the shallot to the pan and sauté briefly, until translucent. Add the chicken broth and white wine to the pan; stir with a whisk to loosen any browned bits from the bottom of the pan. Bring to a boil and boil until the liquid is reduced to about ¾ cup—this should take 4 to 5 minutes, depending on the heat and your pan size. Whisk in the remaining 2 tablespoons butter, 1 tablespoon at a time; if you like, add the cream. Cook the sauce to the desired consistency, and season with additional salt and pepper. Arrange the chicken on a serving platter or four dinner plates and spoon the sauce over the chicken breasts. Garnish with snipped fresh parsley and serve.

Prepping Your *Poulet*

Most of the chicken recipes in this chapter call for slicing or pounding chicken breasts to a thickness of 1/4 inch. This is done not only because the chicken cooks faster, but also because it makes for a tastier dish. When you flatten the breasts, you widen them, too; that allows more of the surface of the chicken to get nicely browned. And don't the browned parts always taste best?

That said, I must admit that pounding chicken breasts is one of my least favorite things to do in the kitchen. Fortunately, there are better ways to achieve a similar result.

The easiest alternative is to buy a product labeled as boneless, skinless *thin-sliced* breasts; while they're already sliced admirably thin, they may not be *exactly* 1/4 inch thick, so adjust cooking time as needed.

When I can't find thin-sliced breasts, I simply slice the chicken breasts in half horizontally through the middle to form two equal-size thin cutlets, and serve each diner two cutlets if the breast is small, one if it is large.

Note that if you halve or butterfly the breasts as directed below, they may not be exactly 1/4 inch thick, so you will need to adjust the cooking time.

TO SLICE A CHICKEN BREAST INTO TWO THIN CUTLETS:

1. Start with firm, very cold chicken breasts. Ideally, pop them in the freezer for 15 to 20 minutes before slicing. Room-temperature chicken is difficult to cut.
2. Place one boneless, skinless chicken breast half on a large cutting board. Lay one hand over the breast to hold it firm while you cut it.
3. Position a sharp, long-bladed slicing knife parallel to the cutting board, along the thicker of the two long sides of the breast, halfway up from the cutting board.
4. Slice through the meat, using gentle sawing motions while you continue to hold the breast steady with the other hand. When you get almost to the other side, open up the breast like a book and then slice all the way through.

TO BUTTERFLY A CHICKEN BREAST:

One glitch you might come across is the way chicken breasts can come packaged in a maddening array of sizes. You might get three breasts, two large and one small. Or four breasts, three tiny ones and one large one. When this happens, butterfly the smallest breasts to make one larger piece to serve one diner. To do this, proceed as above, but stop about 1/2 inch before you slice all the way through. Then open up the breast like a book to form one large, thin piece. Place the breast between two sheets of plastic wrap and pound the middle seam—the part of the breast that wasn't cut—until it is of even thickness with the rest of the breast.

Chicken with Sherry-Mushroom Sauce

This wine-and-mushroom-laced dish is a little like a French version of that Italian classic, chicken Marsala. I prefer using a pale, *fino quinta* style of sherry; refrigerate any leftover sherry to serve as an apéritif. **Makes 4 servings**

4 boneless, skinless chicken breast halves (about 1¼ pounds total)

Salt and freshly ground black pepper to taste

1 tablespoon vegetable oil

3 tablespoons unsalted butter

1 large shallot, finely chopped (about ¼ cup)

1½ cups sliced fresh mushrooms

¾ cup low-sodium chicken broth

¾ cup dry sherry, such as *fino quinta*

2 tablespoons snipped fresh parsley

1. Place the chicken breasts, one at a time, between two sheets of plastic wrap and pound to ¼-inch thickness. (Alternatively, you can halve each breast horizontally, or butterfly them, as described opposite.) Season both sides with salt and pepper.

2. In a large skillet, heat the vegetable oil over medium-high heat until it shimmers. Add the chicken and cook, turning once, until cooked through (internal temperature 165°F), 6 to 8 minutes (reduce the heat to medium if the meat browns too quickly). Transfer the chicken to a platter and cover with foil to keep warm.

3. Melt 1 tablespoon of the butter in the skillet. Add the shallot and sauté briefly, until translucent. Add the mushrooms and cook, stirring, until slightly softened, about 2 minutes. Remove the pan from the heat and carefully add the broth and sherry. Return the pan to the heat and stir with a whisk to loosen any browned bits from the bottom of the pan. Bring to a boil and boil until the liquid is reduced to about ¾ cup, 4 to 5 minutes. Whisk in the remaining 2 tablespoons butter, 1 tablespoon at a time. Season the sauce with additional salt and pepper. Arrange the chicken on four dinner plates, spoon the sauce over the chicken, sprinkle with the parsley, and serve.

Chicken Tarragon

Still skeptical about whether such simple recipes with so few ingredients can really bring inspired results to the table? Please—try this recipe. It's proof that fresh, vivid, beautiful cooking can be very simple indeed. The key here is that supremely French herb, tarragon—in this case, fresh is definitely best.

Makes 4 servings

- 4 boneless, skinless chicken breast halves (about 1¼ pounds total)
- Salt and freshly ground black pepper to taste
- 3 tablespoons unsalted butter
- 1 large shallot, finely chopped (about ¼ cup)
- 2 medium-size tomatoes, seeded and chopped (1 cup)
- ¾ cup dry white wine
- 1 tablespoon tarragon vinegar or white wine vinegar
- 2 tablespoons snipped fresh tarragon
- Fresh tarragon sprigs (optional)

1. Place the chicken breasts, one at a time, between two sheets of plastic wrap and pound to ¼-inch thickness. (Alternatively, you can halve each breast horizontally, or butterfly them, as described on page 78.) Season both sides with salt and pepper.

2. In a large skillet, melt 1 tablespoon of the butter over medium-high heat. Add the chicken (in batches, if necessary) and cook, turning once, until cooked through (internal temperature 165°F), 6 to 8 minutes (reduce the heat to medium if the meat browns too quickly). Transfer the chicken to a platter and cover with foil to keep warm.

3. Add the shallot and tomatoes to the skillet and sauté briefly, until the shallot is translucent. Add the wine, stirring with a whisk to loosen any browned bits from the bottom of the pan. Bring to a boil and boil until the wine is reduced by about half—this should take 2 to 3 minutes, depending on the heat and your pan size.

4. Add the vinegar and cook, stirring, for 1 minute. Whisk in the remaining 2 tablespoons butter, 1 tablespoon at a time, until the butter is melted and the sauce is thickened. Season the sauce with additional salt and pepper, if needed. Stir in the snipped tarragon. Arrange the chicken on a serving platter or four dinner plates, and spoon the sauce over the chicken. Garnish with fresh tarragon sprigs, if you like, and serve.

Chicken *Francese*

Francese is the Italian word for French, and I love the Italians for giving the French credit for this bright lemony-garlicky dish. However, we should probably tip our *chapeaux* to Italian-Americans. I've never seen this dish in either Italy or France; in fact, I first fell in love with it at Queen, a little Italian restaurant in New York's Brooklyn Heights. French, Italian, or Franco-Italian-American, I couldn't resist including it here, since it serves the sauté-deglaze-serve mode of French home cooking just fine.   **Makes 4 servings**

4 boneless, skinless chicken breast halves (about 1¼ pounds total)

Salt and freshly ground black pepper to taste

¼ cup all-purpose flour

2 tablespoons extra-virgin olive oil

1 tablespoon finely chopped fresh parsley or chives

4 tablespoons (½ stick) unsalted butter

3 large garlic cloves, minced

¾ cup dry white wine

3 tablespoons fresh lemon juice

1. Place the chicken breasts, one at a time, between two sheets of plastic wrap and pound to ¼-inch thickness. (Alternatively, you can halve each breast horizontally, or butterfly them, as described on page 78.) Season both sides with salt and pepper. Dredge the chicken in the flour, patting off the excess.

2. Heat the olive oil in a large skillet over medium-high heat until it shimmers. Add the chicken (in batches, if necessary) and cook, turning once, until cooked through (internal temperature 165°F), 6 to 8 minutes (reduce the heat to medium if the meat browns too quickly). Transfer the chicken to a platter, sprinkle with the parsley, and cover with foil to keep warm.

3. Drain off any fat from the skillet. Add 1 tablespoon of the butter to the skillet; when melted, add the garlic and sauté until fragrant, about 30 seconds. Add the wine and lemon juice; stir with a whisk to loosen any browned bits from the bottom of the pan. Bring to a boil and boil until the liquid is reduced by half—this should take 2 to 3 minutes, depending on the heat and your pan size. Reduce the heat to low and whisk in the remaining 3 tablespoons butter, 1 tablespoon at a time, to thicken the sauce. Arrange the chicken on four dinner plates, spoon the sauce over the chicken, and serve.

Chicken Calvados

Calvados is the famous apple brandy of Normandy, and the French cooks of Normandy often use the spirit to flavor their cooking. But don't feel you have to buy a bottle of the real thing for this recipe. If there's an apple brandy made in your region, reach for that over Calvados. As for the apples, use the best locally grown apples you can find. After all, the more local your products, the more true-to-France your cooking will be.   **Makes 4 servings**

4 boneless, skinless chicken breast halves (about 1¼ pounds total)

Salt and freshly ground black pepper to taste

1 tablespoon unsalted butter

1 large shallot, finely chopped (about ¼ cup)

½ cup low-sodium chicken broth

½ cup dry white wine

¼ cup Calvados or apple brandy

2 small tart apples, cored and cut into ¼-inch slices

½ cup heavy cream, plus more if needed

2 tablespoons snipped fresh parsley or chives, or a combination

1. Place the chicken breasts, one at a time, between two sheets of plastic wrap and pound to ¼-inch thickness. (Alternatively, you can halve each breast horizontally, or butterfly them, as described on page 78.) Season both sides with salt and pepper.

2. In a large skillet, melt the butter over medium-high heat. Add the chicken (in batches, if necessary) and cook, turning once, until cooked through (internal temperature 165°F), 6 to 8 minutes (reduce the heat to medium if the meat browns too quickly). Transfer the chicken to a platter and cover with foil to keep warm.

3. Stir in the shallot and sauté briefly, until translucent. Remove the pan from the heat and carefully add the broth, wine, and Calvados.

Return the pan to the heat and bring to a boil, stirring with a wire whisk to loosen any browned bits from the bottom of the pan. Add the apples. Let the mixture boil until the liquid is reduced to ½ cup, turning the apples occasionally—this should take about 4 minutes, depending on the heat and your pan size.

4. Stir in ½ cup cream and boil until the sauce thickens and the apples are crisp-tender. For a creamier sauce, add more cream, 1 tablespoon at a time, and continue to boil until the sauce thickens to the desired consistency. Season the sauce with additional salt and pepper. Arrange the chicken on four dinner plates, spoon the sauce and apples over the chicken, sprinkle with the parsley, and serve.

Filet (or Faux Filet)
with Cherry and Red Wine Sauce

For a special occasion, a French cook might pick up a couple of *tournedos* (beef tenderloins) from the butcher shop. But a great option for a Tuesday night meal is a *faux filet* (false fillet), a cut that comes from the section right next to the tenderloin but isn't as tender—or as expensive. In my experience, American cuts that stand in best for a *faux filet* include top sirloin and top loin (strip) steaks, though the French versions are usually cut thinner.

While a sirloin may not have the divine tenderness and melt-in-the-mouth appeal of filet mignon, it can be a chic little piece when you dress it up with this sweet-tart pan sauce.   **Makes 4 servings**

---

4 (6-ounce) sirloin, top loin, or tenderloin steaks (1 inch thick)

Salt and freshly ground black pepper to taste

3 tablespoons unsalted butter

1 large shallot, finely chopped (about ¼ cup)

¾ cup low-sodium beef broth

¾ cup dry red wine

⅓ cup dried tart cherries

1 tablespoon balsamic vinegar

1 tablespoon fresh thyme leaves

1. Season both sides of the steaks with salt and pepper. In a large skillet, melt 1 tablespoon of the butter over medium-high heat. Add the steaks and cook, turning as needed, to the desired doneness (10 to 12 minutes for medium [145°F]); reduce the heat as necessary if the meat browns too quickly. Transfer steaks to a platter and cover with foil to keep warm.

2. Add the shallot to the skillet and sauté briefly, until translucent. Add the beef broth and red wine to the pan and cook, stirring with a whisk to loosen any browned bits from the bottom of the pan. Add the cherries and vinegar and bring to a boil. Boil until the liquid is reduced to ¾ cup—this should take 4 to 5 minutes, depending on the heat and your pan size. Whisk in the remaining 2 tablespoons butter, 1 tablespoon at a time. Stir in the thyme. Season the sauce with additional salt and pepper.

3. Divide the steaks among four dinner plates, spoon the sauce over the steaks, and serve.

Sauté, Deglaze, and Serve: The Basics

A few minor tricks and thoughts to keep in mind when you cook the recipes in this chapter:

Think *mise en place*. This term, meaning "put in place," comes by way of professional chefs, and the step is essential here. That is, get all of your ingredients measured and ready to go before you start cooking. Once the sauté part is complete, the deglaze and serve steps go really fast.

Pan size is critical. If your pan is too large, the drippings will burn, which will make your pan sauce dark-colored and bitter. If your pan is too small, the meat won't brown nicely. I generally call for a large skillet, but look at your meat, then look at your pans, and decide which one will best accommodate the pieces of meat in one layer without too much space between them. I find that for four servings of chicken breasts, a 12-inch skillet is ideal.

If you do burn your pan drippings—and it happens to the best of us—scrape the burned drippings away, discarding anything black. Melt a tablespoon of butter in the pan to replace the fat you've lost, then proceed with the recipe. It may not be perfect, but it will still be very good.

Avoid overbrowning meat. If you find that your meat is browning too quickly (that is, getting dark brown on the outside before cooking through on the inside), reduce the heat a tad. It also helps to shift the pieces around in the pan a bit while they're cooking.

Stock up on aluminum foil. When tightly covered with foil, the meats you sauté will stay warm for quite some time—at least as long as it takes you to make your pan sauce. The standing time also allows the juices to redistribute throughout the meat, making for a more succulent outcome.

Not enough sauce? The phone rings or something else distracts you and, suddenly, the sauce has reduced too much; you're left with a syrupy spoonful in the pan. If this happens, stir in 1/2 cup wine, chicken broth, or water and let it boil down a little. Add a tablespoon of cream or butter if it still seems dry.

Cooking for two? Use half the amount of meat called for, but make the entire amount of sauce. It can be tricky to reduce such small amounts of liquid; plus, no one will complain about extra sauce!

Flank Steak with *Beurre au Choix*

Here, instead of making a sauce in the pan, you simply top a cooked steak with *beurre au choix*—your choice of one of the flavored butters here. The warm steak melts the butter and wilts the herbs just a little bit, making a kind of sauce. Best of all, you can keep the butter in the freezer and have a bistro-quality dish any time. **Makes 4 servings**

FOR THE LEMON-HERB BUTTER:

8 tablespoons (1 stick) unsalted butter, softened

4 tablespoons snipped fresh *fines herbes* (see page 164) or snipped fresh parsley and chives

½ teaspoon freshly grated lemon zest

4 teaspoons fresh lemon juice

Salt and freshly ground black pepper to taste

FOR THE STEAK:

1 flank steak (1¼ pounds)

Salt and freshly ground black pepper to taste

1 tablespoon extra-virgin olive oil

1. Make the lemon-herb butter: In a medium-size bowl, combine the butter, *fines herbes*, lemon zest, lemon juice, and salt and pepper; blend well. Spoon the butter onto a piece of plastic wrap and wrap the plastic around the butter, shaping it into a log. Twist the ends of the wrap to seal. Refrigerate the butter until firm and use within 2 days, or freeze for up to 2 months.

2. Season both sides of the steak with salt and pepper. In a large skillet over medium-high heat, heat the olive oil until shimmering. Add the steak and brown quickly on both sides; reduce the heat to medium and continue to cook the meat, turning occasionally, to the desired doneness (10 to 12 minutes for medium [145°F]). Transfer the steak to a cutting board, cover with foil, and let stand for 5 minutes.

3. Thinly slice the steak across the grain. Divide the steak among four dinner plates, top with slices of lemon-herb butter, and serve. Alternatively, you can present the steak and lemon-herb butter on a platter and allow diners to serve themselves. Freeze any leftover butter for later use.

Variations

Blue Cheese and Pine Nut Butter. Combine 8 tablespoons (1 stick) softened unsalted butter, ½ cup crumbled blue cheese, 2 tablespoons toasted and cooled pine nuts, and salt and freshly ground black pepper to taste; blend well. Shape and chill as directed in step 1 above.

Anchovy-Garlic Butter. Combine 8 tablespoons (1 stick) softened unsalted butter, 1 tablespoon fresh lemon juice, 2 teaspoons anchovy paste, 2 minced garlic cloves, and salt and freshly ground black pepper to taste; blend well. Shape and chill as directed in step 1 above.

Garlic-Chive Butter. Combine 8 tablespoons (1 stick) softened unsalted butter, 4 minced garlic cloves, 4 tablespoons snipped fresh chives, and salt and freshly ground black pepper to taste; blend well. Shape and chill as directed in step 1 above.

Steak with Brandy and Mustard Sauce

This classic French dish reminds me of something one might have ordered in the sort of elegant, old-school French restaurant of generations past. Consider it retro-romantic, but like many great French classics, it is *so* worth revisiting. Here it is served with Pan-Fried Potatoes (page 168) and Green Beans with Shallots (page 172). **Makes 4 servings**

4 (6-ounce) top loin or tenderloin steaks (1 inch thick)

Salt and freshly ground black pepper to taste

3 tablespoons unsalted butter

1 large shallot, finely chopped (about ¼ cup)

¾ cup low-sodium beef broth

½ cup brandy

1 tablespoon Dijon mustard

1 teaspoon Worcestershire sauce

2 tablespoons snipped fresh parsley

1. Season both sides of the steaks with salt and pepper. In a large skillet, melt 1 tablespoon of the butter over medium-high heat. Add the steaks and cook, turning as needed, to the desired doneness (10 to 12 minutes for medium [145°F]); reduce the heat as necessary if the meat browns too quickly. Transfer the steaks to a platter and cover with foil to keep warm.

2. Add the shallot to the skillet and sauté briefly, until translucent. Remove the pan from the heat and add the broth and the brandy, taking care not to let the liquid spatter.

Return the pan to the heat and bring to a boil, stirring with a whisk to loosen any browned bits from the bottom of the pan. Boil until the liquid is reduced to ½ cup—this should take 2 to 3 minutes, depending on the heat and your pan size. Whisk in the mustard and Worcestershire sauce. Whisk in the remaining 2 tablespoons butter. Season the sauce with additional salt and pepper, if needed.

3. Arrange the steaks on four dinner plates, spoon the sauce over the steaks, sprinkle with the parsley, and serve.

Some Thoughts on Butter

You may raise an eyebrow at the use of butter in so many of the recipes on these pages. Rest assured, the recipes don't call for nearly as much butter (or cream) as this style of cooking traditionally did in the past. These changes were made not only for health reasons, but also because today we have such a greater variety of terrifically fresh, vivid, and interesting ingredients to use, we don't have to rely so much on cream and butter to flavor up a dish.

Still, most recipes in this chapter do call for some butter or cream, though rarely more than 1 tablespoon per person, and quite often less than that. It's worth it for the enjoyment that a touch of pure richness it adds.

Lamb Chops with Olives and Garlic

Among the most joyful and colorful spots at the morning markets in the south of France, olive stands rank right up there with the flowers. You can smell the garlic and spices of their marinades before you even spot the olives. I love getting a random handful or two, and cozying them up to lamb, another favorite south-of-France ingredient. As you'll see, the two marry beautifully together—the spark of the briny olives contrasts with the rich meat. By the way, you can use any combination of green and black olives that you like best. I love Cerignolas (though they're difficult to pit), Nyons, and Niçoise, but kalamata olives are great, and on a budget, the common green manzanilla olives (sometimes called Spanish olives) will work, too. **Makes 4 servings**

8 lamb rib or loin chops (about ⅓ pound each)

Salt and freshly ground black pepper to taste

2 tablespoons extra-virgin olive oil

2 garlic cloves, minced

1 teaspoon dried thyme, crushed

½ cup dry white wine

2 tablespoons fresh lemon juice

⅓ cup pitted green olives, with or without pimientos, chopped

⅓ cup pitted imported black olives, chopped

3 tablespoons snipped fresh parsley

1. Season the chops with salt and pepper. Using a skillet that's large enough to accommodate the chops without crowding (see Note), heat 1 tablespoon of the oil over medium-high heat until shimmering. Add the chops and brown on the short sides to render the fat. Reduce the heat to medium, turn the chops onto one flat side, and cook, turning once to the other flat side, to the desired doneness (about 5 minutes per side per inch of thickness for medium [160°F]). Transfer the chops to a large serving platter and cover with foil to keep warm.

2. Pour off the fat from the skillet. Heat the remaining 1 tablespoon olive oil in the skillet. Add the garlic and thyme and cook until the garlic is fragrant, about 30 seconds. Add the white wine, taking care not to let it spatter. Bring to a boil, stirring to scrape up any browned bits from the bottom of the pan, and boil until reduced by half, about 2 minutes. Add the lemon juice, olives, and parsley; cook and stir until heated through.

3. Spoon the olive sauce evenly over the chops and serve.

Note: If necessary, use two skillets to brown the chops. Cook the olive sauce in just one of the skillets.

Pork Chops with Orange and Thyme

I once enjoyed the flavors of orange and thyme on a sumptuous roast rack of pork in a white tablecloth venue in Paris. Here, I've restyled the irresistible trio into a quick sauté that's more in the spirit of everyday French cooking. **Makes 4 servings**

4 bone-in pork loin chops
(1/2 inch thick)

Salt and freshly ground black
pepper to taste

1 tablespoon unsalted butter

1 large shallot, finely chopped
(about 1/4 cup)

1/4 cup fresh orange juice

2 tablespoons fresh lemon juice

1/2 cup heavy cream

1 tablespoon fresh thyme leaves,
or 1/2 teaspoon dried thyme,
crushed

1 teaspoon grated orange zest

1. Season both sides of the pork chops with salt and pepper. In a large skillet, melt the butter over medium-high heat. Add the pork chops, reduce the heat to medium, and cook, turning once, until done (internal temperature 145°F), 6 to 8 minutes. Transfer the pork chops to a platter and cover with foil to keep warm.

2. Add the shallot to the pan and sauté briefly, until translucent. Add the orange and lemon juices, stirring with a wire whisk to loosen any browned bits from the bottom of the pan. Bring to a boil and boil until the liquid is nearly gone—this should take just a minute or two, depending on the heat and your pan size. Whisk in the cream. Boil until the sauce reaches the desired consistency. Season the sauce with salt and pepper. Whisk in the thyme and orange zest.

3. Divide the chops among four dinner plates, spoon the sauce over the chops, and serve.

Shallots in the French Kitchen

Most French cooks I've met have a basket of shallots (les échalotes) in their kitchens. Somewhat oniony, somewhat garlicky, and a little bit mellow like leeks, shallots add great aroma and flavor to a sauce; in these recipes, they're about as essential as salt and pepper.

However, if you find yourself bereft of shallots, use a combination of yellow onion and garlic. For each 1/4 cup finely chopped shallots called for, use 1/4 cup finely chopped onion and 2 minced garlic cloves. It's not exactly the same, but it will still be very good.

Pork Chops with Mustard Sauce

This is the sort of simple but slightly refined dish you'd spot as a *plat du jour* on a 15-euro menu in some charming little town you happened to pass through during lunchtime in the French countryside. You might forget the name of the town, but you'd always remember how tickled you were at finding such a simple, satisfying dish in the proverbial middle of nowhere—such is traveling the back roads of France. Be sure to also try the variations—the Mustard-Caper Sauce (shown opposite) is one of my favorites in this chapter.   **Makes 4 servings**

4 bone-in pork loin chops (½ inch thick)

Salt and freshly ground black pepper to taste

1 tablespoon extra-virgin olive oil

1 large shallot, finely chopped (about ¼ cup)

¾ cup low-sodium chicken broth

¾ cup dry white wine

1 tablespoon Dijon mustard

2 tablespoons unsalted butter

1 tablespoon heavy cream (optional)

2 tablespoons snipped fresh parsley

1. Season both sides of the pork chops with salt and pepper. In a large skillet, heat the oil over medium-high heat until it shimmers. Add the pork chops, reduce the heat to medium, and cook, turning once, until done (internal temperature 145°F), 6 to 8 minutes. Transfer the pork chops to a platter and cover with foil to keep warm.

2. Drain off all but a sheen of fat from the skillet. Add the shallot to the pan and sauté briefly, until translucent. Add the broth and the wine to the skillet, stirring with a whisk to loosen any browned bits from the bottom of the pan. Bring to a boil and boil until the liquid is reduced to ¾ cup, 4 to 5 minutes. Whisk in the mustard and butter. Bring to a boil and whisk in the cream (if you like) and the parsley. Boil until the sauce reaches the desired consistency.

3. Divide the chops among four dinner plates, spoon the sauce over the chops, and serve.

Variations

Pork Chops with *Cornichon*-Mustard Sauce. Stir ¼ cup julienned *cornichons* into the finished sauce and gently heat through.

Pork Chops with Mustard-Caper Sauce. Add ¼ teaspoon crushed dried *herbes de Provence* when you add the shallot. Stir ¼ cup drained capers into the finished sauce.

Pork Medallions with Apricot-Sage Sauce

We think of thyme and rosemary as Provençal herbs, and tarragon as ultra-French in general. Yet sage also has a prominent spot in French home cooking—especially as a flavoring for pork. And you may be shocked by how good sage tastes with the flavors of apricot. The sweetness of the fruit diminishes the herb's mustiness, bringing its more peppery spark to life. In fact, for a dish that sounds rather straightforward, the flavors, when combined, emerge as quite extraordinary. And while substituting dried herbs for fresh can work in some instances, it's not the case here—fresh sage leaves are a must.

This sauce works equally well served over four bone-in pork chops; just cook the chops 6 to 8 minutes per ½ inch, turning once; after the chops have cooked, drain off the excess fat, if necessary. **Makes 4 servings**

---

1 (1- to 1¼-pound) pork tenderloin, cut into ½-inch-thick medallions (see Note)

Salt and freshly ground black pepper to taste

2 tablespoons unsalted butter

1 small shallot, finely chopped (about 2 tablespoons)

¾ cup low-sodium chicken broth

¾ cup dry white wine

¼ cup apricot preserves

2 tablespoons snipped fresh sage leaves

1. Pat the pork medallions dry with paper towels and season both sides with salt and pepper. In a large skillet, melt 1 tablespoon of the butter over medium-high heat. Add the medallions, reduce the heat to medium, and cook, turning once, until done (internal temperature 145°F), 6 to 8 minutes. (Do not crowd the medallions—if needed, cook them in two batches to allow them to brown nicely.) Transfer the medallions to a platter and cover with foil to keep warm.

2. Add the shallot to the pan and sauté briefly, until translucent. Add the chicken broth and the wine to the pan. Bring to a boil, stirring with a whisk to loosen any browned bits from the bottom of the pan. Boil until the liquid is reduced to ½ cup—this should take 4 to 5 minutes, depending on the heat and your pan size. Add the remaining 1 tablespoon butter, the apricot preserves, and the sage and whisk until the preserves are melted. Season the sauce with additional salt and pepper.

3. Divide the pork medallions among four dinner plates, spoon the sauce over the medallions, and serve.

Note: Try to find a naturally raised, hormone-free pork tenderloin—it will have so much more flavor than the average supermarket variety.

Poisson Meunière

Here, in one of the all-time best ways to serve a sparkling-fresh piece of fish in minutes, we follow the lead of the proverbial miller's wife (*la meunière*). As culinary legend has it, *la meunière* was the lady with access to plenty of fish from the stream that powered her husband's flour mill, and, of course, she had plenty of flour for dredging it in, too.

Speaking of culinary lore, *sole meunière* was the first dish that Julia Child enjoyed after she disembarked from the ship on her very first trip to France in 1949. More than five decades later, toward the end of her life, this *grande dame* of French cooking in America rhapsodized about that unforgettable dish in her lovely memoir, *My Life in France.*

In this classic preparation, you quickly sauté some flour-coated fish fillets, sprinkle with parsley, then with lemon and browned butter, and serve. That's it, and the results are truly legendary. **Makes 4 servings**

4 (6- to 8-ounce) skinless white fish fillets, such as haddock, halibut, grouper, sole, flounder, or cod (½ inch thick; see Note)

Salt and freshly ground black pepper to taste

¼ cup all-purpose flour

¼ cup vegetable oil

4 tablespoons (½ stick) unsalted butter

2 tablespoons snipped fresh parsley, chives, or chervil, or a combination

2 tablespoons fresh lemon juice

1. Season both sides of each fish fillet with salt and pepper. Dredge the fillet in the flour to lightly coat, shaking off the excess. Repeat with the remaining fillets.

2. Using a skillet that's large enough to accommodate the fillets in one layer, heat the vegetable oil over medium-high heat. Add fillets and cook, turning once, until fish is golden-brown on both sides and flakes easily with a fork, about 5 minutes (reduce the heat to medium if fish browns too quickly). Transfer fish to four dinner plates.

3. Drain off any fat from the skillet and—taking care not to burn your fingers—wipe out the pan with paper towels. Add the butter and melt it over medium heat until nut-brown and frothy. Remove the pan from the heat.

4. Scatter the herbs over the fish fillets, sprinkle with lemon juice, and pour the browned butter on top. Serve immediately.

Note: Though lean white fish fillets are a classic choice, salmon also benefits from this preparation.

Fish with Buttery Parsley and Garlic

If you're not convinced that parsley deserves a place alongside basil or thyme as a serious flavor booster, try this recipe. As a quick sauce for delicate fish, its spring-green freshness just sings with butter and garlic. You'll never relegate parsley to mere garnish status again. By the way, the French call the mixture of garlic and parsley *persillade*.   **Makes 4 servings**

- **4 (6- to 8-ounce) skinless white fish fillets, such as haddock, halibut, grouper, sole, flounder, or cod (½ inch thick)**
- **Salt and freshly ground black pepper to taste**
- **¼ cup all-purpose flour**
- **2 tablespoons vegetable oil**
- **2 tablespoons unsalted butter**
- **¼ cup snipped fresh parsley**
- **2 garlic cloves, minced**

1. Season both sides of the fillets with salt and pepper. Dredge the fillets in the flour to lightly coat, shaking off the excess. In a large nonstick skillet, heat the oil over medium-high heat until it shimmers. Add the fillets and cook, turning once, until the fish is golden-brown on both sides and flakes easily with a fork, about 5 minutes (reduce the heat to medium if the fish browns too quickly). Transfer the fillets to a platter.

2. Drain off any fat from the skillet and—taking care not to burn your fingers—wipe out the pan with paper towels. Lower the heat to medium. Melt the butter in the skillet and add the parsley and garlic; cook for 1 minute, without letting the garlic brown.

3. Spoon the parsley and garlic mixture over the fish and serve.

Sauté, Deglaze, and Serve—Discovered

My love for the sauté-deglaze-serve way of cooking matured in France, but it had more humble origins during my salad days in Brooklyn in the mid-1980s.

Throughout the five years I lived in New York City, I never missed the Wednesday food pages of the *New York Times*, as that's when Pierre Franey's "60-Minute Gourmet" column would run.

Each week, Franey would offer one main course and one side dish that, together, could be put on the table within 60 minutes. The recipes were generally French in nature—after all, French-born Franey was a classically trained chef who had overseen the kitchen of New York's esteemed Le Pavillon restaurant. Yet his recipes revealed an everyday-easy side of French cooking that most cooks never imagined they could pull off so simply and beautifully at home.

Franey never called for ingredients that I couldn't find in my not-so-posh neighborhood in Brooklyn. I could read his column on the subway home and figure out my shopping list; then, on the way from the subway to my apartment, I would stop at the butcher or fish market, the greengrocer, and the wine shop. Once home, I'd have dinner on the table in 60 minutes—usually less.

As I cooked from Franey's columns, I began to notice that many of his dishes were variations on the same theme: You'd sauté the meat, deglaze the pan with a liquid, stir in a few extra touches, and serve. It was so easy, but so good.

In subsequent years, when I'd summer in France, again and again I'd come upon fresh, vivid meals made using the same sort of technique. Whether in the homes of French families, in humble corner bistros, or in charming *maman-et-papa* inns, I was never disappointed; in fact, I was delighted by the wide range of flavor that could be wrought through this simple approach.

When I started cooking in the summer apartments I'd lease in France, I'd follow that approach for many of the meals I made. After all, who wants to spend time cooking when there's café dwelling and beach hopping to do? And yet, it was France, where we came to eat well. With sauté-deglaze-serve cooking, we did.

Many of the recipes on these pages are simply classics—it just wouldn't do to leave out Pork Chops with Mustard Sauce (page 92), *Poisson Meunière* (page 95), or Steak with Brandy and Mustard Sauce (page 89). Others are my takes on ideas I've spotted in France or in French cookbooks and cooking magazines or in bistro-style restaurants. Still others I've come up with through heading to the market, seeing what looked good, and bringing it home with the sauté-deglaze-serve style of cooking in mind.

All point the way to getting a modern, true-to-France meal on the table in minutes.

Trout "Ménage à Trois"

A tip I gleaned while eating in France is that sometimes the less celery you use, the better it tastes. In this dish, consider it almost like an herb. It makes a delightful *ménage à trois* when combined with the mellow browned garlic and rich pistachios   **Makes 2 servings**

2 (8-ounce) boned, pan-dressed trout (heads and tails removed)

Salt and freshly ground black pepper to taste

¼ cup all-purpose flour

5 tablespoons extra-virgin olive oil, plus more if needed

½ cup very thinly sliced celery

3 large garlic cloves, thinly sliced

1 tablespoon snipped fresh parsley

2 tablespoons pistachio nuts, coarsely chopped

¼ teaspoon red pepper flakes (optional)

1. Rinse the trout and pat dry. Spread each trout open and season both sides with salt and pepper. Dredge each trout in the flour to lightly coat, shaking off the excess. In a large skillet, heat 3 tablespoons of the olive oil over medium-high heat until it shimmers. Add the trout, skin side down, and cook, turning once, until the fish is golden and flakes easily with a fork, about 7 minutes (reduce the heat to medium if the fish browns too quickly). Transfer to a platter. (If your skillet is not large enough to hold two trout, cook one at a time; transfer the first cooked trout to a warm ovenproof platter and keep it warm in a 300°F oven while the second cooks. Add more oil to the pan if needed.)

2. Taking care not to burn your fingers, wipe out the pan with paper towels. Add the remaining 2 tablespoons olive oil and heat over medium heat. Add the celery and garlic and cook until the celery is tender and the garlic is golden brown, 2 to 3 minutes. Add the parsley and cook briefly. Add the pistachios and, if you like, the red pepper flakes. Spoon the garnish over the trout and serve.

Fish with Mushroom-Saffron Cream

Saffron is as expensive for the French cook as it is for an American cook; even so, it's worth calling on a pinch here or there for elegant meals. In most recipes, this luxury ingredient is used to flavor the most delicate foods, such as fish and shellfish; that way, the little pinch can make a notable impact, as it does here. While you can easily double this recipe for four, I prefer to make this for two—it's a great dish for romance.   **Makes 2 servings**

1/4 **cup heavy cream**

Small pinch of saffron, crushed

12 **to** 16 **ounces skinless white fish fillets, such as halibut, haddock, grouper, sole, flounder, or cod**

Salt and freshly ground black pepper to taste

1/4 **cup all-purpose flour**

3 **tablespoons vegetable oil**

1 **tablespoon unsalted butter**

1/2 **cup thinly sliced fresh mushrooms**

1 **tablespoon finely chopped shallot**

1. Heat the cream to steaming in a small saucepan over low heat. Remove from the heat and stir in the saffron; set aside to infuse for 30 minutes.

2. Season both sides of each fish fillet with salt and pepper. Dredge each fillet in the flour to lightly coat on both sides, shaking off the excess. In a medium skillet, heat the vegetable oil over medium-high heat until it shimmers. Add the fish and cook, turning once, until the fish is golden and flakes easily with a fork, about

5 minutes total per half inch of thickness. Transfer to a platter.

3. Taking care not to burn your fingers, wipe out the skillet with paper towels. Add the butter and melt over medium heat. Add the mushrooms and shallot; cook until the mushrooms are tender, 2 to 3 minutes. Add the saffron cream and bring to a boil; boil until the sauce reaches the desired consistency. Season the sauce with additional salt and pepper. Spoon the sauce over the fish and serve.

Shrimp *Verte*

There are countless everyday French recipes for sautéed shrimp with fresh herbs, but the ones I enjoy most are those in which the herbs are used in abundance. The spring-green windfall provides an intensely fresh and vivid foil for the rich, sweet shrimp—not to mention a beautiful bright green color to complement the pretty pink seafood. Here it is served with Glazed Carrots the French Way (page 169) and Any-Night Baked Rice (page 163). **Makes 4 servings**

½ **cup extra-virgin olive oil**

2 **scallions (white portion and some tender green tops), minced**

1 **small shallot, chopped (about 2 tablespoons)**

½ **cup snipped fresh parsley**

2 **tablespoons snipped fresh chives**

⅛ **teaspoon ground cayenne pepper**

Salt and freshly ground black pepper to taste

1½ **pounds jumbo shrimp, peeled and deveined**

1 **tablespoon unsalted butter**

1. Combine the olive oil, scallions, shallot, parsley, chives, cayenne, and salt and pepper in a blender or food processor; process until everything is finely chopped. Place the marinade in a large bowl. Add the shrimp and toss to coat. Cover; refrigerate for 1 to 2 hours to meld the flavors.

2. Heat a large skillet over medium-high heat; add the shrimp and all of the marinade; cook, stirring, until the shrimp is opaque throughout, about 5 minutes. Remove from heat; stir in butter until melted. Serve the shrimp with the sauce drizzled over.

A Word About French Pan Sauces

French pan sauces are usually thin but intense. That's because they have not been thickened with flour or cornstarch, which can plump up a sauce but mask its flavors. In these sauces, you'll taste pure flavor—the brightness of the herbs, the depth brought by the pan drippings, the intensity of reduced wine, and the richness of a pat or two of butter all combine for a powerhouse of flavor that cornstarch-thickened sauces usually don't have. In fact, beware of restaurants that serve plumped-up sauces on *piccata* and *marsala* dishes—they may look richer (thanks to thickeners and stabilizers), but they're often lacking in flavor intensity compared to the sauces you make at home.

BRAISE, STEW, OR ROAST

Many recipes in the French cook's repertoire call for braising, stewing, or roasting the meat, often as a way to turn less-expensive cuts into bold and succulent dishes. These recipes include some classic braises, stews, and roasts, such as *boeuf bourguignon*, *coq au vin*, and *choucroute garnie*, as well as lesser-known ways—both classic and modern—to call on these beloved cooking techniques.

OPPOSITE: Beef Stew with Orange and Balsamic Vinegar, page 125

Basque-Style Chicken

Tomatoes, onions, *jambon de Bayonne*, and *piment d'Espelette* are the hallmark ingredients of this lively, classic *plat mijoté* (simmered dish), which I discovered when traveling through France's Basque region. *Piment d'Espelette* is a mild, smoky-sweet red pepper that gets ground into a paprika-like powder. If you can't find it at a gourmet shop, a little paprika and a pinch of cayenne pepper make an admirable stand-in—especially with roasted red peppers in the mix to add some sweetness. As for the *jambon de Bayonne*, that's France's answer to *prosciutto di Parma*. Simply use a good-quality prosciutto. **Makes 4 servings**

8 bone-in, skin-on chicken thighs

Salt and freshly ground black pepper to taste

3 tablespoons extra-virgin olive oil

1 medium-size onion, halved and sliced

6 garlic cloves, minced

½ cup sweet vermouth

½ cup low-sodium chicken broth

1 (14.5-ounce) can whole tomatoes, drained and puréed in a food processor

½ teaspoon dried thyme, crushed

½ teaspoon *piment d'Espelette*, or ½ teaspoon Spanish paprika and ⅛ teaspoon cayenne pepper

1 (7-ounce) jar roasted red bell peppers, drained and thinly sliced (about 1 cup)

¼ cup thinly sliced prosciutto or *jambon de Bayonne* (about 1 ounce)

1. Season the chicken thighs with salt and pepper. Heat 2 tablespoons of the olive oil in a Dutch oven or braiser over medium-high heat until it shimmers; add the chicken and cook, turning occasionally, until brown on all sides, 10 to 15 minutes (reduce the heat to medium if the chicken browns too quickly). Transfer the chicken to a plate. Drain off all but 1 tablespoon of fat from the pan.

2. Reduce the heat to medium and add the onion. Cook, stirring, until tender, 4 to 5 minutes; add the garlic and cook, stirring, until fragrant, about 30 seconds more. Remove the pan from the heat and add the vermouth and chicken broth, taking care not to let the liquid spatter. Return the pan to the heat and cook, stirring to loosen any browned bits from the bottom of the pan. Return the chicken to the pan, skin side up, and add the puréed tomatoes, thyme, and *piment d'Espelette*. Bring to a boil and then reduce the heat. Cover and simmer until the internal temperature of the chicken registers 180°F on an instant-read thermometer, 30 to 35 minutes. Add the sliced roasted red peppers about 5 minutes before the end of the cooking time.

3. Meanwhile, heat the remaining 1 tablespoon oil in a small skillet until it shimmers. Add the prosciutto and cook, stirring, until crisp, 1 to 2 minutes. With a slotted spoon, remove the prosciutto from the pan and drain on paper towels.

4. With a slotted spoon, divide the chicken and peppers among four shallow bowls. Boil the pan sauce over medium-high heat until it reduces to the desired consistency. Top the chicken with the sauce, sprinkle with the crisped prosciutto, and serve.

Vermouth-Braised Chicken
with Black Olives and Prosciutto

Though vermouth is wine-based, when you add vermouth to a recipe, you add much more than wine. Vermouth is made with all kinds of herbs, spices, and other flavorings. Noilly Prat, for example—a famous vermouth from the Languedoc region in the south of France—combines chamomile, coriander, bitter orange peel, and nutmeg, as well as other non-divulged ingredients. It's a secret weapon in the French cook's kitchen (and, conveniently, it keeps well in the refrigerator).

It's interesting that I've seen French recipes that call for Noilly Prat by name (not "vermouth," and not even "Noilly Prat vermouth"—just Noilly Prat, period). I sense that these French recipe writers are subtly saying, "Use a French vermouth." Noilly Prat is indeed excellent, but I've successfully made this dish with Italian vermouths, too.

If you really want to underscore this recipe's South-of-France angle, go to a gourmet market with an olive bar and purchase a variety, including France's wrinkly-skinned Nyons olives. If you get a few green olives in the mix, *tant mieux*—so much the better! **Makes 4 servings**

---

8 bone-in, skin-on chicken thighs

Salt and freshly ground black pepper to taste

2 tablespoons extra-virgin olive oil

½ cup finely chopped onion

1 tablespoon minced garlic

½ cup dry vermouth

½ cup low-sodium chicken broth

1 teaspoon dried *herbes de Provence*, crushed

1 tablespoon grated lemon zest

3 tablespoons fresh lemon juice

½ cup pitted imported black olives, such as Nyons and Niçoise

¼ cup thinly sliced prosciutto or cooked and crumbled pancetta (about 1 ounce)

1. Preheat the oven to 350°F.

2. Season the chicken thighs with salt and pepper. Heat the olive oil in an ovenproof Dutch oven or braiser over medium-high heat; add the chicken and cook, turning occasionally, until brown on all sides, 10 to 15 minutes (reduce the heat to medium if the chicken browns too quickly). Transfer the chicken to a plate and drain off all but a sheen of fat from the pan.

3. Reduce the heat to medium and add the onion. Cook, stirring, until the onion is tender, about 3 minutes; add the garlic and cook, stirring, until fragrant, about 30 seconds more. Remove the pan from the heat and add the vermouth and chicken broth, taking care not to let the liquid spatter. Return the pan

to the heat and bring to a boil; boil, stirring with a wire whisk to loosen any browned bits from the bottom of the pan, until reduced by about ¼ cup, about 1 minute. Stir in the *herbes de Provence*, lemon zest, and lemon juice.

4. Return the chicken to the pan; cover and transfer to the oven. Bake for 20 minutes. Uncover; add the olives and sprinkle the prosciutto on top of the chicken. Re-cover, return to the oven, and bake until the internal temperature of the chicken registers 180°F on an instant-read thermometer, about 15 minutes more.

5. Divide the chicken, olives, and prosciutto bits among four shallow bowls, pour a spoonful of sauce over each, and serve.

Coq au Vin Assez Rapide

Chicken with wine is one of those special dishes I've found everywhere in my travels through Burgundy. Classic *coq au vin* can be fussy and time-consuming, as some recipes call for marinating the chicken in wine overnight and peeling a lot of *petits oignons* (here, frozen pearl onions are just so much easier). This *assez rapide* (pretty quick) recipe gets right to the heart of the classic dish without a lot of fuss.

Serve the chicken with Any-Night Baked Rice (page 163). Follow the main course with a tartly dressed green salad and a few slices of *fromage* for a classic cheese course. And end with something refreshing, like a scoop of ice cream and a scoop of sorbet accompanied by a few *Sablés* (page 218).   **Makes 6 servings**

---

3 to 4 pounds bone-in, skin-on chicken breast halves and/or thighs

Salt and freshly ground black pepper to taste

½ cup plus 2 tablespoons all-purpose flour

4 slices bacon, cut into ½-inch pieces

1 tablespoon vegetable oil

1 medium-size carrot, peeled and diced

3 large shallots, thinly sliced (about ¾ cup)

4 garlic cloves, minced

2 cups cru Beaujolais, such as Beaujolais Villages, Moulin-à-Vent, Fleurie, Morgon, or Brouilly (not Beaujolais Nouveau); you can also use Pinot Noir

1 cup low-sodium chicken broth, plus more if needed

1 tablespoon snipped fresh parsley, plus additional snipped fresh parsley or chives, or a combination, for the garnish

½ teaspoon dried thyme, crushed

1 bay leaf

1½ cups frozen pearl onions

3 tablespoons unsalted butter

8 ounces fresh mushrooms, stems trimmed, left whole if small, quartered or halved if larger

1. Preheat the oven to 350°F.

2. Season the chicken with salt and pepper. Dredge the chicken in ½ cup of the flour, pat off the excess, and set aside. Cook the bacon in a braiser or oven-safe Dutch oven over medium heat until crisp; remove with a slotted spoon and drain on paper towels. Add the vegetable oil to the bacon fat left in the braiser; heat over medium-high heat until it shimmers. Add the chicken and cook, turning occasionally, until brown on all sides, 10 to 15 minutes (reduce the heat to medium if the chicken browns too quickly). Transfer the chicken to a plate and pour off all but 2 tablespoons of fat from the braiser.

3. Reduce the heat to medium. Add the carrot and shallots to the braiser; cook, stirring, until the carrots soften somewhat and the shallots are tender, about 4 minutes. Add the garlic and cook, stirring, until fragrant, about 30 seconds more. Add the wine and chicken broth and bring to a boil, stirring to loosen any browned bits from the bottom of the pan. Add the parsley, thyme, and bay leaf. Return the chicken, skin side up, to the braiser and add the bacon.

4. Cover the braiser and transfer to the oven. Bake until the chicken is tender and cooked through (the internal temperature should register 170°F for breasts, 180°F for thighs), about 1 hour.

5. About 15 minutes before the end of the cooking time, cook the frozen pearl onions in a large saucepan according to the package directions. Drain and leave in the colander. In the same saucepan, melt 1 tablespoon of the butter over medium-high heat; add the mushrooms and cook, stirring, until tender and lightly browned, 4 to 5 minutes. Return the onions to the pan. Remove the pan from the heat and cover to keep warm.

6. With a slotted spoon, transfer the chicken pieces to a large platter; cover with foil to keep warm. Discard the bay leaf. Pour the juices and solids from the braiser into a large measuring cup and skim off the fat. You want a total of 2 cups of liquid, including the bacon, carrot, shallots, and garlic in the liquid. If you have more, boil the liquid in the pot over medium-high heat until reduced to 2 cups. If you have less, add additional chicken broth to make 2 cups, return the liquid to the pot, and bring to a boil.

7. In a small bowl, mix the remaining 2 tablespoons butter and 2 tablespoons flour together to make a paste (a *beurre manié*). Add the *beurre manié* bit by bit to the cooking liquid, stirring with a wire whisk to blend away any lumps. Cook, stirring, until the mixture boils and thickens, then continue to cook and stir for 2 minutes more. Add the onions and mushrooms and heat through.

8. Divide the chicken among six shallow bowls. Pour the sauce over the chicken, dividing the bacon, mushrooms, and onions evenly. Top each serving with a sprinkling of parsley and/or chives and serve.

Braise, Stew, or Roast: The Basics

Here are a few thoughts to keep in mind as you cook your way through the recipes in this chapter.

BRAISING AND STEWING

Use the cut called for: Braising and stewing were invented for tough, unwieldy, and often nicely marbled cuts. Substituting another cut—especially a more tender cut—may not work. For example, if you use beef tenderloin in a stewing recipe, you won't be doing either the stew or the tenderloin a favor—the meat will become stringy and dry.

Brown in batches, if needed: Appetizingly browned meat is part of the appeal of these dishes. Be sure to pat the meat dry before the browning process and avoid overcrowding the pan with the meat—depending on how wide the base of your pan is, you may need to brown the meat in batches. Overcrowded meat steams rather than browns.

Use a tight-fitting lid: If steam escapes, you'll lose too much liquid—and it's the moist heat from the liquid that brings out the flavor and tenderness of the meat.

Go low and slow: Check the dish once in a while to make sure the liquid is simmering, not boiling—slow cooking is the key to delectable results. Even tight-fitting lids can let steam escape if the liquid is rapidly boiling, and you don't want any extra liquid to evaporate. However, don't lift the lid any more than needed or you'll lose heat and steam.

ROASTING

Use the specific meat called for: Roasting works best for tender meats—save tougher cuts for braising and stewing.

Preheat the oven as directed: This helps the interior of the meat get done before the exterior gets overdone.

Use a meat thermometer: Timing for roasted meat and poultry, in my experience, is less exact than for other cooking methods. My recipes offer a range for the timing; be sure to check the meat's internal temperature with an instant-read meat thermometer at the beginning of the range. If more roasting is needed, remove and wash the thermometer well, then check the meat periodically as needed until the temperature has risen to the recommended doneness.

Allow cooked meats to stand: When specified in the recipe, let the meat stand after roasting and before serving. This helps the juices distribute throughout the flesh, resulting in moister results. Keep in mind that the internal temperature of the meat will continue to rise about 5 degrees during this standing time.

Poulet Bijoutière

I call this dish "the jeweler's chicken" not just because it's rich, but because of its beautiful ruby-garnet color, contributed by the pomegranate juice. This amazing ingredient has a deep flavor that's brightened with just a hint of astringency—think of it, poetically, like the sparkle in a dark-colored ruby. If you really want the dish to glitter, sprinkle on some glistening pomegranate seeds when you serve it.

Do French cooks use pomegranate juice? Yes, and they call it *jus de grenade*. If that sounds a little like *grenadine*, there's a reason for that. The famous cocktail syrup was originally made from pomegranates from the island of Grenada. (But don't substitute that sweet cocktail syrup for the real juice in this recipe.) **Makes 4 servings**

---

8 bone-in, skin-on chicken thighs

Salt and freshly ground black pepper to taste

5 garlic cloves, crushed

2 tablespoons vegetable oil

4 large shallots, quartered

¼ cup semi-sweet white wine, such as an off-dry German Riesling

¾ cup pomegranate juice

¼ cup low-sodium chicken broth

2 sprigs fresh thyme, or ¼ teaspoon dried thyme, crushed

2 tablespoons red currant jelly

Hot cooked basmati rice

1. Season the chicken thighs with salt and pepper. Rub the inside of a large, deep skillet or braiser with one of the garlic cloves; discard the clove. Heat the oil in the pan over medium-high heat until it shimmers; add the chicken and cook, turning occasionally, until brown on all sides, 10 to 15 minutes (reduce the heat to medium if the chicken browns too quickly). Transfer the chicken to a plate and drain off all but a sheen of fat from the pan.

2. Reduce the heat to medium and add the remaining garlic and the shallots. Cook, stirring, until the garlic and shallots are soft and beginning to brown lightly, 1 to 2 minutes. Return the chicken to the skillet, skin side up.

3. Add the wine; stir with a whisk to loosen any browned bits from the bottom of the pan. Bring to a boil and boil briefly, until reduced by half. Add the pomegranate juice, chicken broth, and thyme and bring to a boil. Reduce the heat and simmer for 10 minutes, turning the chicken now and then so that both sides become colored by the juice.

4. Discard the thyme sprigs (if using) and stir in the red currant jelly. Continue to cook at an active simmer until the internal temperature of the chicken registers 180°F on an instant-read thermometer, 15 to 17 minutes, shifting the chicken and stirring the sauce occasionally. Stir in a tablespoon or so of water if the sauce becomes overly thick before the chicken is done (the sauce should be the consistency of a spoonable glaze).

5. Arrange two thighs on each of four dinner plates and spoon the sauce over the chicken. Serve with hot cooked rice.

Parsley in the French Kitchen

Basil is minty and clovelike; rosemary has a piney smell; tarragon reminds us of licorice. But what does parsley smell like?

Parsley is what the color green would smell like if it had a fragrance. It's a little like fresh-cut grass; or, if you closed your eyes at a farmers' market herb stand and took in all of its smells at once—basil, marjoram, watercress, mint—that would be parsley. The humble herb brings out a lot of flavor dimensions at once, yet in a mild, unobtrusive way. Perhaps that's why it's called for so much in French cooking; it can invigorate a dish in so many ways without ever becoming a monotonous, one-note flavor. It is the essence of freshness—and what dish can't benefit a little from that?

While many chefs and cooks prefer flat-leaf parsley (also known as Italian parsley) over curly-leaf parsley, both varieties are available in France, and both make their way into French home cooking. In many markets, parsley is free—a little bonus given away by vendors when you purchase fish, meat, or vegetables.

Which one should you use? I like flat-leaf parsley—it seems more intensely flavored to me. However, if curly-leaf parsley grows in abundance in your area, use it—fresh, local curly-leaf parsley trumps trucked-in, flavor-drained flat-leaf parsley any day. Especially if you've snipped it fresh from your own window box or garden.

Lemony Mustard Roast Chicken *Ce Soir*

Lapin rôti à la moutarde (rabbit roasted with mustard) is a grandmotherly French recipe at its simple, rustic best—the cook simply slathers a mixture of wine, mustard, and *crème fraîche* over rabbit pieces, then roasts them. This recipe borrows from that simple technique, omitting the *crème fraîche* and using lemon juice instead of wine for a sunny, bright-tart flavoring for chicken.

This is a good weeknight choice. Cutting the chicken in half before roasting it allows you to get it to the table in much less time than it would take to roast a whole, uncut bird. **Makes 4 servings**

---

1 (3½-pound) whole chicken

2 tablespoons fresh lemon juice

2 tablespoons extra-virgin olive oil

Salt and freshly ground black pepper to taste

2 tablespoons Dijon mustard

1. Preheat the oven to 400°F.

2. Set the chicken, breast side down, on a cutting board. Use heavy kitchen shears to cut along both sides of the backbone to remove it. Press down on both sides of the chicken to open and flatten it, then whack the breastbone with a heavy chef's knife (be careful of your fingers). Finish by cutting through the breastbone with kitchen shears. Place the chicken halves, skin side up, on a rack in a shallow roasting pan. Brush the chicken all over with the lemon juice and olive oil. Season both sides with salt and pepper.

3. Roast the chicken until an instant-read thermometer inserted in the thickest part of the thigh registers 175°F, 40 to 50 minutes (see Note). Brush the skin all over with the mustard. Roast for 5 minutes more. Remove the chicken from the oven and transfer to a cutting board; let stand for 10 minutes before carving (the temperature of the thighs should rise 5 degrees as it stands, to 180°F).

4. To serve, cut each chicken half into two pieces (to make a total of two breast/wing pieces and two thigh/leg hindquarters).

Note: Having roasted many a chicken, I find that overall roasting times can vary, depending on how thick the meat is around the bones. I give a range, but be sure to use a meat thermometer to determine doneness.

Pot-Roasted Chicken
with Mushrooms and Chervil

I came across a version of this recipe in a delightful provincial French cookbook from the 1960s that I found at a flea market in the village of Collioure. What intrigued me most was the method—the way the chicken is "roasted," without any liquid (except what gets rendered from the chicken), in a covered pot on top of the stove. The method results in beautifully browned skin, super-moist meat, and, best of all, a windfall of terrific pan juices, which become a delectably rich sauce. It's been a favorite of mine ever since.

Makes 4 servings

2½ to 3 pounds bone-in, skin-on chicken breast halves, legs, and/or thighs

Salt and freshly ground black pepper to taste

1 tablespoon unsalted butter

1 tablespoon vegetable oil

2 cups sliced fresh mushrooms

½ cup dry white wine

½ cup heavy cream

2 tablespoons snipped fresh chervil, or 1 tablespoon snipped fresh tarragon and 1 tablespoon snipped fresh parsley

1. Season the chicken with salt and pepper. Melt the butter with the oil in a braiser or large Dutch oven over medium-high heat; add the chicken and cook, turning occasionally, until brown on all sides, 10 to 15 minutes (reduce the heat to medium if the chicken browns too quickly). Transfer the chicken to a plate and pour off all but a sheen of fat from the pan.

2. Return the chicken pieces to the pan, skin side down. Reduce the heat to low. Cover the pot and let the chicken cook for 8 minutes. By this time, there will be some fat in the pot; turn the chicken pieces skin side up and spoon the fat over them. Adjust the heat to a point between low and medium-low (you want the chicken to continue cooking, but not to brown too much more). Cover the pot and cook the chicken until it is done (the internal temperature should register 170°F for breasts, 180°F for thighs and drumsticks), about 30 minutes more, uncovering the pot to spoon the fat over the chicken after 10 minutes, then again after 20 minutes.

3. Transfer the chicken to a serving platter and cover with foil to keep warm. Increase the heat to medium-high. Add the mushrooms to the juice in the pot and cook, stirring, until tender, 4 to 5 minutes. Add the white wine to the pan; stir with a whisk to loosen any browned bits from the bottom of the pan. Bring to a boil and boil until the wine is reduced to a few spoonfuls, about 1 minute. Stir in the cream and cook briefly, until thickened. Remove from the heat and stir in the chervil.

4. Arrange the chicken pieces on four plates, spoon the sauce on top, and serve.

Roast Chicken Breasts
Stuffed with Ricotta, Shallots, and *Fines Herbes*

Cheese and well-chosen herbs help the French cook transform some inexpensive chicken pieces into an impressive dinner-party dish. I've seen a number of recipes that call on this winning combination, but here I take the lead from Richard Olney, a highly respected American-born cookbook author who lived and worked in France most of his life. His cheese of choice for this dish was ricotta, and it works beautifully.

Serve this with a nice lemon-sparked salad in summer—put the chicken and the salad on the same plate so that the lemony salad dressing acts as a sauce for the entire dish. In winter, a good accompaniment is Angel Hair Pasta with Fresh Grape Tomato Sauce (page 165), as shown here.   **Makes 4 servings**

---

3 tablespoons extra-virgin olive oil

1 large shallot, minced (about ¼ cup)

2 garlic cloves, minced

2 tablespoons snipped fresh parsley

1 tablespoon snipped fresh chives

1 tablespoon snipped fresh tarragon

½ cup whole-milk ricotta cheese

Salt and freshly ground black pepper to taste

4 bone-in, skin-on chicken breast halves (6 to 8 ounces each)

1. Preheat the oven to 425°F.

2. Heat 1 tablespoon of the olive oil in a medium-size skillet over medium heat until it shimmers. Add the shallot and cook, stirring, until tender but not brown, 4 to 5 minutes. Add the garlic, parsley, chives, and tarragon; cook, stirring, until the garlic is fragrant, about 30 seconds more. Transfer to a bowl; cool slightly.

3. Stir the ricotta cheese into the shallot mixture; season with salt and pepper. Slide your fingers under the skin of each chicken breast half to separate it from the meat while leaving it attached on one side. Spoon one-fourth of the filling onto the meat under the skin of each breast. Pull the skin back over the breast to cover the filling. Season the breasts with salt and pepper and brush with the remaining 2 tablespoons olive oil. Place the breasts, skin side up, in a baking pan large enough to hold them in one layer.

4. Bake until the internal temperature of the chicken registers 170°F on an instant-read thermometer, 35 to 40 minutes. Allow the chicken breasts to stand for 5 minutes before serving.

Panko-Breaded Oven-Baked Chicken

I adapted this dish from a brochure of recipes created to feature Comté cheese. Believe it or not, the original called for *les corn-flakes* (yes, the French have corn flakes—and they call them exactly that), but I think panko (Japanese bread crumbs) offers a more softly nubbly crust. You'll find this a little like good ol' oven-fried chicken—but with French *je ne sais quoi*. Serve with a composed green salad and you'll never be quite satisfied with a chicken Caesar salad again.   **Makes 4 servings**

- 4 boneless, skinless chicken breast halves (about 1¼ pounds total)
- Salt and freshly ground black pepper to taste
- ¼ cup all-purpose flour
- 1 large egg
- ½ cup finely grated Comté, Gruyère, or Emmental cheese (about 2 ounces)
- ¾ cup panko crumbs
- ⅓ cup finely chopped walnuts or pecans
- 1 tablespoon extra-virgin olive oil
- 1 tablespoon unsalted butter, melted

1. Preheat the oven to 425°F.

2. Generously grease a shallow baking pan with olive oil and set aside. Place the chicken breasts, one at a time, between two sheets of plastic wrap and pound to ¼-inch thickness. (Alternatively, you can halve each breast horizontally, or butterfly them, as described on page 78.) Season both sides with salt and pepper.

3. Place the flour in one shallow bowl. Beat the egg in another shallow bowl. Combine the cheese, panko crumbs, and walnuts in a third shallow bowl. Dip the chicken breasts in the flour, patting off the excess, and then in the egg, allowing the excess to drip off. Then coat each breast with the cheese-crumb mixture, patting to help the coating adhere. Place the chicken in the baking pan. Combine the olive oil and butter in a small bowl. Drizzle over the top of the chicken.

4. Bake the chicken for 8 minutes; turn the chicken over and cook until tender and cooked through (internal temperature 165°F), about 6 minutes more. Serve.

Braise, Stew, or Roast

Braising, stewing, and roasting result in some of France's most traditional and cherished home-cooked meals, from beef *bourguignon* to *coq au vin* to cassoulet. While these styles of cooking take more time than the quick sauté-deglaze-serve mode of cooking in the previous chapter, many of the recipes themselves are quite simple, requiring just a little prep before the "hands off" simmering or roasting time. In my experience, they're also among the best dishes to serve for entertaining, as most of the work is done well before the guests arrive.

The differences between braising, stewing, and roasting can basically be defined as wet, wetter, and dry, respectively. Here's an overview:

BRAISING AND STEWING

These methods are quite similar, in that recipes for both generally begin with browning the meat, then cooking it in liquid—a small amount for braises, a little more for stews—tightly covered and at low temperatures. The "low and slow" style of cooking is the secret to coaxing bold flavors and velvety, spoon-tender textures out of less expensive cuts of meat that might be tough when cooked by other methods.

ROASTING

To roast, you cook the food in the oven in an uncovered pan. At its best, the dry-heat method results in meat, poultry, or fish that finishes up nicely browned on the outside and moist on the inside. This style of cooking requires tender cuts.

Beef *Bourguignon*

Until recently, many American recipes for this French classic simply called for stew meat, which works well for many stews but never quite resembled the larger pieces of soft, velvety meat I'd enjoyed when traveling through Burgundy. What was this marvelous cut? French women's magazines sometimes called for *boeuf pour bourguignon*—beef for Burgundy stew; other recipes called for *boeuf à braiser*—beef for braising. No help there.

Some trial and error once home steered me in the direction of boneless short ribs. Now, short ribs may not be precisely the cut used by a Burgundian cook (French butchers often cut their meats differently than Americans), but it is a near-perfect soul mate: lusciously moist, tender, yielding in all the right ways, and never stringy. Sometimes, I can't believe how easy this stew really is, especially considering all of the "wows" I get when I serve it. **Makes 6 servings**

2½ pounds boneless beef short ribs, cut into 2-inch chunks

Salt and freshly ground black pepper to taste

2 slices thick-cut bacon, cut into ½-inch pieces

Olive oil or vegetable oil, if needed

1 large yellow onion, chopped (about 1 cup)

3 garlic cloves, minced

2 cups Beaujolais Villages, red Burgundy, or Pinot Noir

1 cup low-sodium beef broth, plus more if needed

1 teaspoon dried thyme, crushed

1 bay leaf

1½ cups frozen pearl onions

3 tablespoon unsalted butter, at room temperature

8 ounces fresh mushrooms, stems trimmed, left whole if small, quartered or halved if larger

2 tablespoons all-purpose flour

1 recipe Any-Night Baked Rice (page 163)

1. Preheat the oven to 350°F.

2. Pat the beef dry with paper towels and season with salt and pepper; set aside. In a large ovenproof Dutch oven, heavy enameled pot, or braiser, cook the bacon over medium heat until crisp. Remove the bacon with a slotted spoon and drain on paper towels. Pour off all but 1 tablespoon of bacon drippings (or add oil to equal 1 tablespoon total) and turn the heat to medium-high. Brown the beef in batches in the hot drippings, turning as necessary to brown evenly, 5 to 7 minutes per batch (reduce the heat to medium if the meat browns too quickly). Transfer the beef to a plate as it is done.

3. Drain off all but 1 tablespoon of fat from the pot. Reduce the heat to medium. Add the onion to the pot and cook, stirring, until tender, 4 to 5 minutes; add the garlic and cook, stirring, until fragrant, about 30 seconds more. Return the meat to the pot; add the bacon, wine, beef broth, thyme, and bay leaf and bring to a boil, stirring to loosen any browned bits from the bottom of the pot. Cover and bake until the meat is very tender, about 2 hours.

4. About 15 minutes before the end of the cooking time, cook the frozen pearl onions in a large saucepan according to the package directions. Drain and leave in the colander.

In the same saucepan, melt 1 tablespoon of the butter over medium-high heat; add the mushrooms and cook, stirring, until tender and lightly browned, 4 to 5 minutes. Return onions to the pan; remove from the heat and cover to keep warm.

5. Use a slotted spoon to transfer the beef from the pot to a bowl; cover to keep warm. Remove and discard the bay leaf. Pour the juices and solids from the pot into a large measuring cup and skim off the fat. You want 2 cups of pan liquid total, including the bacon, onions, and garlic in the liquid. If you have more, boil the liquid in the pot over medium-high heat until reduced to 2 cups. If you have less, add additional beef broth to make 2 cups, return the liquid to the pot, and bring to a simmer.

6. In a small bowl, work the remaining 2 tablespoons butter and the flour together to make a paste (a *beurre manié*). Add the *beurre manié* bit by bit to the cooking liquid, stirring with a wire whisk to blend away any lumps. Bring to a boil, stirring, and continue to cook and stir for 2 minutes more to thicken. Return the beef to the pot, add the onions and mushrooms, and heat through.

7. Serve the stew in shallow bowls with the baked rice.

Beef Stew
with Orange and Balsamic Vinegar

When I think of the times I've enjoyed *le vinaigre balsamique* most in France, it's been in a *plat mijoté*—a simmered dish, such as braised beef. That's the way I use it here—but with a bit of orange to brighten the depth of flavor balsamic brings to this stew.   **Makes 4 servings**

1½ **pounds beef stew meat, cut into** ¾**-inch pieces**

Salt and freshly ground black pepper to taste

¼ **cup all-purpose flour**

2 **tablespoons extra-virgin olive oil, plus more if needed**

½ **cup chopped onion**

2 **garlic cloves, minced**

½ **cup fresh orange juice**

½ **cup dry red wine**

¼ **cup low-sodium beef broth**

2 **tablespoons Grand Marnier or other orange liqueur**

¼ **cup balsamic vinegar**

½ **teaspoon dried thyme, crushed**

1 **tablespoon grated orange zest**

4 **carrots, peeled and cut into** ¼**-x-2-inch sticks**

1 **recipe Any-Night Baked Rice (page 163), Noodles with *Fines Herbes* (page 164), or whipped potatoes**

1. Season the beef with salt and pepper. Place the flour in a plastic bag and add the meat, a few pieces at a time, shaking to coat. In a large saucepan or medium-size Dutch oven, heat the oil over medium-high heat. Add half of the meat and cook, turning as needed, until browned on all sides, about 5 minutes (reduce the heat to medium if the meat browns too quickly). Transfer the meat to a plate and repeat with the remaining meat, adding more oil if needed. Remove all of the meat from the pan.

2. Reduce heat to medium; add the onion (along with a touch more olive oil if the pan seems too dry) and cook, stirring, until tender, 4 to 5 minutes. Add the garlic; cook, stirring, until fragrant, 30 seconds more. Remove pan from heat.

3. Combine the orange juice, red wine, beef broth, Grand Marnier, and balsamic vinegar; add these liquids to the pan and cook, stirring, to loosen any browned bits from the bottom of the pan. Return the meat to the pan and add the thyme. Bring to a boil. Reduce the heat and simmer, partially covered, for 1 hour. Uncover and simmer until the meat is tender, 30 to 45 minutes more, adding the orange zest during the last 10 minutes of cooking.

4. Meanwhile, in a small saucepan, boil the carrots in lightly salted water to cover until just tender, about 4 minutes. Drain and reserve. Just before serving, stir the carrots into the stew and cook until heated through.

5. Serve the stew with the baked rice, noodles, or whipped potatoes.

Stew of Provence *Tout Simple*

What will turn this simple, gratifying stew into a dynamite Provençal-style Sunday night supper is what you serve with it. A bright, perky salad with tender greens, chopped grape tomatoes, and scallions, dressed with Vinaigrette *Maison* (page 242), will do the trick. And if you have a half-glass of wine and some baguette left over after you finish up the stew, bring out a wedge of cheese for an impromptu cheese course.   **Makes 4 servings**

1½ **pounds beef stew meat, cut into** 3/4-**inch pieces**

Salt and freshly ground black pepper to taste

1/4 **cup plus 1 tablespoon all-purpose flour**

2 **tablespoons extra-virgin olive oil, plus more if needed**

3/4 **cup chopped onion**

3 **garlic cloves, minced**

1/2 **teaspoon dried** *herbes de Provence,* **crushed**

1½ **cups dry red wine, such as Syrah or Côtes-du-Rhône**

1/2 **cup low-sodium beef broth**

1 **tablespoon unsalted butter, at room temperature**

1 **recipe Any-Night Baked Rice (page 163), whipped potatoes, or Noodles with** *Fines Herbes* **(page 164)**

1. Season the beef with salt and pepper. Place ¼ cup of the flour in a plastic bag and add the meat, a few pieces at a time, shaking to coat. In a large saucepan or medium-size Dutch oven, heat the oil over medium-high heat until it shimmers. Add half of the meat and cook, turning as necessary, until browned on all sides, about 5 minutes (reduce the heat to medium if the meat browns too quickly); transfer to a plate and repeat with the remaining meat, adding more oil if needed. Remove all of the meat from the pan.

2. Reduce the heat to medium; add the onion (along with a touch more olive oil if the pan seems too dry) and cook, stirring, until tender, 4 to 5 minutes. Add the garlic and *herbes de Provence* and cook, stirring, until the garlic is fragrant, about 30 seconds. Add the wine and beef broth and cook, stirring to loosen any browned bits from the bottom of the pan. Return the meat to the pan and bring to a boil. Reduce the heat, cover, and simmer until the meat is tender, 1½ to 1¾ hours.

3. Work the butter and the remaining 1 tablespoon flour together to make a paste (a *beurre manié*). Add the *beurre manié* bit by bit to the stew, stirring with a wire whisk to blend away any lumps. Cook and stir until thickened and bubbly; continue to cook and stir for 2 to 3 minutes more.

4. Serve the stew in shallow bowls with the baked rice, whipped potatoes, or noodles.

Pomegranate *Pot-au-Feu*

Pot-au-Feu (literally, "pot on the fire") refers to a dish of meat and vegetables cooked in water. Usually, the resulting broth is served as a first-course soup, followed by a main dish of the meat and vegetables. It's classic French comfort food at its grandmotherly best.

In my updated version of *pot-au-feu*, I use pomegranate juice instead of water. And instead of serving the broth as a first course, I boil it down into a deeply rich, vaguely fruity sauce. The result is still comfort food, but with a modern touch. **Makes 4 to 6 servings**

---

1 (2-pound) boneless beef chuck pot roast

Salt and freshly ground black pepper to taste

2 tablespoons canola oil, plus more if needed

2 medium-size leeks (white and pale green parts only), halved lengthwise, rinsed, and sliced crosswise (about 1 cup)

6 garlic cloves, minced

2 cups pomegranate juice

1 cup low-sodium beef broth

2 to 3 teaspoons dried *herbes de Provence*, crushed

1 bay leaf

1 tablespoon unsalted butter (optional)

Any-Night Baked Rice (page 163), whipped potatoes, or Noodles with *Fines Herbes* (page 164)

1. Preheat the oven to 325°F.

2. Season the meat with salt and pepper. Heat the oil in a large ovenproof Dutch oven over medium-high heat until it shimmers. Add the roast and cook, turning as needed, until browned on all sides, about 10 minutes. Transfer the meat to a plate.

3. Reduce the heat to medium. If the pan is dry, add another tablespoon of oil. Add the leeks and cook, stirring, until slightly softened, about 2 minutes; add the garlic and cook, stirring, until fragrant, about 30 seconds more. Add 1 cup of the pomegranate juice to the pot and bring to a boil, stirring to loosen any browned bits from the bottom of the pot. Boil gently until the liquid is reduced by half, 2 to 3 minutes. Add the remaining 1 cup pomegranate juice, the broth, *herbes de Provence*, and bay leaf. Return the meat to the pot and bring to a boil. Cover the pot, transfer to the oven, and bake until the meat is tender, about 2 hours.

4. Transfer the roast to a cutting board and cover with foil to keep warm. Strain the cooking liquid through a fine-mesh sieve into a bowl; discard all of the solids, including the bay leaf. Skim the fat from the cooking liquid and return the liquid to the pot. Boil until reduced to a sauce-like consistency, then stir in the butter to further thicken and enrich the sauce, if you like.

5. Slice the meat and arrange it on a serving platter. Pour a little of the sauce over the meat and pass the rest of the sauce at the table. Serve with the rice, whipped potatoes, or noodles.

Choucroute Garnie Mardi Soir

When you don't have time to chase down the great variety of meats often found in a classic version of *choucroute garnie*, try this scaled down, yet immensely satisfying, *mardi soir* (Tuesday night) version of the dish. **Makes 4 servings**

1 (2-pound) bag sauerkraut

8 juniper berries

2 whole cloves

2 bay leaves

2 tablespoons unsalted butter

1 medium-size onion, chopped

1 cup dry white wine

1 cup low-sodium chicken broth

2 slices thick-cut bacon, cut into 1-inch pieces

Freshly ground black pepper and salt to taste

2 boneless smoked pork chops, each cut in half

4 good-quality, natural-casing frankfurters, or 4 fully cooked Knockwurst or smoked sausages

4 medium-size red-skinned potatoes, peeled and halved

Dijon mustard, for serving

1. Preheat the oven to 350°F.

2. Rinse and drain the sauerkraut well in a colander under cold running water. Rinse again and drain; set aside. Tie the juniper berries, cloves, and bay leaves in a piece of cheesecloth or a spice bag; set aside.

3. Melt 1 tablespoon of the butter in an oven-safe Dutch oven or braiser over medium heat. Add the onion and cook, stirring, until tender but not browned, 4 to 5 minutes. Add the wine, chicken broth, bacon, pepper, and spice bundle. Stir in the drained sauerkraut. Bring to a simmer. Cover the pot, transfer to the oven, and bake for 30 minutes.

4. Add the smoked pork chops and frankfurters to the pot, burying them in the sauerkraut. Cover and return to the oven; bake until the meats are heated through, about 30 minutes more.

5. Meanwhile, put the potatoes in a saucepan. Cover with water by at least an inch, add salt, and bring to a boil. Reduce the heat and cook at an active simmer until tender, about 20 minutes; drain. Return the potatoes to the pot along with the remaining 1 tablespoon butter. Remove from the heat and cover to keep warm.

6. Discard the spice bundle. With a slotted spoon, transfer the sauerkraut, smoked chops, and frankfurters to a platter. Toss the potatoes with the butter; arrange the potatoes around the platter and serve, passing the Dijon mustard at the table.

Gascony Pork Chops

Prunes grown around the city of Agen, then soaked in Armagnac (the regional brandy), are a famed delicacy of the historical region known as Gascony. These delightfully drunken prunes make their way into Gascon cooking in recipes from pâté to dessert. In fact, if you ever travel to the region, be sure to try prune-Armagnac ice cream; it is sublime.

I once enjoyed the famed prunes in a recipe for pork, and soon thereafter, I developed this recipe. I just love the interplay of the sweetness of the prunes and the savory qualities of the other ingredients, all enlivened by a spark of vinegar. **Makes 4 servings**

---

4 bone-in pork chops (1 inch thick)

Salt and freshly ground black pepper to taste

1 tablespoon extra-virgin olive oil

2 large shallots, thinly sliced (about ½ cup)

2 large garlic cloves, slivered

1 teaspoon dried summer savory, crushed

½ cup low-sodium chicken broth

¼ cup Armagnac, Cognac, or brandy

⅓ cup thinly sliced pitted prunes

1 tablespoon white wine vinegar

2 tablespoons unsalted butter

1. Preheat the oven to 350°F.

2. Season the pork chops with salt and pepper. Heat the olive oil in an oven-safe skillet (with a tight-fitting lid) or braiser over medium-high heat until it shimmers. Add the chops and cook, turning once, until browned on both sides, 4 to 6 minutes (reduce the heat to medium if the meat browns too quickly). Transfer the chops to a plate.

3. Reduce the heat to medium. Add the shallots and cook, stirring, until tender, about 4 minutes. Add the garlic and summer savory and cook, stirring, until fragrant, about 30 seconds more. Remove the pan from the heat. Add the chicken broth and Armagnac. Return the pan to the heat and bring to a boil, stirring to loosen any browned bits from the bottom of the pan.

4. Return the chops to the pan and scatter the prunes around them. Cover, put the pan in the oven, and bake until the internal temperature of the chops registers 145°F on an instant-read thermometer, about 15 minutes. Transfer the pork chops and prunes to a plate; cover with foil to keep warm.

5. Set the pan over medium-high heat and add the vinegar. Bring to a boil and continue to cook, stirring, until the liquid is thickened and reduced to about ⅔ cup. Whisk in the butter to finish the sauce.

6. Arrange the chops and prunes on four dinner plates, spoon the sauce on top, and serve.

Braised Pork Meatballs
with Dijon Cream Sauce

Though France's meatballs are not nearly as familiar to us as, say, Swedish, Vietnamese, or Italian-American meatballs, French cooks do make some great versions. These include *boules de picolat* (French Catalonian meatballs in a tomato sauce with green olives) as well as many versions of *boulettes provençales*, presented in a sauce featuring ingredients such as sweet peppers, black olives and/or sun-dried tomatoes. Taking inspiration from further north and marrying white wine and Dijon mustard in a rich cream sauce, this is one of my favorites.   **Makes 6 servings**

1½ pounds ground pork

1 cup finely chopped parsley

1 egg

2 cloves garlic, finely minced

Salt and freshly ground black pepper to taste

½ cup vegetable oil

1 cup finely chopped onion

½ cup dry white wine

3 tablespoons Dijon mustard

1½ cups heavy cream

Snipped fresh parsley

1 recipe Any-Night Baked Rice (page 163), or whipped potatoes

1. In a bowl, mix the pork, parsley, egg, and garlic. Season with salt and pepper (though go easy on the salt, as the Dijon mustard that you'll add later can be quite salty). Shape the mixture into 12 meatballs.

2. Heat the oil in a large, deep skillet or braiser over medium-high heat until it shimmers. Add the meatballs and cook, turning once, until they are light brown on both sides, about 6 minutes total.

3. Reduce the heat to medium-low; continue to cook the meatballs, turning occasionally until nicely brown on all sides. Transfer the meatballs to a plate and set aside.

4. Drain off all but a sheen of fat from the pan. Increase the temperature to medium and add the onion; cook, stirring, until tender, about 3 minutes. Add the wine and cook, stirring to loosen any browned bits from the bottom of the pan. Cook and stir until the wine is reduced to ¼ cup, about 3 minutes.

5. Whisk in the mustard until incorporated. Add the heavy cream and cook, stirring, until the liquid is reduced to about 1 cup. Return the meatballs to the pan; reduce the heat to low, cover, and simmer until the meatballs are cooked through (160°F), about 20 minutes.

6. Divide the meatballs among six shallow bowls, spoon the sauce over the meatballs and sprinkle each serving with parsley. Serve with baked rice or whipped potatoes.

Pork and White Bean Cassoulet *Ce Soir*

This is my any-night take on cassoulet, that famous southwestern-France stew of white beans simmered with sausages, lamb or pork, and duck confit—rich, salty pieces of duck that have been cooked and preserved in their own fat. A traditional cassoulet can take days to make, especially if you preserve your own confit.

While not the extravaganza that is a true cassoulet, this version is more in the everyday spirit of this book. It offers a good helping of the warmth and well-being that cassoulet brings, but it can be done in a day (especially if you use the boiling method to soak the beans). It does take a little time—but most of it is hands-off simmering.   **Makes 6 servings**

---

2 cups dried Great Northern beans, rinsed and picked over

8 cups water

2 to 2½ pounds bone-in country-style pork ribs, cut in half crosswise (see Note)

Salt and freshly ground black pepper to taste

1 tablespoon plus 2 teaspoons extra-virgin olive oil

3 slices thick-cut bacon, cut into ½-inch pieces

1 red bell pepper, cored, seeded, and chopped (about ¾ cup)

1 small onion, chopped (about ½ cup)

3 large garlic cloves, minced

½ teaspoon dried *herbes de Provence*, crushed

½ cup dry sherry

3 cups low-sodium chicken broth

1 (14.5-ounce) can diced tomatoes, drained

12 ounces sweet Italian sausage links, pricked all over with a fork and cut crosswise into 6 pieces

1. Soak the beans in the water overnight; drain and set aside. Alternatively, place the beans and the water in a large Dutch oven. Bring to a boil and boil for 2 minutes. Remove from the heat, cover, and let stand for 1 hour. Drain the beans and set aside.

2. Season the ribs with salt and pepper. Heat 1 tablespoon of the olive oil over medium-high heat in a large Dutch oven. Add the ribs and cook, turning occasionally, until brown on all sides, 8 to 10 minutes (reduce the heat if the meat browns too quickly). Transfer the ribs to a plate. Cook the bacon in the pan until crisp. Using a slotted spoon, transfer the bacon to paper towels to drain.

3. Drain off all but 1 tablespoon of fat from the pan. Add the bell pepper and onion and cook, stirring, until tender, 4 to 5 minutes. Add the garlic and *herbes de Provence* and cook, stirring, until fragrant, about 30 seconds.

4. Remove the pan from the heat. Add the sherry and return the pan to the heat. Bring to a boil and boil, stirring to loosen any browned bits from the bottom of the pan, until the sherry is reduced by half, about 1 minute. Add the beans, bacon, chicken broth, and drained tomatoes to the Dutch oven; top with the ribs. Bring to a boil. Reduce the heat, cover tightly, and simmer for about 1 hour (the ribs will not quite be done at this point).

5. After the ribs have cooked for about 45 minutes, heat the remaining 2 teaspoons oil in a medium-size skillet over medium-high heat. Cook the sausage pieces, turning as needed to brown evenly, for about 5 minutes (the sausage will not be cooked through at this point).

6. After the ribs have cooked for 1 hour, add the sausage pieces to the Dutch oven, pushing them down into the stew so that they are submerged. Bring back to a boil. Reduce the heat, cover, and simmer

until the sausage is cooked through, the ribs are nearly tender, and the beans are tender, about 15 minutes more.

7. Uncover the pot and increase the heat so that the stew comes to an active simmer. Cook, stirring occasionally, until the liquid is reduced, the ribs are tender, and the stew has thickened, 10 to 15 minutes. Taste and adjust the seasonings.

8. Serve in wide, shallow bowls with a piece of sausage, a piece of pork, and plenty of beans in each bowl.

Note: Depending on where the bone falls on the rib, you might not be able to cut all of the ribs in half before you cook them. If that is the case, cook any uncut ribs whole; after the ribs have finished cooking, you'll be able to coax the meat off the uncut bones, getting two servings from each bone.

Tuna Steaks Braised
with Tomatoes, Olives, and Fennel

It's easy to think of Provence as perennially sunny and warm—likely because most Americans visit in summer. Yet anyone who has ever ventured there in cooler months knows that the mistral wind is fierce and cold in winter and spring. Minnesota it's not, but it's still time to turn from light, bright, and simple foods to something heartier. That's the appeal of this recipe. With Pernod, tomatoes, and olives, it features favorite south-of-France flavors, yet meaty tuna makes for a warm, hearty braise geared toward cooler months.

The ¼ cup of olive oil may seem like a lot, but it's an important part of the flavor profile, making the dish rich and delectable. This is one of those times to bring out that bottle of really good olive oil.

Makes 4 servings

¼ **cup extra-virgin olive oil**

1 fennel bulb, trimmed, halved, and sliced (snip and reserve fronds; discard tough core)

1 medium-size onion, halved and thinly sliced

2 garlic cloves, minced

1 (14.5-ounce) can diced tomatoes, undrained

½ **cup pitted mixed imported olives (both green and black)**

¼ **cup Pernod, Ricard, Pastis 51, or ouzo**

4 (6-ounce) tuna or swordfish steaks (1 inch thick)

Salt and freshly ground black pepper to taste

1. Heat the oil in a large skillet over medium heat until it shimmers. Add the fennel and onion and cook, stirring, until crisp-tender, about 5 minutes; add the garlic and cook, stirring, until fragrant, about 30 seconds more. Remove the pan from the heat. Stir in the tomatoes and their juices, the olives, and the Pernod. Return to the heat and bring to a boil.

2. Season the tuna steaks with salt and pepper and place on top of the tomato mixture. Cover and reduce the heat. Simmer for 5 minutes; turn the steaks and simmer, covered, until the tuna flakes easily when tested with a fork, about 5 minutes more. Divide the tuna and sauce among four shallow bowls, garnish with the reserved fennel fronds, and serve.

Roasted Fish with Sauce *au Choix*

Roasting is a technique that would be in any French cook's repertoire for preparing fish. You can serve the fish topped simply with a finishing drizzle of olive oil. Or, if you've thought ahead, top it with a pat of flavored butter, such as Garlic-Chive Butter. If you have a few minutes more to spare, serve with one of the sauces in the Basics chapter or the *Pipérade*.

This technique works best for thicker fillets and steaks from fish with dense flesh, such as salmon, snapper, haddock, halibut, and sea bass.   **Makes 4 servings**

---

1 to 1½ pounds fish fillets or steaks

Extra-virgin olive oil

Salt and freshly ground black pepper to taste

1 recipe sauce of your choice, such as Beurre Blanc, Hollandaise Sauce, Saffron-Vermouth Sauce, or Tartar Sauce *Chez Vous* (see Basics chapter for recipes); or *Pipérade* (page 171) or Garlic-Chive Butter (page 86)

1. Preheat the oven to 450°F.

2. Measure the thickness of the fish. Brush a shallow baking dish with olive oil. Place the fish in the dish, and brush the fish all over with additional olive oil. Season with salt and pepper. Tuck any thin edges underneath the fish so that the fillets are as uniform in thickness as possible. Roast until the fish flakes easily with a fork, 4 to 6 minutes for every ½ inch of thickness.

3. Divide the fish into four portions (if they didn't already come that way) and place on warmed individual plates. Top with the sauce and serve.

Roasted **Salmon** with Pernod Sauce

Pernod is a heady spirit flavored with star anise and other herbs that's usually served mixed with ice and water and sipped as an apéritif. I love the bright, flavorful effects the spirit brings to this elegant one-dish meal. It's perfect for a cozy dinner for two, and while it looks and tastes like something you'd pay top dollar for at a corner bistro, it comes together very easily. Just get the vegetables and sauce going before you start roasting the salmon, and you can likely have this dish on the table in half an hour. **Makes 2 servings**

4 small red-skinned potatoes (about 8 ounces), scrubbed and quartered

1 large carrot, peeled and cut into matchstick-size pieces

1/3 cup frozen pearl onions

1 tablespoon unsalted butter

1 small garlic clove, minced

1/4 cup dry white wine

1/4 cup clam juice or chicken broth

2 tablespoons plus 1 teaspoon Pernod, Ricard, Pastis 51, or ouzo

2 (6-ounce) salmon fillets, skin removed

Salt and freshly ground black pepper to taste

2 teaspoons extra-virgin olive oil

2 teaspoons snipped fresh *fines herbes*, plus additional for garnish (see page 164)

1/4 cup heavy cream

1. Preheat the oven to 450°F.

2. Put the potatoes in a medium-size saucepan with enough lightly salted water to cover by an inch. Bring to a boil, then cook at an active simmer for 10 minutes. Add the carrot and onions and cook until all of the vegetables are just tender, about 5 minutes more. Drain and rinse with cool water to stop the cooking process. Drain well.

3. Meanwhile, melt the butter in a small saucepan over medium heat; add the garlic and cook, stirring, until fragrant, about 30 seconds. Remove the pan from the heat. Add the white wine, clam juice, and 2 tablespoons of the Pernod. Bring to a boil and boil until the mixture is reduced to about 2 tablespoons, about 7 minutes. Remove from the heat and set aside.

4. While the vegetables are cooking and the sauce is reducing, measure the thickness of the salmon and season with salt and pepper. Combine the olive oil, the remaining 1 teaspoon Pernod, and the *fines herbes*; rub the mixture all over the salmon. Place in a shallow baking dish, tucking under any thin edges so that the fillets are as uniform in thickness as possible. Roast until the fish flakes easily with a fork, 4 to 6 minutes per 1/2 inch of thickness.

5. When the fish is just about done, reheat the sauce. Stir in the cream and bring to a boil. Add the vegetables. Cook, gently tossing, until the vegetables are warm.

6. Spoon the vegetables and sauce into two warmed shallow bowls, arranging the vegetables toward the rim. Place the salmon in the center of the bowl. Sprinkle with *fines herbes* and serve.

Salmon with Wine, Leeks, and Garlic

With mellow leeks, garlic, and wine to infuse the fish with flavor, and the barest touch of cream to finish the sauce, this dish tastes and feels like elegant classic French fare, but it's pleasantly light on its feet. I enjoy serving this with Any-Night Baked Rice (page 163) for a wholly satisfying main course that nevertheless leaves open the possibility of a cheese course or dessert (or better yet, both). **Makes 4 servings**

4 (4- to 6-ounce) pieces skinless salmon fillet (about 1 inch thick)

Salt and freshly ground black pepper to taste

1 tablespoon unsalted butter

1 large leek (white and pale green part only), halved lengthwise, rinsed, and sliced crosswise (about 3/4 cup)

2 garlic cloves, minced

3/4 cup dry white wine

2 tablespoons snipped fresh *fines herbes* (see page 164)

2 tablespoons heavy cream

1. Season the salmon with salt and pepper; set aside.

2. Melt the butter in a large skillet over medium heat. Add the leek and cook, stirring, until tender but not brown, 4 to 5 minutes; add the garlic and cook, stirring, until fragrant, about 30 seconds more.

3. Add the wine and bring to a boil; place the salmon fillets in the pan.

Return the wine to a boil and reduce the heat. Cover and simmer until the salmon flakes easily when tested with a fork, 8 to 10 minutes.

4. Transfer the salmon to a plate and cover with foil to keep warm. Increase the heat and boil the sauce until reduced to about 1/3 cup. Swirl in the *fines herbes* and cream. Season the sauce with salt and pepper. Serve the salmon with the sauce.

Making a Menu

To stay true to the character of the recipes in this book, keep the menu simple. Here's how a French cook might approach a meal anchored by one of the braises, stews, or roasts in this chapter.

If serving a sit-down first course, the French home cook would likely kick off the meal with a tempting starter to get everyone in the mood for more good things to come. Consider a salad, such as One *Bonne* Starter Salad (page 30), Belgian Endive Salad with Blue Cheese and Walnuts (page 32), or Melty Goat Cheese Salad with Honey and Pine Nuts (page 38). Soups would likely not appear before stews or most braises, but a French cook might serve a bowl of something vivid and fresh before a roast. Good options include Roasted Tomato and Garlic Soup (page 67) and Roasted Vegetable Soup *Classique* (page 63).

Braises, stews, and roasts are usually served with sides that are thoughtful, yet not too complicated. Choose one that won't detract from the main recipe; see page 162 for ideas.

Traditionally, most recipes in this chapter would be followed by a cheese course that includes a creamy, bulging choice such as Camembert.

Following such meaty, hearty fare, the French host might serve something smooth and refreshing for dessert, such as Lemon Curd *Crème Brûlée* (page 215) or French Lemon Tartlets (page 222). For simple family meals, ice cream, fruit, or sweetened *fromage blanc* would be a typical any-night finale.

CASSEROLES AND PASTA

We often think of pasta as Italian and casseroles as midcentury American. And yet, French cooks have their own takes on everything from shepherd's pie to lasagna. Like us, they often rely on pasta as the base of a quick, nourishing meal. Of course, by using quintessential French ingredients—from shallots and *fines herbes* to favorite French cheeses—these dishes become unmistakably French.

OPPOSITE: "Butcher's Day Off" Mushroom Pasta, page 155

Chicken and Noodle *Gratin*

To a creamy and comforting chicken-noodle bake, I've added classic French ingredients: tarragon, shallots, and Comté cheese. The result? French elegance and American comfort in one warming (and wonderfully easy) dish.   **Makes 4 to 6 servings**

---

1 pound boneless, skinless chicken breasts, or 1¾ cups cubed rotisserie chicken (skip step 1)

Salt to taste

4 ounces thin egg noodles

½ cup fresh bread crumbs

1 tablespoon snipped fresh parsley

1 tablespoon extra-virgin olive oil

4 tablespoons (½ stick) unsalted butter

1 cup chopped celery

2 large shallots, sliced into thin rings (about ½ cup)

¼ cup all-purpose flour

1 teaspoon dried tarragon, crushed

⅛ teaspoon cayenne pepper

Freshly ground black pepper to taste

2 cups 2 percent or whole milk

1 cup cubed Comté, Gruyère, or Emmental cheese

1. Place the chicken breasts in a medium-size saucepan. Add water to cover by 1 inch; season with salt. Bring to a boil; reduce the heat to an active simmer and cook until the internal temperature of the chicken registers 170°F on an instant-read thermometer, about 20 minutes. Drain, cool slightly, and cut into bite-sized pieces. Transfer to a large bowl.

2. Preheat the oven to 350°F.

3. Cook the noodles according to the package directions; drain and add to the bowl with the chicken. In a bowl, stir together the bread crumbs, parsley, and olive oil and set aside.

4. Melt the butter in a medium-size saucepan over medium heat. Add the celery and shallots and cook, stirring, until tender but not brown, 4 to 5 minutes. Stir in the flour, tarragon, cayenne, and salt and pepper, making sure all of the flour is moistened by the butter in the pan. Cook and stir for 1 minute. Do not allow flour mixture to brown. Gradually add the milk, stirring with a wire whisk until combined. Cook and stir until thick and bubbly, then cook and stir 1 minute more.

5. Scrape the sauce into the bowl with the chicken and noodles, stir in the cheese, and mix well. Pour into a 1½-quart casserole dish or divide evenly among six 10-ounce individual casserole dishes. Sprinkle the top(s) evenly with the bread crumb mixture.

6. Bake until the casserole(s) bubble and the topping is golden, about 25 minutes for one large casserole or about 20 minutes for the individual dishes. Allow the casserole(s) to stand for 5 minutes before serving.

Poulet Pot Pie

Do the French make pot pies? Indeed they do, although French cooks usually use puff pastry (*pâte feuilletée*) rather than short pastry (*pâte brisée*—roughly, what we call pie dough). For special meals, individual cassolettes feuilletées arrive at the table bubbling with fillings made from everything from *escargots* to shellfish. For more everyday fare, the home cook might use duck confit (preserved duck) from the *traiteur*; and rather than fussing with individual *cassolettes*, the cook would prepare the dish as one larger *plat familial* (family dish). In this plat *familial*, I use chicken, as it's easier to find. Using frozen puff pastry makes the dish easy enough for a weeknight, but it's anything but ordinary, thanks to the classic French flavorings.   **Makes 4 to 6 servings**

½ package frozen puff pastry sheets (1 sheet)

1⅓ pounds boneless, skinless chicken breasts, or 2 cups cubed rotisserie chicken (skip step 2)

Salt to taste

4 medium-size carrots, peeled and bias-cut into ½ inch slices (1¼ cups)

4 tablespoons unsalted butter

4 medium-size leeks (white and pale green parts only), halved lengthwise, rinsed, and thinly sliced crosswise (about 2 cups)

1 small yellow onion, chopped (⅓ cup)

2 garlic cloves, minced

¼ cup all-purpose flour

1 cup low-sodium chicken broth

½ cup 2 percent or whole milk

½ cup dry white wine

½ cup heavy cream

1½ tablespoons snipped fresh tarragon, or 2 tablespoons snipped fresh parsley and 1½ teaspoons dried tarragon, crushed

Freshly ground black pepper to taste

1 egg, beaten with 1 tablespoon water

1. Thaw the puff pastry according to the package directions.

2. Meanwhile, place the chicken breasts in a medium-size saucepan. Add water to cover by about 1 inch; season with salt. Bring to a boil; reduce the heat to an active simmer and cook until the internal temperature of the chicken registers 170°F on an instant-read thermometer, about 20 minutes. Drain, cool slightly, and cut into bite-size pieces. Transfer to a bowl.

3. Preheat the oven to 400°F.

4. Bring a saucepan of lightly salted water to a boil. Add the carrots, bring back to a boil, and cook for 3 minutes. Drain, rinse under cool running water, and drain again. Add the carrots to the chicken in the bowl.

5. Melt the butter in a large saucepan over medium heat. Add the leeks and onion and cook, stirring, until the onion is tender but not brown, 4 to 5 minutes. Add the garlic and cook, stirring, until fragrant, about 30 seconds more. Stir in the flour, making sure all of the flour is moistened by the butter in the pan. Cook and stir for 1 minute. Do not allow the flour mixture to brown. Whisk in the chicken broth, milk, and white wine. Cook and stir until thickened and bubbly; cook and stir 1 minute more. Stir in the cream. Stir in the chicken and carrots, the tarragon, and salt and pepper. Bring to a boil, stirring occasionally. Transfer the mixture to a 2-quart round casserole or deep-dish pie plate.

6. Unfold the puff pastry sheet and place it atop the casserole. Roll up any overhanging pastry to make it even with the edges of the casserole dish. Brush the top of the pastry with the egg and water mixture.

7. Bake until the filling is bubbly and the pastry is golden and cooked through, 15 to 20 minutes. Serve.

Chicken and Rice *Plat au Four*

Rice baked with garlic, onions, butter, and chicken broth is one of my all-time favorite French side dishes (see Any-Night Baked Rice, page 163). This recipe adds mushrooms and a little cheese to the casserole, with chicken thighs baked alongside, to make a wholly satisfying *plat au four* (oven main dish) that's great for a weeknight family meal. Incidentally, sautéed fresh spinach goes beautifully with this.   **Makes 4 servings**

8 bone-in, skin-on chicken thighs

Salt and freshly ground black pepper to taste

1 tablespoon unsalted butter

1 tablespoon extra-virgin olive oil

1 medium-size onion, finely chopped (about ½ cup)

2 cups sliced fresh mushrooms

1 garlic clove, minced

½ cup dry white wine

4 fresh thyme sprigs or ¼ teaspoon dried thyme, crushed

¾ cup low-sodium chicken broth

½ cup uncooked long-grain white rice

¼ cup grated Gruyère, Emmental, or Parmigiano-Reggiano cheese (about 1 ounce)

¼ cup snipped fresh chives

1. Preheat the oven to 425°F.

2. Season the chicken thighs with salt and pepper. In a large skillet, melt the butter with the olive oil over medium-high heat; add the chicken thighs, skin side down, and cook until the skin is browned, about 5 minutes. Turn and cook the opposite side for 1 minute more (the chicken will not be done at this point). Place the chicken in a single layer in a shallow baking pan; set aside. Drain off all but 2 tablespoons fat from the skillet.

3. Add the onion and mushrooms to the same skillet and cook until the onions are tender, 4 to 5 minutes. Add the garlic and cook, stirring, until fragrant, about 30 seconds more. Season with salt and pepper. Add the wine and thyme and cook until the wine is reduced by half, about 1 minute. Add the chicken broth and rice and bring to a boil, stirring up any browned bits in pan.

4. Transfer the rice mixture to a 1½-quart casserole dish. Cover the casserole and slide it into the oven. Place the baking pan with the chicken alongside the rice casserole in the oven. Bake the rice until tender, about 20 minutes. Remove from oven and let stand while the chicken continues to bake until the internal temperature registers 180°F on an instant-read thermometer, about 5 minutes more.

5. Divide the chicken thighs and the rice casserole among four dinner plates. Sprinkle with the cheese and chives and serve.

Curried Chicken Comté

One of the things I learned when traveling through the Franche-Comté region of eastern France is that Comté cheese goes marvelously with curry; even the tiniest bit of the spice blend has an impact. I saw the combination often on restaurant menus, and when I returned home I was eager to experiment with it. This recipe brings the dynamic Comté-curry duo to a spin on chicken Florentine for a modern update to the classic. Serve with Any-Night Baked Rice (page 163). And this may be one of those meals where you'll want to freshen up the palate with a good garlicky green salad before heading on to dessert.   **Makes 4 servings**

4 boneless, skinless chicken breast halves (about 1¼ pounds total)

Salt and freshly ground black pepper to taste

2 tablespoons unsalted butter

1 large shallot, finely chopped (about ¼ cup)

1 tablespoon all-purpose flour

½ teaspoon sweet curry powder

1 cup 2 percent or whole milk

¾ cup shredded Comté, Gruyère, Emmental, or cheddar cheese (about 3 ounces)

1 tablespoon extra-virgin olive oil

9 ounces fresh spinach, washed and drained, tough stems removed

1. Place the chicken breasts, one at a time, between two sheets of plastic wrap and pound to ¼-inch thickness. (Alternatively, you can halve each breast horizontally, or butterfly them, as described on page 78.) Season both sides with salt and pepper.

2. In a large skillet, melt 1 tablespoon of the butter over medium-high heat. Add the chicken and cook, turning once, until cooked through (internal temperature 165°F), 6 to 8 minutes (reduce the heat to medium if the chicken browns too quickly). Transfer to a platter and cover with foil to keep warm. Cool the skillet and wipe it out with paper towels; set aside.

3. Melt the remaining 1 tablespoon butter in a small saucepan over medium heat. Add the shallot and cook, stirring, until tender but not brown, 2 to 3 minutes. Add the flour and curry powder; cook and stir to form a paste, then cook and stir for 1 minute more. Do not allow the flour mixture to brown. Slowly add the milk, whisking until combined. Cook and stir until the mixture boils and thickens, then cook and stir for 2 minutes more. Add ½ cup of the cheese and stir until melted. Remove from the heat and set aside.

4. Preheat the broiler.

5. Heat the olive oil in the skillet over medium-high heat. Add the spinach, cooking and turning for just a few seconds until wilted (you may need to do this in two batches). Do not overcook—a few remaining unwilted leaves is fine.

6. Transfer the spinach to a shallow flameproof baking pan. Top with the chicken breasts. Spoon the sauce over the chicken and sprinkle with the remaining ¼ cup cheese. Watching carefully, broil 4 to 5 inches from the heat until the cheese and sauce bubble and begin to brown, 4 to 6 minutes.

7. Divide the chicken, spinach, and sauce among four dinner plates and serve.

Great Grating Cheeses

Often, French recipes for dishes from pastas to *gratins* simply call for *fromage râpé* (grated cheese) without specifying the exact cheese to use. In such instances, the French cook will usually reach for Comté (a French Gruyère) or Emmental (versions from France, not Switzerland, of course). (For more information on these cheeses, see page 202.) Though these cheeses are made in the eastern part of the country, they're generally considered the go-to grating cheeses all over France, unless a regional cheese is specifically called for in a recipe.

It should be noted that one of the world's best grating cheeses, Italy's Parmigiano-Reggiano, is also widely available in France. However, it's expensive. A frugal home cook might use it, but is likely do so sparingly.

Pappardelle *alla Bolognese Francese*

French Bolognese sauce? But of course! French home cooks often prepare Italian food, sometimes doing straight-on versions of Italian dishes, but often adding characteristically French ingredients and seasonings. That France-meets-Italy melding inspired this recipe, which calls for Comté (or a similar) cheese instead of Parmigiano-Reggiano and Provençal seasonings instead of basil and oregano.   **Makes 4 servings**

½ ounce dried porcini mushrooms

¼ cup extra-virgin olive oil

1 carrot, peeled and diced (about ½ cup)

1 medium-size onion, chopped (about ½ cup)

3 garlic cloves, minced

1 teaspoon dried *herbes de Provence*, crushed

8 ounces lean ground beef

8 ounces ground pork

½ cup dry white wine

½ cup low-sodium chicken broth

2 tablespoons snipped fresh parsley, plus additional for garnish

Salt and freshly ground black pepper to taste

1 (14.5-ounce) can whole tomatoes, undrained, puréed in a food processor

1 tablespoon tomato paste

8 ounces dried pappardelle, tagliatelle, or fettucine

½ cup freshly grated Comté, Gruyère, or Emmental cheese (about 1 ounce), plus additional for serving

1. Put the mushrooms in a heatproof bowl. Cover with boiling water and soak for 20 minutes. Lift the mushrooms out of the soaking liquid; rinse, chop, and set aside.

2. Bring a large pot of water to a boil for the pasta.

3. Heat the oil in a Dutch oven over medium heat until it shimmers. Add the carrot and onion and cook, stirring, until the onion is tender but not brown, 4 to 5 minutes. Add the garlic and *herbes de Provence* and cook, stirring, until fragrant, about 30 seconds more. Add the beef and pork; cook, stirring with a wooden spoon to break up the meat into tiny bits, until the meat is no longer pink but not browned, about 3 minutes. Add the wine and broth and cook until the liquid is reduced by half. Stir in the chopped porcini and parsley, salt, and pepper. Add the puréed tomatoes and the tomato paste and bring to a boil. Reduce the heat and simmer, stirring occasionally, until the sauce is thickened, about 5 minutes; taste and add more salt and pepper if needed. Remove from the heat and cover to keep warm.

4. Meanwhile, cook the pasta according to the package directions; drain and return to the pan. Add all but about 1 cup of the sauce to the pasta; toss to coat. Add the cheese and toss again. Divide the pasta among wide, shallow bowls. Spoon the remaining sauce over each serving and sprinkle with parsley. Pass additional cheese at the table.

Pasta in France

It's true that pasta is the quintessential Italian staple. However, the French love their *pâtes* (pasta—not to be confused with pâté) as much as Americans do, and French cooks use it in many of the same ways we do: with red or white sauces; in soups, salads, and baked dishes; as well as in quick improvisations that cooks on both sides of the Atlantic have come to appreciate as a great way to get a meal on the table after a long day.

When possible, French cooks use fresh pasta, and while some make their own from scratch, excellent versions of fresh pasta are readily available in many markets. Yet keep in mind that French supermarket shelves brim with many of the same shapes and styles of dried pasta as ours. So you can cook with dried pasta and still cook French.

To add extra French finesse to your pasta dishes, try seeking out tagliatelle—fresh or dried—made with eggs. Widely used in France, these long, thin noodles originally hail from the Emilia-Romagna region of Italy. (Emilia-Romagna's food is among the most refined in Italy—so is it any surprise that their noodle is among the most popular in France?)

Fettucine, which is preferred in southern Italy and more readily found in the United States, can also be used. Indeed, it's probably what a French cook would substitute if unable to snag some tagliatelle.

Roasted Shrimp Capellini
with Shallots and *Fines Herbes*

Roasting is a sublime way to prepare shrimp. Here, the roasted seafood gets tossed with fragrant *fines herbes* and thin, delicate pasta for a clever—and very French-flavored—way to turn one pound of shrimp into an elegant entrée for four.   **Makes 4 servings**

1 pound large shrimp, peeled and deveined

2 scallions (white portion and some tender green tops), sliced (about ¼ cup)

1 large shallot, finely chopped (about ¼ cup)

1 garlic clove, minced

¼ cup snipped fresh *fines herbes* (see page 164), or 1 teaspoon dried *fines herbes*, crushed

¼ cup extra-virgin olive oil

1 tablespoon fresh lemon juice

Salt and freshly ground black pepper to taste

8 ounces dried capellini (angel hair pasta)

1 cup frozen peas

½ teaspoon chicken base or crumbled high-quality chicken bouillon cube

¾ cup freshly grated Parmigiano-Reggiano cheese (about 3 ounces)

Red pepper flakes (optional)

1. Preheat the oven to 400°F. Bring a large pot of water to a boil for the pasta. Lightly coat a 9-inch square or round baking dish with olive oil.

2. Place the shrimp in one layer in the baking dish. Sprinkle the scallions, shallot, garlic, and herbs over the shrimp. Whisk together the olive oil and lemon juice and pour evenly over the shrimp. Season with salt and pepper. Roast until the shrimp are opaque throughout, about 10 minutes.

3. When the shrimp are done, cook the pasta according to the package directions, adding the peas during the last minute of cooking time and scooping out ¼ cup of the pasta cooking water before draining. Drain the pasta and peas. Return the reserved pasta cooking water to the pot over medium heat and swirl in the chicken base to dissolve. Remove pan from heat. Add the pasta and peas and half of the cheese. Toss.

4. Add the roasted shrimp to the pasta, including the seasonings and any juices in the pan, and toss. Add the remaining cheese, salt and pepper, and, if you like, some red pepper flakes. Toss again; reheat gently to make sure the peas are cooked through. Divide among four wide, shallow bowls and serve immediately.

Tagliatelle with Bacon and Gruyère

Pâtes aux lardons—creamy pasta studded with thick, luscious cubes of pork belly and sauced simply with *crème fraîche* and sometimes egg yolk—is a popular any-night dish in France. It's similar to Italy's pasta carbonara, though the French often include one of their own cheeses (such as Gruyère or Emmental) to make the dish. Here, I've followed that lead, but I've substituted American slab bacon for the hard-to-find French-style *lardons*.   **Makes 4 servings**

6 slices thick-cut bacon, chopped

4 large egg yolks

1 cup shredded Gruyère, Emmental, or Comté cheese (about 4 ounces)

1 cup freshly grated Parmigiano-Reggiano cheese

1 cup *crème fraîche*

Salt and freshly ground black pepper to taste

8 ounces dried tagliatelle or fettucine

¼ to ½ cup 2 percent or whole milk

¼ cup snipped fresh parsley or chives

1. Bring a large pot of water to a boil for the pasta.

2. In a large saucepan, cook the bacon over medium heat until crisp but not hard. Using a slotted spoon, transfer the bacon to a paper towel–lined plate.

3. In a large bowl, whisk the egg yolks slightly. Stir in the Gruyère, Parmigiano-Reggiano, *crème fraîche*, and salt and pepper.

4. Meanwhile, cook the pasta according to the package directions; drain and return to the pot. Set the pot over medium-low heat.

5. Toss the cooked bacon with the pasta in the pot. Add the egg-cheese mixture. Gently heat and stir, adding milk ¼ cup at a time until the sauce coats the pasta and everything is cooked through, 1 to 2 minutes. Divide among four wide, shallow bowls, sprinkle with parsley, and serve.

"Butcher's Day Off" Mushroom Pasta

Often in the smaller French coastal towns in which I've set up house, the butcher shops are open on Sundays, yet shuttered one day in the middle of the week. This allows these family-run businesses to take advantage of the crowds that come on the weekend, but also to get their weekly day in the sun, too.

Until I get into the rhythm of the openings and closings of businesses, I sometimes head to the butcher with grand plans to make something meaty, only to realize I've come on their day off. More than once when this has happened, I've headed to a greengrocer displaying baskets of beautiful fresh mushrooms. I bring them back to my French kitchen and make this simple but thoroughly pleasure-packed dish. **Makes 4 servings**

1 pound assorted fresh mushrooms, such as cremini, white, shiitake, chanterelle, and/or morels, or 2 ounces assorted dried mushrooms

8 ounces dried tagliatelle or linguine

2 tablespoons unsalted butter

2 large shallots, sliced (about ½ cup)

2 large garlic cloves, minced

½ cup dry white wine

Salt and freshly ground black pepper to taste

1 cup heavy cream, plus more if needed

1 cup freshly grated Gruyère, Comté, or Emmental cheese (about 4 ounces)

¼ cup toasted walnuts

¼ cup snipped fresh parsley

1. If using fresh mushrooms, trim the stems from the mushrooms; clean and slice the caps. If using shiitakes, remove and discard the woody stems before slicing; if using morels, just halve them lengthwise. If using dried mushrooms, place them in a heat-proof bowl; cover with boiling water and allow to stand for 30 minutes. Rinse and drain. Cut any large mushroom pieces into bite-size pieces; set mushrooms aside.

2. Cook the pasta according to the package directions; drain.

3. Meanwhile, melt the butter in a large skillet over medium heat; add the shallots and cook until the shallots are just softened, about 3 minutes. Add the fresh mushrooms (if using); cook and stir until the mushrooms are softened, about 5 minutes. Add the garlic and cook, stirring, until fragrant, about 30 seconds. Add the wine and drained dried mushrooms (if using); bring to a boil and boil gently until the liquid has almost evaporated, about 1 minute. Add salt and pepper. Stir in the heavy cream and bring to a boil; cook until slightly thickened, about 2 minutes. Remove from heat; add the Gruyère, stirring just until melted.

4. Add the drained pasta to the skillet. Toss to coat and heat through. If the pasta seems dry, add a touch more heavy cream. Taste and add more salt and/or pepper if needed. Divide among four wide, shallow bowls and sprinkle with the walnuts and snipped fresh parsley to serve.

Market Day Tagliatelle with Goat Cheese

The scenario: You come home from your farmers' market, basket brimming with all kinds of vegetables, but now you're really hungry and you just don't have it in you to prepare anything time-consuming or complicated. This is it: the recipe you're looking for. It's a recipe I often use in France; quickly, simply, and lusciously, it showcases whatever fresh produce I found at the market.

I don't recommend making this dish unless you can get locally grown, picked-within-a-day-or-two vegetables for it. They are the star here, and freshness will make all the difference in this vibrant pasta.

Makes 4 servings

- 8 ounces dried tagliatelle or fettucine
- 2 tablespoons extra-virgin olive oil
- 4 cups fresh vegetables (see Note)
- 1 cup halved cherry or grape tomatoes
- ½ cup dry white wine
- 2 scallions (white portion and some tender green tops), sliced (about ¼ cup)
- 2 tablespoons snipped fresh parsley, chives, or chervil, or a combination
- Salt and freshly ground black pepper to taste
- 4 ounces soft-ripened goat cheese, crumbled or cubed

1. Bring a large pot of water to a boil and cook the tagliatelle according to the package directions; drain.

2. Meanwhile, heat the olive oil in a large skillet over medium heat; add the vegetables and cook until barely tender-crisp, about 4 minutes. Add the tomatoes, wine, and scallions. Cook at an active simmer until the liquid has nearly evaporated, about 5 minutes; stir in the fresh herbs. Season with salt and pepper.

3. Combine the drained pasta, goat cheese, and vegetables in a large bowl. Toss until everything is combined and the cheese partially melts (a few warm, solid chunks are desirable). Divide among four wide, shallow bowls and serve.

Note: Good vegetable choices include julienned carrots, trimmed snow peas, sliced summer squash, trimmed and sliced asparagus, and small, tender green beans. The size of the cuts should be somewhat similar so that all of the vegetables cook at the same rate. Fresh spinach is a great addition, but wait to stir it in with the fresh herbs—you want it to just wilt slightly.

Summer Tomato and Olive Pasta
with Fresh French Herbs

This vibrant, no-cook sauce is another recipe I turn to when I return from a late-summer market in France with a basket of tomatoes—only ripe, locally grown, in-season summer tomatoes will do—and fresh herbs. You can fiddle with the varieties and amounts of herbs you use according to what's freshest and best at the market or in your garden, but please don't substitute dried.   **Makes 4 servings**

8 ounces rotini or fusilli pasta

12 ounces assorted ripe summer tomatoes, such as heirloom tomatoes and red and yellow cherry and pear-shaped tomatoes, chopped

¼ cup pitted, chopped imported black olives

2 tablespoons snipped fresh parsley

2 tablespoons snipped fresh chives

1 teaspoon snipped fresh thyme

2 tablespoons extra-virgin olive oil

⅔ cup crumbled feta cheese (preferably French) or soft-ripened goat cheese

Salt and freshly ground black pepper to taste

1. Bring a large pot of water to a boil and cook the pasta according to the package directions.

2. Meanwhile, in a large bowl, combine the tomatoes, olives, parsley, chives, thyme, and olive oil. Stir to combine. Gently stir in the cheese.

3. Drain the pasta and add to the bowl with the sauce; toss gently to combine. Season with salt and pepper. Serve in wide, shallow bowls.

Herbs by the Handful

Recipes in French cookbooks and magazines often call for *une poignée d'herbes*—a handful of herbs. Sometimes the herbs are vaguely specified, such as *une poignée d'herbes de Provence* or *une poignée de fines herbes*, but often, it's just *une poignée d'herbes fraîches* (a handful of fresh herbs), or even *une poignée d'herbes selon goût* (a handful of herbs according to what you like).

While I give more specific measurements and recommendations for herbs, you should know that you can vary the herbs *selon goût*—according to taste—always using more of what's fresh and available, and whichever herb you like best.

15-Minute Tagliatelle
with Smoked Salmon and Fresh French Herbs

Though this dish is something you'll see on countless casual French restaurant menus, it's also the French home cook's answer to that "oops, forgot about dinner" dilemma. Most of the ingredients have long shelf lives in the pantry or refrigerator (except the fresh herbs—and you can substitute dried chives or dillweed, if you wish). Keep everything on hand to get a truc-to-France meal on the table quickly.

If you prefer the drier hard-smoked salmon over the soft and moist lox-style salmon, you could use that, though the latter is more true to France. **Makes 4 servings**

---

8 ounces dried spinach tagliatelle or fettucine and/or dried plain tagliatelle or fettuccine

1 cup *crème fraîche*

4 ounces lox-style smoked salmon, cut into small strips

¼ cup snipped fresh dillweed and/or chives, or 2 teaspoons dried dillweed and/or chives

Salt and freshly ground black pepper to taste

1. Bring a large pot of water to a boil and cook the pasta according to the package directions, scooping out ½ cup of the pasta cooking water before draining; drain the pasta. Set the pasta water and pasta aside separately.

2. In the same pot you used to cook the pasta, whisk together the *crème fraîche* and the reserved pasta water until smooth. Bring to a boil over medium heat. Add the pasta to the pot and cook until the sauce thickens a bit. Add the salmon and stir gently to heat through. Add the dillweed or chives (or both). Season with salt and pepper (be sure to taste first, as smoked salmon can be salty in itself).

3. Divide among four wide, shallow bowls and serve.

FRENCH SIDE DISHES

French cooks take as much care in choosing their side dishes as they do anything else that comes to the table. Sometimes, all the main dish needs is a pair of simple but thoughtfully prepared accompaniments, such as Any-Night Baked Rice or Pan-Fried Potatoes, alongside some green beans, asparagus, or carrots made in favorite French ways. At other times, the side becomes something of a star in itself—as when *Pipérade* or *Gratin Dauphinois* makes an appearance.

OPPOSITE: *Gratin Dauphinois Ce Soir,* page 166

Side Dishes the French Way

French home-cooked meals often come with either a starch or a vegetable, and sometimes both. Generally, if the family is dining in courses (that is, enjoying a starter, main course, and cheese or dessert), and the first course stars vegetables, then another vegetable need not be served with the main course. Yet sometimes it is—if you're going that route, choose one of this chapter's vegetable dishes according to your tastes.

Here are a few ways to go about choosing the starch for your main courses.

For Sauté-Deglaze-Serve recipes: The last thing you want for these quick main dishes is a complicated side dish. Three that are easy to get to the table include Any-Night Baked Rice (page 163), Pan-Fried Potatoes (page 168), and couscous.

For Stews and Braises: It would be rare for a French cook to serve a saucy side dish alongside these already-saucy dishes. I always serve Any-Night Baked Rice (page 163) with the classic wine-braised dishes Beef *Bourguignon* (page 122) or *Coq au Vin Assez Rapide* (page 110). Though hefty enough to stand up to meaty dishes, the delicate flavor of the rice complements the bold dishes well. Any-Night Baked Rice also goes well with stews, as do Noodles with *Fines Herbes* (page 164) and Celery Root and Potato Purée (page 168).

For Roasts: When you have a not-very-saucy dish, that's when you bring on the nicely creamy or saucy side dishes. For casual meals, consider Angel Hair Pasta with Fresh Grape Tomato Sauce (page 165) or whipped potatoes; when you are serving guests, try the Celery Root and Potato Puree (page 168) or the *Gratin Dauphinois Ce Soir* (page 166).

Any-Night Baked Rice

Make this recipe once, and I'm willing to bet you will make it again and again for the rest of your life. It is the perfect way to make moist (but never sticky), buttery (but not cloying), flavorful (but goes-with-anything) rice. It's infinitely easier than risotto, and much, much tastier than boiled rice.

I adapted this from a recipe by Pierre Franey, the French-born chef who wrote the "60-Minute Gourmet" column in the *New York Times* in the 1970s and '80s. I've probably made it more than a thousand times in my life. The basic ingredients are butter, onions, garlic, rice, chicken stock, and thyme. You can vary the seasonings and ingredients, just as Franey did: He'd toss in apple and curry for *riz à l'Indienne*, turmeric for *riz au turmérique*, pimiento or roasted red pepper for *riz aux piments*, Parmesan (after the rice is cooked) for *riz au Parmesan*, and pine nuts (after cooking) for *riz avec pignons*. You get the idea—though the basic recipe is exquisite in itself.   **Makes 4 to 6 servings**

1 tablespoon unsalted butter

¼ cup finely chopped onion

1 garlic clove, minced

1 cup long-grain rice

¼ teaspoon dried thyme, crushed

1½ cups low-sodium chicken broth

1 bay leaf

1. Preheat the oven to 425°F.

2. Melt the butter in a flameproof, ovenproof pot with a heavy lid (I use Le Creuset's 18-cm enameled cast-iron French oven, which holds almost 2 quarts) over medium heat. Add the onion and cook until tender but not brown, 4 to 5 minutes. Add the garlic and cook, stirring, until fragrant, about 30 seconds. Add the rice and thyme; cook and stir about 1 minute more (the rice should be nicely coated with butter and starting to cook, but not yet brown) Add the chicken broth and the bay leaf; stir to break up any clumps of rice. Bring to a boil.

3. Cover the pot tightly and slide it into the oven. Bake the rice for 15 minutes. Remove from the oven and let stand, covered, for 5 minutes.

4. Remove and discard the bay leaf, stir the rice with a fork, and serve immediately—or let stand, covered, in a warm place (such as on an unheated back burner) for up to 20 minutes more.

Noodles with *Fines Herbes*

Most French apartments that I've stayed in have flower boxes in the windowsills, and when in France, I do as the French do—I reserve a few spots in the boxes for fresh herbs. I always pick up a pot of parsley and chives, and sometimes chervil and tarragon (which are a bit trickier to grow). When you're flush with fresh herbs, you can make just about anything sing—which is exactly what fresh herbs do to packaged noodles here.   **Makes 4 to 6 servings**

8 ounces wide egg noodles

2 tablespoons unsalted butter

2 tablespoons fresh snipped *fines herbes* (see box below)

Freshly ground black pepper to taste

1. Bring a large pot of water to a boil and cook the noodles according to the package directions. Drain well.

2. In the same pot, melt the butter over medium heat; add the fresh herbs and cook briefly to release their fragrance. Remove from the heat. Toss the noodles with the melted herb butter and add salt and pepper to taste. Serve warm.

Fines Herbes à la Tricheuse

Much loved by French cooks, *fines herbes* are a blend of finely chopped chervil, parsley, chives, and tarragon. Few ingredients add an unmistakably French flavor to a recipe more than this refined mix, which brings a nip of oniony sharpness from the chives, a touch of licorice from the chervil and tarragon, and a spark of spring-green freshness from the parsley. It tastes best with poultry, fish and shellfish, and eggs (an omelet with *fines herbes* is a classic quick-fix dinner in France).

If you can easily gather all the herbs called for in the *fines herbes* blend—either from a garden or window box, or inexpensively at the market—then by all means use all four. You can also get a similar effect using just parsley, chives, and tarragon, if you can't find fresh chervil (elusive in many parts of this country).

However, if you don't have these three or four herbs in fresh form, try this cheater's (*à la tricheuse*) option: For each tablespoon of *fines herbes* called for, substitute 1 tablespoon chopped fresh parsley and ½ teaspoon of a dried *fines herbes* blend, crushed between your fingers. That way, you'll get that nice freshness brought by the fresh parsley, with the dried mix adding the appropriate flavor angles.

Angel Hair Pasta with Fresh Grape Tomato Sauce

This is a great dish to serve with simply roasted meats or other main dishes that don't have their own sauce, because the juices from the tomatoes, butter, and olive oil here kind of create a little sauce. It's particularly good with Roast Chicken Breasts Stuffed with Ricotta, Shallots, and *Fines Herbes* (page 119).

Makes 4 servings

1 cup grape tomatoes, halved or quartered depending on size

Salt and freshly ground black pepper to taste

4 ounces angel hair pasta

2 tablespoons unsalted butter

2 tablespoons extra-virgin olive oil, plus more if needed

¼ cup chopped onion

1 garlic clove, minced

1 tablespoon snipped fresh parsley, chives, or chervil, or a combination

¼ cup freshly grated Parmigiano-Reggiano or other cheese that grates easily, such as Gruyère (about 1 ounce)

1. Sprinkle the tomatoes with salt and pepper to taste; set aside. Bring a large pot of water to a boil and cook the pasta according to the package directions; drain and keep warm.

2. Wipe the pot dry. Melt the butter with the oil in the same pot over medium heat; add the onion and cook until tender but not brown, 4 to 5 minutes Add the garlic and parsley and cook until fragrant, about 30 seconds. Add the tomatoes and cook, stirring, until the tomatoes are warmed through and becoming juicy, about 2 minutes.

3. Remove from the heat. Toss the pasta with the tomato sauce, adding a little more olive oil if the pasta seems dry. Serve warm with cheese sprinkled over each serving.

Gratin Dauphinois Ce Soir

There are countless recipes out there for French scalloped potatoes, which are the best in the world. Some require cutting the potatoes into paper-thin slices with a mandoline and baking the dish at a low temperature for hours. Let's let professional chefs go that route—they get paid for their time in the kitchen.

This everyday French version gets right to the pleasures of the dish without the fuss. You start by boiling the potatoes with the cream and milk, which helps everything thicken to the right consistency. This recipe also goes easy on the cheese, which is used here as a flavor enhancer, not the main ingredient. The star of the dish is the earthy potatoes, in a robe of creamy lusciousness.   **Makes 4 to 6 servings**

---

1 garlic clove, crushed

2 teaspoons unsalted butter, softened

2 pounds russet potatoes, peeled and thinly sliced

1½ cups 2 percent or whole milk

½ cup heavy cream

½ teaspoon salt

¼ teaspoon freshly ground black pepper

Freshly grated nutmeg

½ cup shredded Comté, Gruyère, or Emmental cheese (about 2 ounces)

1. Preheat the oven to 375°F. Rub the inside of a 2-quart baking dish all over with the garlic and discard the garlic. Coat the inside of the dish with the butter.

2. In a large saucepan, combine the potatoes, milk, cream, salt, pepper, and a few gratings of nutmeg. Bring to a simmer over medium heat. Simmer until the liquid thickens slightly, about 5 minutes, gently turning the potatoes once or twice with a slotted spoon. Spoon the potatoes evenly into the baking dish and pour the milk mixture over the potatoes. Sprinkle the cheese evenly over the top.

3. Bake until the cheese is golden and the potatoes are tender, 30 to 40 minutes. Let stand for 10 minutes before serving.

Celery Root and Potato Purée

There are many reasons why French puréed potatoes often taste so different than ours. Sometimes, the secret is simply that the potatoes have been puréed with another root vegetable, such as turnips or, as in this case, celery root. **Makes 4 to 6 servings**

1 celery root (1¼ to 1½ pounds)

1 teaspoon salt, plus additional to taste

2 medium-size russet potatoes (about 1 pound), peeled and cut into 2-inch chunks

3 tablespoons unsalted butter, melted

Heavy cream or whole milk

Freshly ground black pepper to taste

1. Use a sharp paring knife to trim and peel the celery root. Cut into 2-inch chunks. Place the celery root in a large pot. Add the salt and water to cover and bring to a boil. Boil for 10 minutes, then add the potatoes, adding more water if necessary to cover. Boil until the celery root and potatoes are tender, about 20 minutes more.

2. Drain well and return the celery root and potatoes to the pot; add the butter. Blend with an immersion blender or beat with a hand mixer, adding the cream, a couple of tablespoons at a time, as needed to reach the desired consistency. Season to taste with salt and pepper.

Pan-Fried Potatoes

In French home cooking, this dish makes a satisfying and reliable partner to easygoing weeknight entrées like flank steak, Hamburgers with Figs and Leeks (page 176), and Pork Chops with Mustard Sauce (page 92). Note that you can use all butter, all olive oil, or a combination; whichever you choose, these potatoes will fry up beautifully and simply; just get them cooking and keep a casual eye on them while you're fixing everything else. **Makes 4 servings**

3 tablespoons unsalted butter or extra-virgin olive oil, or a combination

3 to 4 large russet potatoes, cut into ¾-inch dice (4 cups)

Salt and freshly ground black pepper to taste

Snipped fresh parsley (optional)

Melt the butter in a large nonstick skillet over medium heat; add the potatoes and cook, stirring occasionally, until browned, 20 to 25 minutes. Season with salt and pepper. If you like, sprinkle parsley over all. Serve immediately, as they start to soften upon standing too long.

Glazed Carrots the French Way

This classic French way with carrots will be an epiphany to anyone who thinks a side dish of carrots is boring. The trick is that rather than adding butter to boiled carrots, you add the butter and a little sugar to the cooking water. The buttery flavor works its way throughout the carrots as they cook, uncovered, and you end up with just enough liquid to make a fine little sauce. **Makes 4 servings**

---

5 to 7 medium-size carrots,
   peeled and sliced (2½ to 3 cups)

¾ cup water

1 tablespoon sugar

1 tablespoon unsalted butter

Pinch of salt

Place the carrots, water, sugar, butter, and salt in a 2-quart saucepan. Bring to a boil. Reduce the heat and cook at an active simmer, stirring occasionally, until the water is nearly gone and the carrots are tender and glazed, 12 to 14 minutes. Serve hot.

Roasted Asparagus

Olive oil, salt, and freshly ground pepper are sometimes all you need to make so many foods—roast chicken, steaks, fish, tomatoes—really come alive. Roasted asparagus is another case in point. Sometimes, a French cook might add another ingredient, such as chopped hard-boiled egg, a poached egg, shavings of Gruyère, crumbled *chèvre*, or strips of roasted red pepper; in such cases, the asparagus would likely be served as a first course. However, the beauty of this dish is that you don't have to do anything more than what's right here, and you'll have something special every time you make it. One more note: This tastes fine at room temperature, so no need to rush it to the table. **Makes 4 servings**

---

1 pound asparagus, trimmed

2 tablespoons extra-virgin olive oil

Salt and freshly ground black
   pepper to taste

1. Preheat the oven to 450°F. Place the asparagus spears in a large, shallow roasting pan. Drizzle with the olive oil, season with salt and pepper, and roll the asparagus around to coat each spear in oil. Spread the asparagus into a single layer.

2. Roast until tender and lightly browned, 8 to 10 minutes. Serve warm or at room temperature.

Pipérade

Pipérade is like a Basque take on *ratatouille*, minus the eggplant and zucchini. It's usually flavored with the region's famous *piment d'Espelette*, a powdered spice made of peppers grown in and around Espelette, in the Basque region of France. If you search gourmet shops or online, you can find a little jar of *piment d'Espelette*; however, a combo of paprika and cayenne, as I suggest in the recipe, will do.

I've enjoyed *pipérade* in many ways in the Basque country. I've seen it served over a slice of ham and alongside grilled fish—it's shown here with Roasted Fish with Sauce *au Choix* (page 135). However, this sweet, fresh sauce seems tailor-made for eggs—I give some serving suggestions below.

Makes 4 servings (about 2½ cups)

---

2 tablespoons extra-virgin olive oil

1 red bell pepper, seeded and cut into very thin strips

1 green bell pepper, seeded and cut into very thin strips

½ cup chopped onion

2 garlic cloves, minced

1 (14.5-ounce) can diced tomatoes, undrained

½ teaspoon *piment d'Espelette*, or ½ teaspoon mild paprika and ⅛ teaspoon cayenne pepper, plus more if desired

Salt and freshly ground black pepper to taste

1. Heat the oil in a large skillet over medium heat. Add the bell peppers and onion and cook, stirring frequently until tender, 8 to 10 minutes; add the garlic and cook, stirring, until fragrant, about 30 seconds more. Add the tomatoes and their juices and the *piment d'Espelette*. Simmer until the *pipérade* thickens, about 3 minutes. Season with salt and black pepper; add more *piment d'Espelette* if you like.

2. You can serve the *pipérade* now, in its chunky form. However, if you want a smoother *pipérade*, cool the mixture slightly, then pulse in a food processor to the desired thickness (a saucy mixture with chunks of red and green pepper is especially nice for egg dishes). Reheat if needed, then serve.

Serving Suggestions

- Tuck a scant ½ cup warm *pipérade* into a Rolled French Omelet (page 195), omitting the *fines herbes*.
- Top fried or scrambled eggs with warm *pipérade*.
- Use in Baked Eggs with *Pipérade* (page 201).
- Spoon warm *pipérade* over slices of baked ham as a main course. Serve with Any-Night Baked Rice (page 163).
- Serve *pipérade* alongside Roasted Fish with Sauce *au Choix* (page 135).

French Green Beans *Classique*

I'll never forget when I stumbled on the French way to prepare green beans. I was dining in St. Rémy de Provence at a small family-run inn; halfway through the meal, when I meant to go to the restroom, I inadvertently walked into the kitchen instead.

Before me was a cook at a sauté station standing near a towering pile of cooked green beans. He grabbed a meaty handful of the beans and put them into a sauté pan slick with melted butter. In the five or so seconds that I stood there saying, *"Oh, pardon, excusez-moi, au revoir,"* I figured it out. You blanch the beans to near doneness, then finish them off by sautéing them. This double-cook method is green bean perfection. **Makes 4 servings**

---

12 ounces fresh green beans, trimmed

1 tablespoon unsalted butter

1 tablespoon extra-virgin olive oil

Salt and freshly ground black pepper to taste

1. Fill a saucepan with enough lightly salted water to cover the green beans, and bring to a boil. Add the beans and boil until nearly crisp-tender, 8 to 10 minutes. Drain, rinse well under cool running water to prevent further cooking, and drain again.

2. Melt the butter with the olive oil in a skillet over medium heat; add the green beans and cook, tossing, until crisp-tender, heated through, and coated with the butter and olive oil, 1 to 2 minutes. Season to taste with salt and pepper and serve.

Variations

Green Beans with Shallots. Blanch the beans as directed. After heating the butter and olive oil in the skillet, cook 1 large shallot, sliced into rings (about ¼ cup) for 1 minute. Add the green beans; cook, stirring, until the shallot is tender but not brown and the green beans are crisp-tender, heated through, and coated with the butter and olive oil, 1 to 2 minutes more. Season to taste with salt and pepper and serve.

Green Beans *Persillade*. Blanch the beans as directed. After heating the butter and olive oil in the skillet, cook 2 minced garlic cloves until fragrant, about 30 seconds. Add 2 tablespoons snipped fresh parsley; cook, stirring, until the parsley releases its fragrance. Add the green beans and cook, tossing, until crisp-tender, heated through, and coated with the butter and olive oil, 1 to 2 minutes more. Season to taste with salt and pepper and serve.

Peas with Pearl Onions and Thyme

Peas with pearl onions go especially well with sautéed fish dishes, such as *poisson meunière*. In season, a French cook would use fresh peas and fresh "*oignons nouveau*," (spring onions, with small, mellow-tasting bulbs), but for everyday, year-round cooking, frozen pearl onions will work just fine. And of course, it would be best if you could use fresh thyme, but you will be forgiven—at least by me—if you use dried. Besides, a little bit of the perfumey herb, crushed between your finger and thumb, will release plenty of the delicate aroma you're after here. But use only a smidgen—too much can bring overly perfumed notes to the dish.   **Makes 4 servings**

1 (10-ounce) package frozen peas

1 tablespoon unsalted butter

¼ cup water

½ cup frozen pearl onions

1 teaspoon snipped fresh thyme, or a very small pinch of dried thyme, crushed

Salt and freshly ground black pepper to taste

1. Cook the peas according to the package directions; rinse under cold water to stop the cooking process. Set aside.

2. Place the butter and water in a medium-size skillet over medium-high heat; heat until the butter melts. Add the frozen onions and dried thyme (if using). Bring to a boil and cook until the water has evaporated, 4 to 5 minutes. Continue to cook, stirring, until the onions begin to turn light golden brown, about 1 minute more. Add the peas and fresh thyme (if using); cook and stir briefly until the peas are warmed and the fresh thyme has released its aroma. Season to taste with salt and pepper and serve.

Variation

To use fresh shelled peas: Substitute 2 cups shelled peas (1½ to 2 pounds unshelled) for the frozen peas. Cook the shelled peas in a small amount of boiling salted water until just tender, 3 to 5 minutes. Drain, rinse with cold water, and set aside. Continue with step 2 above.

SANDWICHES, PIZZAS, AND SAVORY TARTS

The French make amazing savory things with breads, flatbreads, and various doughs. Many of these dishes are distinctly regional, from *Pan Bagnat* sandwiches casually munched on the beaches of the Côte d'Azur to Alsace's warming bacon-and-onion tart to sandwiches made from one-of-a-kind local cheeses. Others, such as Pizza *la Reine* and the *Croque Monsieur*, are enjoyed throughout France. Enjoy them as the French would—as satisfying ways to savor great French ingredients in a quick, stylish package.

OPPOSITE: Pizza *Bergère*, page 184

Hamburgers with Figs and Sautéed Leeks

This knife-and-fork burger melds two ingredients that harmonize beautifully on a cheese tray—figs and Gruyère cheese—with humble hamburger patties, and seals the deal with a sauce that's sweet, fruity, and tart.   **Makes 4 servings**

¼ **cup slivered dried figs**

½ **cup dry white wine**

1 **pound lean ground beef, shaped into four ¾-inch-thick patties**

Salt and freshly ground black pepper to taste

1 **tablespoon unsalted butter**

1 **medium-size leek (white and pale green parts only), halved lengthwise, rinsed, and sliced (about ½ cup)**

1 **teaspoon honey**

1 **teaspoon Dijon mustard**

4 **ounces Gruyère, Comté, or Emmental cheese, sliced**

4 **(¾-inch-thick) slices from a crusty country-style round bread, toasted**

1. In a small bowl, combine the figs and wine. Allow to stand until the figs are softened somewhat, about 30 minutes.

2. Season the patties with salt and pepper. Lightly grease a nonstick skillet. Heat the skillet over medium-high heat; add the patties and sear on both sides. Reduce the heat to medium or medium-low and cook, turning as needed to prevent overbrowning, 12 to 15 minutes (the internal temperature should register 160°F on an instant-read thermometer). Transfer the patties to a broiler pan; cover with foil to keep warm.

3. Preheat the broiler.

4. Drain off the fat and drippings from the skillet. Melt the butter in the skillet over medium heat. Add the leek and cook, stirring, until tender but not brown, 4 to 5 minutes. Carefully add the reserved wine and figs; cook until the liquid is reduced by half, about 1 minute. Stir in the honey and Dijon mustard and cook briefly, until the sauce is thickened. Remove the pan from the heat and cover to keep the sauce warm.

5. Top the burgers with the cheese; broil until the cheese is melted, about 1 minute (watching constantly). Place one slice of toast on each dinner plate, top each with a patty and some of the sauce, and serve.

A True *Croque Monsieur*

It pains me to think that there could someday be a generation of people who believe that a *croque monsieur* is simply a grilled ham and Swiss sandwich. Indeed, that's often what comes to the table when you order one at American bistros. It's even sadder that some French cafés have resorted to doing the same. *Aux armes*, diners! Let's revolt. It's time to bring back the béchamel—the lavish slather of white sauce that transforms an otherwise simple snack into a knife-and-fork wonder.

Make it at home, and you can enjoy it the way it was always meant to be. Yes, with the béchamel, the real version takes longer than simply grilling a sandwich, but don't think of it as merely a sandwich. When served with a bright and sprightly vinaigrette-tossed salad to contrast with the richness of the cheese and sauce, the *croque monsieur* makes a stylish weeknight supper. Enjoy it with a glass of crisp wine, such as a good white Burgundy. This recipe serves two, but you can easily double it for more.   **Makes 2 servings**

---

1 tablespoon unsalted butter

1 tablespoon all-purpose flour

3/4 cup 2 percent or whole milk

Salt and freshly ground black pepper to taste

4 slices thin white sandwich bread, toasted until crisp

4 thin slices baked or smoked ham

3/4 cup shredded Gruyère, Comté, or Emmental cheese (about 3 ounces)

1. Preheat the broiler. Lightly grease a baking sheet.

2. For the béchamel, in a small saucepan, melt the butter over medium heat. Whisk in the flour to form a smooth paste; cook and stir for 1 minute. Do not allow the flour mixture to brown. Gradually pour in the milk, whisking as you pour. Cook and stir over medium heat until the sauce is thickened and bubbly. Cook and stir for 1 minute more. Season with salt and pepper. Remove from the heat.

3. Place 2 toasted bread slices on the baking sheet; top each with 2 slices of ham and divide 1/4 cup of the cheese atop the ham. Top each with the remaining toast slices. Divide the béchamel over the tops of both sandwiches (it's fine if some streams down the sides). Scatter the remaining cheese atop the sauce.

4. Broil the sandwiches about 4 inches from the heat until heated through and the tops are irresistibly golden and speckled with polka dots of browned cheese, 4 to 6 minutes (watching constantly). Transfer to individual plates and serve.

Tartine with Brie and Salami

So often we pair cheeses like Brie and Camembert with sweet things, like fruit, but in a rustic little sandwich shop in the Franche-Comté region of France, I found a *tartine* that combined Brie with savory black Nyons olives and a local hard salami—with unbelievably good results. **Makes 2 servings**

2 tablespoons chopped pitted imported black olives, such as Nyons, kalamata, or Niçoise

2 tablespoons drained and thinly sliced roasted red bell peppers

1/2 cup diced salami, such as rosette de Lyon, Genoa, or soppressata

2 (3/4-inch-thick) slices from a crusty country-style round bread (preferably long slices from the center of the loaf), toasted

Extra-virgin olive oil

1/2 cup large-diced (1/2-inch) Brie or Camembert cheese

1. Preheat the broiler.

2. In a bowl, combine the olives, roasted peppers, and salami; set aside.

3. Brush one side of each toasted bread slice with olive oil. Arrange the bread slices, oiled sides up, on a baking sheet. Pile the salami mixture on the toasted bread, covering the entire bread surface, including the crusts, so the bread does not burn. Top with the cheese, evenly distributing it across the sandwiches (you don't need to cover the entire sandwich with the cheese—a little goes a long way).

4. Broil the sandwiches 3 to 4 inches from the heat until the cheese is mostly melted and translucent, about 3 minutes (watching constantly). Transfer the sandwiches to individual plates and serve.

Pan Bagnat pour Deux

Pan bagnat is kind of like a Niçoise salad sandwich, though as with the *salade Niçoise*, there are as many versions as there are cooks who make it. Standard ingredients include eggs, capers, and onions, and I've seen plenty of variations with tuna and without. I like this recipe with radishes; they add crispness and a delightful peppery angle.   **Makes 2 servings**

1 small shallot, minced (about 2 tablespoons)

2 canned anchovy fillets, minced, or 2 teaspoons anchovy paste

Freshly ground black pepper and salt to taste

1 tablespoon fresh lemon juice

1 teaspoon Dijon mustard

2 tablespoons extra-virgin olive oil

1 tablespoon drained capers

1 (5-ounce) can chunk light albacore tuna packed in oil, rinsed and drained well

¼ red onion, sliced very thinly

2 crusty sandwich rolls

Salted butter to taste

2 large eggs, hard-cooked, peeled, and sliced

3 to 4 radishes, sliced

1. In a medium-size bowl, use the back of a spoon to crush the shallot, anchovy, and some pepper into a rough paste; stir in lemon juice and mustard. Whisk in the olive oil until blended; stir in the capers. Add the tuna and onion. Taste and add salt, but only if necessary, and additional freshly ground black pepper if needed.

2. Brush the cut side of the top halves of the rolls with a very thin layer of butter. Spread the tuna salad on the bottom halves, arrange an egg and radish slices on top of the tuna, and top with the buttered roll halves. Serve.

Pizza in France

The French adore pizza, and nearly every town has a pizzeria or two. Some French pizzerias offer charming little dining rooms or outdoor café seating for a casual meal; others just have a counter where you can enjoy a quick drink while you wait for your pizza *à emporter* (to go). Pizza delivery is gaining popularity, too.

Most French pizzas are thin crusts topped with a bare coating of tomato sauce and a delicate sprinkling of great ingredients—it's a matter of having little bits of something wonderful rather than massive amounts of nothing special.

Unlike menus of traditional American pizzerias, which offer a list of ingredients that allow you to top your pizza any which way you want, the menus of French pizzerias generally offer a finite set of specialty pizzas. Some go by standard names throughout France. Pizza Neptune, for example, offers seafood toppings. Other combinations are region-specific; for instance, I once came across a *Commingoise* pizza, named for a region in the foothills of the Pyrénées, that included duck gizzards and smoked duck breast. Other popular choices are snagged from the Italians, such as the Marguerite (fresh mozzarella, basil, and tomato).

While the most common pizza cheese is a French Gruyère, I've found that mozzarella, blue cheese, and goat cheese often make their way onto the pie, though usually in combination with the Gruyère. Sometimes, pizza doesn't come with tomato sauce, but rather with a thin slather of *crème fraîche* and ingredients that go well with it, such as smoked salmon. And some pizzas come topped with an egg—which bakes a bit in the oven to add extra texture from the whites and extra richness from the yolk.

Two enormously popular pizzas are Pizza *la Reine* (page 183) and Pizza *Bergère* (page 184). Once you get the hang of these, you can try other French combinations, using those recipes as a template.

Trois Fromages: Tomato sauce, Gruyère, soft-ripened goat cheese, and a small amount of blue cheese.

Quatre Saisons: Tomato sauce, with artichoke hearts, thin-sliced baked or smoked ham, olives, and sliced fresh mushrooms, each placed in separate quadrants, with Gruyère over all.

Provençal: Tomato sauce, onions, green olives, anchovies, dried *herbes de Provence*, Gruyère, and a drizzle of olive oil over all after it comes out of the oven.

Jambon Cru (prosciutto): Tomato sauce, prosciutto, pitted kalamata olives, Gruyère and mozzarella, and fresh basil and oregano. Top with a drizzle of olive oil after it comes out of the oven.

Campagnarde (country-style): Tomato sauce, Gruyère, ham, mushrooms, and cooked bacon pieces. Sometimes this pizza is topped with a cooked egg. The easiest way to go this route is to fry an egg in a skillet just before the pizza is done and place it in the center of the finished pizza.

A note on spices: The French rarely add seasonings to the tomato sauce; rather, they add the herbs on top of the pie, with the other toppings. Good choices include fresh parsley, chives, oregano, basil, or *herbes de Provence*, or dried oregano, dried basil, or dried *herbes de Provence*. If using dried, use much less than you would fresh, and add to the pizza before baking. When using fresh, sprinkle atop the pizza during the last 5 minutes of baking time.

Pizza *la Reine*

Pizza *la Reine*—the queen's pizza—appears in pizzerias all over France, always sporting mushrooms and ham, and sometimes black olives, in addition to the tomato sauce and cheese. French home cooks also make this delight at home. Pressed for time, they use commercial *pâte à pizza* (pizza dough), which is readily available from the supermarket—you can do the same (prebake or not, according to the package directions). However, I nearly always make my own pizza dough—it's not that difficult or time consuming, and I love its fresh flavor. **Makes two 12-inch pizzas, to serve 4**

---

1 recipe Pizza Dough (page 254)

1 recipe Fresh Tomato Sauce for Pizza (page 253), Raw Tomato Sauce for Pizza (page 253), or 1⅓ cups purchased pizza sauce

4 ounces thinly sliced baked or smoked ham, cut into bite-size strips (about 1 cup)

1 cup sliced fresh mushrooms

10 to 12 pitted kalamata olives, halved

1 teaspoon dried oregano, crushed

2 cups freshly grated Gruyère, Comté, or Emmental cheese (about 8 ounces)

1. Prepare the pizza dough, dividing it in half and allowing it to rest for 10 minutes, as directed.

2. Position the racks in the middle and lowest thirds of oven. Preheat the oven to 425°F. Grease two large baking sheets.

3. Roll or pat the dough into two 12-inch rounds on the pans (see Note). Prick all over with a fork. Bake until golden brown, about 10 minutes, switching the positions of the pans after 5 minutes. Remove from the oven; flatten any air bubbles with a fork.

4. Spread a thin layer of tomato sauce on top of the crusts, stopping ½ inch from the edge (use about ⅔ cup sauce per pizza). Divide the ham and mushrooms across the crusts; dot with the black olives and sprinkle with oregano. Scatter the cheese over the top.

5. Bake the pizzas until the toppings bubble, the crusts are cooked through, and the edges are brown, 8 to 10 minutes, switching the positions of the pans after about 5 minutes. Cut each pizza in triangles to serve.

Note: You can also shape the dough into four 6-inch rounds; the baking time will be about the same.

Pizza *Bergère*

Pizza Bergère is another popular French style of pizza. *Bergère* means shepherdess, and in this case it refers to goat cheese—an ingredient that a *bergère* (or her male counterpart) would likely appreciate. If you choose the right goat cheese (use soft-ripened rather than fresh), it will melt slightly into pools of lusciousness that provide wonderfully rich, complex flavor.   **Makes two 12-inch pizzas, to serve 4**

1 recipe Pizza Dough (page 254)

1 recipe Fresh Tomato Sauce for Pizza (page 253), Raw Tomato Sauce for Pizza (page 253), or 1⅓ cups purchased pizza sauce

4 ounces thinly sliced baked or smoked ham, cut into bite-size strips (about 1 cup)

4 ounces soft-ripened goat cheese, thinly sliced into discs (if cut from a log) or cut into small wedges (if not in log form)

1 teaspoon dried *herbes de Provence*, crushed

10 to 12 pitted kalamata olives, halved

1 cup freshly grated Gruyère, Comté, or Emmental cheese (about 4 ounces)

1. Prepare the pizza dough, dividing it in half and allowing it to rest for 10 minutes, as directed.

2. Position the racks in the middle and lowest thirds of oven. Preheat the oven to 425°F. Grease two large baking sheets.

3. Roll or pat the dough into two 12-inch rounds on the pans (see Note). Prick all over with a fork. Bake until golden brown, about 10 minutes, switching the positions of the pans after 5 minutes. Remove from the oven; flatten any air bubbles with a fork.

4. Spread a thin layer of tomato sauce on top of the crusts, stopping ½ inch from the edge (use about ⅔ cup sauce per pizza). Divide the ham, goat cheese, and *herbes de Provence* across the crusts; dot with the olives. Scatter the Gruyère on top.

5. Bake the pizzas until the toppings bubble, the crusts are cooked through, and the edges are brown, 8 to 10 minutes, switching the positions of the pans after about 5 minutes. Cut each pizza in triangles to serve.

Note: You can also shape the dough into four 6-inch rounds; the baking time will be about the same.

Herbes de Provence

Though originally from the south of France, *herbes de Provence* are beloved by cooks all over France. This wonderfully fragrant blend gathers up herbs that grow in abundance in Provence; its cornerstones are rosemary, fennel, and thyme, though the blend usually includes other herbs, such as marjoram, basil, lavender, savory, or oregano.

Provençal cooks can pluck the herbs from their gardens or window boxes; however, dried *herbes de Provence* blends are more common, and make their way into cooking throughout France. In fact, because the hallmark of these herbs is their piney, perfumey aroma, the dried versions work plenty of magic in recipes. Just be sure not to get too enthusiastic: They can overpower a dish if used in abundance.

Pissaladière

Pissaladière is a classic Niçoise onion/anchovy/garlic pizza–like tart. Bakeries sell them by the slice, and I often see people munching them on their way to the beach or after an arduous (ha!) day of staring off into the impossibly blue waters on the Côte d'Azur.

When home, I like to serve *pissaladière* with appetizers or with a main-dish salad for lunch. But it's also something you could serve with a couple of salads, a wedge of cheese, a glass of wine—and call it a summer supper. **Makes 8 appetizer or side-dish servings**

---

1 recipe Pizza Dough (page 254)

3 tablespoons extra-virgin olive oil

1 pound onions, halved and sliced (about 3½ cups total)

2 teaspoons snipped fresh thyme and/or rosemary leaves, or ½ teaspoon dried thyme and/or rosemary, crushed

Salt and freshly ground black pepper to taste

1 to 2 teaspoons anchovy paste

1 garlic clove, minced

¼ cup halved pitted imported black olives, such as Niçoise or kalamata

¼ cup freshly grated Parmigiano-Reggiano cheese (about 1 ounce)

1. Prepare the pizza dough as directed, reserving one-half of the dough for another use (see Note, page 254).

2. Position a rack in the lowest third of the oven. Preheat the oven to 425°F. Grease a large baking sheet. On a lightly floured surface, roll the remaining dough half into an 8 x 12-inch rectangle or a 10-inch round. Transfer to the baking sheet; press indentations all over the surface of the dough with your fingertips and set aside.

3. In a large skillet, heat 2 tablespoons of the olive oil over medium heat; add the onions, dried herbs (if using), and salt and pepper (go easy on the salt as the anchovy paste is salty). Cook, stirring occasionally, until the onions are tender and range from golden to dark brown, about 12 minutes. Add the anchovy paste during the last few minutes of cooking, stirring it in until it is worked into the mixture; stir in the fresh herbs (if using).

4. Combine the remaining 1 tablespoon olive oil and the garlic; brush over the surface of the pizza crust. Spread the onion mixture evenly over the crust, leaving a ½-inch rim around the edges. Top with the olives and sprinkle with the Parmigiano-Reggiano.

5. Bake until the crust is golden, about 14 minutes. Transfer to a cutting board and let cool for about 5 minutes (or up to 1 hour— *pissaladière* can also be served at room temperature). To serve, cut into 8 slices.

Alsatian Bacon and Onion Tart

This recipe is inspired by *tarte flambée*, which is to Alsace what *pissaladière* is to Provence—the classic dressed-up flatbread of the region. Serve it as a creamy and irresistible side to salad in the summer or to soup in the winter. Cut into thinner wedges, it's also great as part of an appetizer party spread.

Makes 8 appetizer or side-dish servings

1 recipe Pizza Dough (page 254)

6 slices bacon, chopped

1 medium onion

1 cup sour cream

1 large egg, beaten

Salt and freshly ground black pepper to taste

1. Prepare the pizza dough as directed, reserving one-half of the dough for another use (see Note, page 254).

2. Position an oven rack in the lowest third of the oven. Preheat the oven to 450°F. Grease a large shallow-rimmed baking sheet. On a lightly floured surface, roll the remaining dough half into a 10-inch round. Transfer to the baking sheet; roll the edges over once to form a rim and set aside.

3. Cook the bacon in a large skillet over medium heat until crisp but not hard. Transfer with a slotted spoon to paper towels to drain. Using a small, sharp knife, cut the onion in half, then slice each half as thinly as you can (you should almost be able to see through the slices). Toss the onions with your fingers to break up the slices (you should have about ¾ cup); set aside. In a small bowl, beat the sour cream and egg together until smooth. Set aside.

4. Prick the dough all over with a fork. Bake for 5 minutes. Remove from the oven; flatten any air bubbles with a fork.

5. Spread the sour cream and egg mixture atop the partially baked crust. Top with the onions and bacon and season well with salt and pepper.

6. Bake until the crust is golden brown on the bottom and edges, about 10 minutes more. Transfer to a cutting board and let cool for 5 minutes. Cut into 8 slices and serve warm.

Mushroom-Asparagus *Vol-au-Vents*

Fresh asparagus, draped in cream sauce and tucked into a pastry shell, is a beloved French first course in spring. It's an especially opulent treat when the season's morels join the dish, too. The pastry shells are called *vol-au-vents*, which means "flying in the wind," because of their light and airy texture. Make these with spring's tastiest asparagus, either as an elegant first-course starter or as a light luncheon dish accompanied by a salad. **Makes 6 first-course or light lunch servings**

1 (10-ounce) package frozen puff pastry shells (6 shells)

8 ounces thin asparagus, trimmed and cut into 1-inch pieces (about 1½ cups)

1 tablespoon unsalted butter

8 ounces earthy-flavored fresh mushrooms, such as cremini (sliced), shiitake (woody stems removed and discarded; caps sliced), or morels (halved)

1 large shallot, finely chopped (about ¼ cup)

1 cup heavy cream

Salt and freshly ground black pepper to taste

2 tablespoons snipped fresh chives

1. Prepare and bake the pastry shells according to the package directions. Set aside.

2. Bring a saucepan of water to a boil. Add the asparagus, bring back to a boil, and boil for 3 minutes. Drain; rinse under cold water. Drain well and pat dry with paper towels. Set asparagus aside.

3. Melt the butter in a large skillet over medium heat. Add the mushrooms and shallot and cook, stirring, until the mushrooms are tender, 8 to 10 minutes. Add the cream and salt and pepper. Simmer until the cream is thickened, 5 to 7 minutes. Stir in the asparagus and heat through.

4. Spoon the mixture into the pastry shells, letting some run over the sides. Garnish with chives and serve.

EGGS AND CHEESE

The omelet and baked egg recipes here show you how French home cooks turn a few eggs into a quick, gratifying any-night dinner. This chapter also covers cheese, another beloved ingredient, of course, of the French table. These pages celebrate the essential three—goat cheese, Gruyère, and Pyrénées sheep's milk cheese—plus give you some great serve-alongs for a beautiful, never-fussy, always-fantastic cheese course.

OPPOSITE: Rolled French Omelet with *Fines Herbes*, page 195, served with *Pipérade*, page 171

Oeufs Durs Mayonnaise

In the more humble cafés and bistros of France, you often see the same starters pop up on simple prix-fixe menus. Choices will include pâté, some sort of puréed vegetable soup, a raw vegetable salad, and *oeufs durs mayonnaise*—hard-cooked eggs with mayonnaise.

While the latter may sound disappointingly plain, the details make it a seriously good little dish to start an informal meal: Usually, the eggs are arranged on some leaves of tender butterhead lettuce and garnished with *cornichons* and olives. When you think about it, it's like a deconstructed deviled egg—a linger-and-relax, knife-and-fork version of the American party classic.

Of course, French mayonnaise is excellent—even when purchased from the supermarket. In fact, it comes in tubes with a star tip, which allows you to pipe the mayonnaise prettily on dishes such as this When I'm home in the States, I doctor supermarket mayonnaise just a bit with mustard, lemon juice, and herbs. If, by chance, you live near a market that imports a good French mayo, use it and omit the mustard and lemon juice here.   **Makes 4 first-course servings**

---

4 large eggs, hard-cooked and shelled

2 tablespoons good-quality mayonnaise

1 teaspoon Dijon mustard

1 teaspoon fresh lemon juice

2 tablespoons snipped fresh parsley, chives, tarragon, or chervil, or a combination, plus additional snipped fresh herbs for serving

8 leaves butterhead lettuce, such as Boston or Bibb

8 *cornichons*, drained

8 black olives, such as Niçoise or kalamata

1. Cut the eggs in half lengthwise. In a small bowl, whisk the mayonnaise, mustard, lemon juice, and herbs until smooth.

2. Arrange 2 leaves of lettuce on each of four salad plates. Top each plate with 1 hard-boiled egg (halved), 2 *cornichons*, and 2 olives. Dollop the mayonnaise on the eggs, garnish with additional fresh herbs, and serve.

Serving Suggestions

- Consider this a stand-in for the usual first-course tossed salad when you're in the mood to eat in courses.
- Serve as an easier-than-deviled eggs appetizer on an appetizer buffet. Cut a small slice from the uncut side of each egg half to prevent them from rolling around. Arrange the eggs on a large platter, dollop with mayonnaise. Serve the cornichons and olives in separate bowls on the platter.
- Add the mayonnaise-dolloped eggs to a platter with cured meats, Roasted Asparagus (page 169), and olives, as pictured above. Pass the platter at the table for a great sit-down starter.

Rolled French Omelet with *Fines Herbes*

French cooks serve omelets flipped, folded, and even flat, like an Italian frittata. However, my favorite French way to serve omelets is rolled. This technique is easier, in my view, than flipping. It also results in a creamy omelet—the outside is sunny yellow and cooked just enough to hold it together, while the interior remains fluffy and moist, like the best scrambled eggs.

Serve omelets café style—with a basket of sliced baguette alongside. If you must have potatoes, Pan-Fried Potatoes (page 168) are perfect (just make sure they're almost finished before you begin to cook the omelet).   **Makes 1 omelet**

---

2 large eggs

1 tablespoon snipped fresh *fines herbes* (see page 164)

Salt and freshly ground black pepper to taste

1 teaspoon unsalted butter

1. In a small bowl, beat the eggs, herbs, and salt and pepper until well blended; set aside.

2. Heat a 7-inch nonstick skillet over medium-high heat. Melt the butter in the skillet until hot but not brown. Add the eggs to the skillet. Shake the pan back and forth while using a fork held with the tines parallel to the pan to gently stir the eggs (the fork should not scrape the bottom of the pan). When the eggs are nearly cooked but still wet, stop stirring or you will tear the omelet; continue cooking until the eggs are set. Tilt the pan and use the fork or a spatula to gently roll the omelet, starting from its top edge. If you prefer your omelet more well done, leave it in the pan on the heat for a few moments more.

3. Roll the omelet out of the pan onto a plate, seam side down. Serve.

Rolled French Omelet
with Tapenade *Verte* and Sheep's Milk Cheese

While the French rarely eat omelets at breakfast, I find omelets to be weekend-morning dining at its leisurely best. I especially love slipping tasty leftovers from the previous night's gatherings into a breakfast omelet.

Consider this recipe a template for making morning-after-the-party omelets with party foods or other ingredients you might have around. This recipe uses tapenade, a great party staple. Prosciutto and Gruyère are a great combo, as are Brie and salami or other hard dry-cured sausage.   **Makes 1 omelet**

2 large eggs

Salt and freshly ground black pepper to taste

1 teaspoon unsalted butter

2 tablespoons finely grated Pyrénées sheep's milk cheese (such as Ossau-Iraty or P'tit Basque), or Manchego, or Gruyere, at room temperature

1 to 2 tablespoons Tapenade *Verte* (page 19), at room temperature, or chopped pitted green olives

1. In a small bowl, beat the eggs and salt and pepper until well blended; set aside.

2. Heat a 7-inch nonstick skillet over medium-high heat. Melt the butter in the skillet until hot but not brown. Add the eggs to the skillet. Shake the pan back and forth while using a fork held with the tines parallel to the pan to gently stir the eggs (the fork should not scrape the bottom of the pan). When the eggs are nearly cooked but still wet, stop stirring or you will tear the omelet; continue cooking until the eggs are set. Tilt the pan and use the fork or a spatula to gently roll the omelet, starting from its top edge. If you prefer your omelet more well done, leave it in the pan for a few moments more.

3. Roll the omelet out of the pan onto a plate, seam side down. Cut a slit down the center of the omelet and fill it with the cheese and the Tapenade *Verte*. Serve.

Variation

Tapenade *Noire* and Goat Cheese Omelet. Prepare as directed, except substitute soft-ripened goat cheese for the sheep's milk cheese and substitute Tapenade *Noire* (page 16) or chopped pitted black olives for the Tapenade *Verte*.

A Goat-Cheese Primer

One of the great pleasures of cooking and eating in France is discovering the abundance and variety of goat cheeses the country has to offer. In addition to the familiar logs, they also come in a variety of other fanciful shapes—from *crottins* (little rounds said to be named after, um, horse droppings) to bells, hearts, flowers, four-leaf clovers, pyramids, wheels, and donuts.

French goat cheeses also come in a range of styles, and much of their character can depend on how long the cheese is aged (or ripened, in goat-cheese parlance). As the cheeses ripen, their rinds develop, and their flavors go from mild to complex to pungent. In broad strokes, here are the three categories of goat cheese most often available in the United States:

Fresh, unripened goat cheeses. Sold soon after they're made, these rindless, chalky-white cheeses are creamy and rather mild-tasting after an initial tartness on the tongue. In French homes, they're often served with fruit for dessert or spread on toasts and topped with other ingredients as an appetizer. They also make their way into recipes, though they don't melt as nicely—nor taste quite as intriguing and complex—as soft-ripened and aged cheeses.

Soft-ripened (also known as semi-ripened) goat cheeses. Depending on how long they're ripened, these cheeses can range from chalky-creamy to smooth-creamy; often they're a bit of both—very soft and creamy near the rind, and more chalky-creamy toward the center. These are my favorite goat cheeses to cook with, because they have a bolder, more complex flavor than unripened fresh goat cheeses; they melt better, too.

Aged goat cheeses. When goat cheeses are fully ripened, they become drier, denser, and firmer, and the rind becomes rough, hard, and inedible. These offer the boldest of flavors, and often work well for grating.

You will find when you shop that many goat cheeses aren't labeled with the words "soft-ripened" or "semi-ripened." It's worth going to a top-quality cheese counter and asking a pro to point them out. If that's not possible, look for a goat cheese with a soft, edible rind. Avoid the rindless versions, labeled "fresh *chèvre*" or "fresh goat cheese" when a soft-ripened cheese is called for.

As the French home cook would shop for local products, so should you; American cheese-makers craft lovely versions of soft-ripened goat cheese. Two widely available producers to look for are Laura Chenel and Cypress Grove; you might even be fortunate enough to find some local versions you love.

Rolled French Omelet with Dill and Feta

Once you get the hang of a classic French rolled omelet (page 195), you'll never lack for a great breakfast, lunch, or light supper dish. Do as a French cook would: Add ingredients according to what's looking good at the market or what's ready and waiting in your refrigerator. Just make sure your ingredients are always chopped into small pieces and at room temperature before you tuck them into the omelet (otherwise, they'll cool the eggs). Here's a variation I enjoy when I bring home bunches of dillweed in summer.   **Makes 1 omelet**

---

2 large eggs

Salt and freshly ground black
   pepper to taste

1 teaspoon unsalted butter

2 tablespoons finely crumbled
   feta cheese (preferably French
   feta), at room temperature

1 teaspoon snipped fresh dillweed

1. In a small bowl, beat the eggs and salt and pepper until well blended; set aside.

2. Heat a 7-inch nonstick skillet over medium-high heat. Melt the butter in the skillet until hot but not brown. Add the eggs to the skillet. Shake the pan back and forth while using a fork held with the tines parallel to the pan to gently stir the eggs (the fork should not scrape the bottom of the pan). When the eggs are nearly cooked but still wet, stop stirring or you will tear the omelet; continue cooking until the eggs are set. Tilt the pan and use the fork or a spatula to gently roll the omelet starting from its top edge. If you prefer your omelet more well done, leave it in the pan for a few moments more.

3. Roll the omelet out of the pan onto a plate, seam side down. Cut a slit down the center of the omelet and fill it with the cheese and the dillweed. Serve.

Omelets for Two—or a Few

Omelets are made one at a time, but cooking takes a matter of moments, so you can easily serve even filled omelets to two or more diners. To do so, follow this plan:

· Bring any filling ingredients to room temperature.
· Have your omelet ingredients—eggs, butter, salt, and pepper—sitting out and ready to go for each omelet.
· After you've made the first omelet, transfer it to a plate, fill as directed, cover with foil, and set in a warm place.
· Wipe out the pan and start the next omelet, beating the eggs as the butter melts. As each omelet is finished, fill, cover, and keep warm as in the preceding step.

Bacon, Chive, and Caramelized Onion Quiche

Though French cooks might prefer using unsmoked *lardons* (bacon's French cousin) in their quiches, the smoky flavor of good American bacon adds so much to the flavor of this dish. And with caramelized onions in the mix, how can you go wrong? Ditto for a great Gruyère or Comté cheese.

This quiche is another case of a rediscovered gem—forget all the mediocre commercial versions of quiche you've endured at lesser restaurants and from the frozen-food aisle. Make it fresh and *chez vous*, and it will once again be a revelation. **Makes 6 to 8 servings**

---

1 recipe Pastry *Rapide* (page 256), prepared for a 9-inch deep-dish pie plate and prebaked

3 large eggs

1 cup heavy cream

½ cup 2 percent or whole milk

½ teaspoon salt

⅛ teaspoon cayenne pepper

4 ounces bacon, chopped (about 4 thick slices)

Extra-virgin olive oil, if needed

1 large sweet onion, such as Vidalia or Walla Walla, chopped (about 2 cups)

1 cup shredded Comté, Gruyère, or Emmental cheese (about 4 ounces)

¼ cup snipped fresh chives or sliced scallions (white portion and some tender green tops)

1. Preheat the oven to 375°F. In a medium-size bowl, whisk the eggs lightly. Whisk in the cream, milk, salt, and cayenne pepper; set aside.

2. In a large skillet, cook the bacon over medium heat until cooked but not crisp, 3 to 5 minutes. Using a slotted spoon, transfer the bacon to paper towels to drain. Drain off all but about 1 tablespoon of the bacon drippings from the pan (or, if needed, add enough extra-virgin olive oil to equal about 1 tablespoon of fat in pan). Add the onion to the pan and cook, stirring, over medium heat until translucent, 3 to 5 minutes. Cover and continue to cook, stirring occasionally, until the onions range from golden to brown, about 10 minutes. Spread the onions and bacon in the baked crust; sprinkle with the cheese and chives.

3. Slowly pour the egg mixture over the onions and bacon, distributing it evenly. Cover the exposed edges of the pastry with foil to prevent overbrowning.

4. Bake until the filling is set in the middle, 35 to 40 minutes. Cool on a wire rack for 5 minutes before slicing.

Baked Eggs with Ham and Gruyère

When it comes to ease, baking eggs is second only to scrambling them. But when it comes to presentation, baked eggs have scrambled eggs beat a few times over.

While the French often serve baked eggs as a first course, known as *oeufs en cocotte*, I consider them one of the easiest ways to bring a lunch or light supper main dish to the table using ingredients I keep on hand. Ham and firm cheeses, like Gruyère, have a long shelf life in the fridge, as do prosciutto and sheep's milk cheese (see the variation below; the Prosciutto and Pyrénées Cheese version is shown here).

I've sized this recipe for an individual serving so that you can make this casual dish for a night when you're home alone. But this recipe is incredibly easy to double, triple, or even quadruple—so you can serve whoever's around.   **Makes 1 serving**

---

2 large eggs

1 tablespoon heavy cream

Salt and freshly ground black pepper to taste

2 tablespoons finely grated Gruyère, Comté, or Emmental cheese

1 to 2 thin slices baked or smoked ham, diced

1 tablespoon snipped fresh parsley or chives

1. Preheat the oven to 375°F. Butter an 8-ounce baking dish (see Note).

2. Break the eggs into the dish. Drizzle the cream over the eggs and sprinkle with salt and pepper. Place the dish on a baking sheet and slide it into the oven; bake for 10 minutes.

3. Sprinkle the eggs with the cheese, ham, and parsley. Return to the oven and bake until the egg whites are completely set and the yolks thickened but not hard, 2 to 5 minutes more. Serve.

Note: I use 8-ounce individual porcelain quiche or *gratin* dishes (not metal tartlet pans with removable bottoms; they will leak). You can also use 8-ounce ramekins, but these aren't as shallow as quiche or *gratin* dishes, so you may need to bake the eggs longer.

Variations

Baked Eggs with Prosciutto and Pyrénées Cheese. Substitute diced, thinly sliced prosciutto for the ham and Pyrénées sheep's milk cheese (such as Ossau-Iraty or P'tit Basque) for the Gruyère.

Baked Eggs with *Pipérade*. Spread a scant ½ cup warm *Pipérade* (page 171) over the bottom of the buttered dish; hollow out an egg-size indentation in the middle of the *pipérade*. Use just one egg per serving; break the egg into the indentation. Omit all of the other ingredients. Bake until the egg white is completely set and the yolk is thickened but not hard, about 20 minutes.

French Cheeses for Cooking

There are more than 350 kinds of cheese made in France, and getting to know as many of them as you can get your hands on may be one of the food lover's greatest pleasures. So, why do most of my recipes call for the same handful of cheeses? After all, French cooks in Burgundy or Champagne in the north might melt a little Chaource into their *gratins*, while one in south-central Auvergne might grate up some Cantal; for a goat-cheese salad, home cooks in the southwest would probably reach for a regional choice, like Rocamadour, while those to the north would more likely choose one of the many famed Loire Valley cheeses in their region.

Yet one of the promises of this book is that you don't have to seek out hard-to-find ingredients to bring life-enhancing everyday French food to your table. That's why many of my recipes call for cheeses that most French cooks use on a regular basis and that are easily found in the United States.

Top on the list are Alpine cheeses such as Gruyère and Emmental, those marvelous cooking, melting, and eating cheeses that are at once fruity, nutty, and sharp. Most versions found stateside are from Switzerland, but the French make their own versions, and they're among the most popular in French home cooking.

French Gruyère, known as Comté, is becoming more widely available stateside. Hailing from the delightfully rustic, unspoiled, and woefully under-celebrated Franche-Comté region on the French-Swiss border, Comté is traditionally aged longer than Swiss Gruyère and, to me, tastes richer, deeper, and more uncommonly wild (akin to a mountain meadow buzzing and chirping and alive with sweet grass smells). However, it is absolutely fine to use a Swiss Gruyère instead of Comté. Swiss Gruyère, too, is one of the world's great cheeses—fruity, nutty, rich, and complex.

Another fantastic French cheese you'll spot often on these pages is Pyrénées sheep's milk cheese. This cheese (known as *brebis Pyrénées)* has been made in the Pyrénées mountains for about 4,000 years; locally, it's most often served on its own as part of a cheese course, or—with cherry jam—for dessert. For many years, these cheeses were hard to find outside of the Pyrénées, even in France.

These days, as Pyrénées sheep's milk cheese is becoming widely available, I've started to see more and more French recipes that call on it. And for good reason: Its complex, nutty-caramel flavor adds so much to so many different types of dishes. And while it's costly, a little goes a long way.

Two of the most widely available Pyrénées sheep's milk cheeses are the young P'tit Basque and the longer-aged Ossau-Iraty. Choose the younger for creamier texture and milder flavor, the more mature cheese for a sharper, "sheepier" taste.

If you can't find a Pyrénées sheep's milk cheese, you have a number of options. Keep your eye out for American versions of sheep's milk cheese—Major Farm's Vermont Shepherd Traditional Sheep's Milk Cheese, for example, is highly recommended. Manchego, a Spanish sheep's milk cheese, is an admirable stand-in. Gruyère is a good option for its complex flavor and meltability.

Goat cheeses are also often used in everyday French cooking, so naturally, they make many appearances in my recipes. Find more info on French goat cheeses on page 197.

But what about Parmigiano-Reggiano, the quintessential Italian cheese that sometimes makes an appearance in this decidedly French cookbook? This beloved world-class cheese is available in France, and French cooks do take advantage, though they use it sparingly, as it's more expensive for them than many French choices. Still, no matter where you live, sometimes a recipe can benefit from the bold snap of flavor that just a bit of that prized cheese can bring.

Something else to keep in mind about cheese: In many cases, you can substitute a cheese you have on hand for one that you don't, as long as you use a cheese with somewhat similar cooking properties. I've used high-quality cheddar when I couldn't find Gruyère. I've grated some Emmental when I've run out of Parmigiano-Reggiano. I've cooked with Gruyère if I can't find Ossau-Iraty. That's not to say that a dish made with cheddar will taste the same as one made with Gruyère—it won't. But if you use a similarly styled, high-quality version of a cheese whose flavor you'll like, you'll most likely enjoy the dish.

Roasted Asparagus and Cheese Tartlets

Served with an array of vegetable salads, these individual-size quiches make a good lunch or a fine light supper. I also enjoy serving them on platters when I want something hearty to anchor an appetizer spread—in this case, I halve or quarter the baked tartlets to make mingling-friendly bites.

A note on the pastry: In keeping with the everyday spirit of this book, I've called for a purchased pie pastry. Purists (and those who love all-scratch baking!) can use the Rich Pastry for Savory Tarts (page 257) for more indulgent results. See Note, below. **Makes 4 tartlets**

1 purchased refrigerated pie pastry (for a 9-inch pie)

8 ounces asparagus, trimmed

2 teaspoons extra-virgin olive oil

¼ cup freshly grated Pyrénées sheep's milk cheese (such as Ossau-Iraty or P'tit Basque), or Manchego, Comté, Gruyère, or Emmental cheese (1 ounce)

Salt and freshly ground black pepper to taste

3 large eggs

⅓ cup heavy cream

1. Bring the pastry to room temperature as directed on the package. Preheat the oven to 450°F.

2. Place the asparagus in a shallow roasting pan, drizzle with the olive oil, and season with salt and pepper; toss to coat the asparagus with the oil. Roast the asparagus until almost tender, about 8 minutes. Cool slightly, then cut the asparagus into 1- to 2-inch pieces. Set aside. Reduce the oven heat to 425°F.

3. Cut the pastry into four equal quadrants. On a lightly floured surface, roll and shape each into a 6-inch circle. Ease each round of pastry into a 4½-inch fluted tart pan with a removable bottom or an 8-ounce individual porcelain quiche or *gratin* dish. With a rolling pin, roll over the top of the tart pans to trim off any extra dough.

4. Place the pans on a baking sheet and bake until lightly brown all over, about 12 minutes. Reduce the oven heat to 375°F.

5. Divide the asparagus and the cheese among the 4 tart shells. In a small bowl, beat the eggs and the cream together; season with salt and pepper. Divide evenly among the tart shells.

6. Bake until the filling is set (it will no longer jiggle when shaken), 15 to 20 minutes, loosely covering the tartlets with a sheet of foil, if needed, during the last 5 to 10 minutes to prevent the pastry edges from overbrowning. Transfer the tartlet pans to a wire rack to cool for 5 minutes. Remove the tartlets from the pans or dishes and serve warm.

Note: To use the Rich Pastry for Savory Tarts, prepare and chill the pastry as directed on page 257 through step 1. Roast the asparagus while the pastry is chilling. Divide the chilled pastry dough into four portions. On a lightly floured surface, roll each portion into a 6-inch circle. Continue as directed above, except in step 4, bake the pastry about 15 minutes.

A Bright Mini Salad for the Cheese Course

In some French homes and restaurants, the cheese course is served with a sparkling little salad, often made simply of a bitter green or two dressed with a tart vinaigrette. This mini salad provides a terrific foil to bold, rich, and often creamy cheeses. In fact, when you've dined on a filling main course, and you think you can't possibly enjoy a cheese course afterward, this little puff of salad does wonders to brighten and lighten the pleasure.

For more humble meals, a mini salad is simply plated with one local cheese. In fancier restaurants, a plate with the salad will be placed in front of you; the server will then wheel up the *chariot de fromages* (the cheese trolley) and let you select a few to go on your plate alongside the salad. There isn't a trolley in French homes, though, so I suggest you do what French hosts often do: Simply offer everyone a plate with the little pile of greens, place a selection of cheeses in the middle of the table, and let everyone help themselves *à volonté* (as they wish). **Makes 4 mini salads**

---

1 small garlic clove, minced

Salt and freshly ground black pepper to taste

2 teaspoons sherry vinegar or rice vinegar

1 tablespoon sunflower oil, walnut oil, or extra-virgin olive oil

Dash of hot pepper sauce

2 cups frisée, tender arugula, or curly endive, or a combination, or 1 cup watercress and 1 cup mild tender lettuce, such as butterhead (Boston or Bibb) or red leaf lettuce

Cheeses for the cheese course (see box, below)

1. Put the garlic clove and salt and pepper in a small bowl; mash with the back of a spoon. Add the vinegar and whisk until the salt is dissolved. Add the oil, whisking until incorporated. Whisk in the hot pepper sauce.

2. In a salad bowl, toss the greens with the dressing. Serve about ½ cup of greens per person alongside the cheese(s) of your choosing.

Cheeses for the Cheese Course

When entertaining, a selection of three cheeses is ideal, and there are many ways to go about choosing which three cheeses. I enjoy "bringing home the barnyard"—that is, serving a cow's milk cheese, a sheep's milk cheese, and a goat's milk cheese. In such a case, Gruyère, Ossau-Iraty, and a soft-ripened goat cheese make a great threesome. Another way to go about it is to head to a cheesemonger and look and taste your way to a trio of stylistically different cheeses; for example, a blue, a soft-rind cheese (such as Camembert), and a firmer cheese (such as Cantal) would be great.

Winter Compote for Cheese

On prix-fixe restaurant menus in France, you'll often see formulas that feature either "*fromage et dessert*" or "*fromage ou dessert*." The difference is key. The former means you'll be getting a cheese course *and* dessert; the latter means you'll have to choose between cheese *or* dessert—and that can be a tough choice!

At home, when serving *fromage et dessert*, a French cook would serve the cheeses quite simply, with bread or perhaps a bit of salad. However, when serving *fromage* without a dessert course to follow, the cook will sometimes bring a little something sweet to the table. In summer, drippingly ripe cherries, peaches, and apricots work well; in fall, crisp apples or tender pears do the trick. In winter, when many fresh, local fruits are hard to come by, a jam or compote like this one brings just enough to the cheese course to make it feel like a justifiably sweet, satisfying finish to the meal. **Makes about 2 cups**

½ **cup finely chopped dried figs**

½ **cup finely chopped dried apricots**

½ **cup chopped dried cherries**

½ **cup fresh orange juice**

¼ **cup sugar**

¼ **cup Cognac or brandy**

1 teaspoon finely chopped orange zest

Pinch of salt

1. In a medium-size saucepan, combine the figs, apricots, cherries, orange juice, sugar, Cognac, orange zest, and salt. Bring to a boil and cook, stirring, until the sugar is dissolved. Reduce the heat and simmer, stirring occasionally, until the liquid is reduced and syrupy, about 10 minutes. Transfer to a bowl and cool to room temperature. Cover and refrigerate.

2. Bring to room temperature before serving.

Serving Suggestions

- I like to place the bowl of compote on a tray with cheeses and breads, set it in the center of the table, and allow diners to serve themselves *à volonté* (as they wish). Be sure to give everyone a salad-size plate, plus a knife and fork (see page 207 for good choices for a cheese course).
- This compote is also heavenly when served warm. For a luscious canapé, spread about a tablespoon on a toasted baguette slice; top with Brie or a Gruyère-style cheese, and run under the broiler until the cheese melts.
- Save some of this compote to make open-face turkey and Brie sandwiches. Spread some compote on toasted bread slices (baguette is perfect), then top with chunks of turkey and a few thin slices of Brie. Run under the broiler until the Brie is oozy.
- Stir a little honey into some of the compote; warm slightly and spoon over ice cream. Top with toasted pine nuts.

LES DESSERTS

We often think of French desserts as elaborate creations—the domain of trained pastry chefs or of cooks who treat baking and confections as a serious hobby. While you'll find a few pastry-shop favorites here, most of the recipes reflect the kinds of desserts that French cooks truly make for family and friends: clafoutis, *crème caramel*, crêpes, *pots de crème*, clever ice cream combos, and other gratifying ways to end any night's meal simply and sweetly.

OPPOSITE: Chocolate *Pots de Crème*, page 236

Cherry Clafoutis

Clafoutis is the classic home-baked dessert. It's the French cook's way of bringing something lovely and sweet to the table any night, and it takes just minutes to stir together before popping in the oven. A bit like a baked custard, a bit like a cake, clafoutis will remind you of everything you love about other sweet, eggy dishes—French toast, bread pudding, and crêpes.

Keep in mind that the sides of the clafoutis may rise while baking, but they will sink and even out nicely once cooled. And if the custard has a few cracks, count them as your badge of honor—you're serving a charmingly rustic and authentic homemade French dessert. **Makes 6 servings**

---

12 ounces pitted fresh sweet cherries or frozen pitted sweet cherries, thawed and drained well

3 large eggs

½ cup granulated sugar

½ teaspoon pure vanilla extract

2 tablespoons kirsch (cherry brandy)

Pinch of salt

½ cup all-purpose flour

1 cup whole milk

¼ cup heavy cream

¼ cup confectioners' sugar

Spiked whipped cream (see Note), for serving

1. Preheat the oven to 375°F. Butter and sugar a 9-inch round nonmetal baking dish with 2-inch sides.

2. Spread the cherries in the baking dish. In the bowl of an electric mixer, beat the eggs, sugar, vanilla, kirsch, and salt on medium speed until well combined. Slowly beat in the flour, milk, and cream until combined. Pour the batter over the cherries.

3. Bake until a thin knife inserted near the center of the clafoutis comes out clean and the top is a deep golden color, about 40 minutes. If the top is brown before the custard is done, loosely cover with a sheet of foil. Place on a wire rack to cool, but serve warm. Just before serving, dust the top of the clafoutis with confectioners' sugar and serve in either scoops or wedges topped with spiked whipped cream.

Note: To make spiked whipped cream, place 1 cup cold heavy cream into a chilled mixing bowl. Add 2 to 4 tablespoons confectioners' sugar. Beat with an electric mixer on medium speed until soft peaks form. Beat in 2 tablespoons kirsch until soft peaks return.

Variation

Peach Clafoutis. Substitute 4 fresh peaches (about 1½ pounds), peeled, pitted, and sliced, for the cherries. Substitute peach brandy for the kirsch.

Lemon Curd Crème Brûlée

I've savored many a *crème brulée* in France. Some of my favorites add the flavor of citrus to liven up the rich, sweet custard. That's the case here—the dessert is rich and wonderful, but just watch your guests' faces light up when they hit that tangy center—a pool of homemade or purchased lemon curd. It's a smashing surprise. **Makes 4 servings**

4 tablespoons lemon curd, purchased or homemade (page 239)

1¾ cups heavy cream

5 large egg yolks

⅓ cup plus 12 teaspoons sugar

1 teaspoon pure vanilla extract

Pinch of salt

1. Position a rack in the middle of the oven. Preheat the oven to 325°F. Put a pot of water on to boil.

2. Spoon 1 tablespoon lemon curd into each of four 8-ounce individual porcelain quiche or gratin dishes, placing each dollop in the center of the dish (see Note). Spread the curd into two-inch circles. Set the dishes into a large baking pan.

3. In a small saucepan, heat the cream over medium-low heat until steaming. In a medium-size bowl, whisk together the egg yolks, ⅓ cup of the sugar, the vanilla, and the salt until well combined. Gradually whisk the hot cream into the egg mixture. Divide the custard evenly among the baking dishes.

4. Slide the oven rack out and place the pan with the baking dishes on the rack. Carefully pour the boiling water into the pan until it comes halfway up the sides of the baking dishes, then slide the rack back in. Bake until the centers barely jiggle when shaken, 25 to 30 minutes. With a steady, oven-mittened hand, remove the baking dishes from the water bath. Transfer to a wire rack to cool for 20 minutes. Cover and refrigerate until well chilled, about 4 hours.

5. Before serving, blot the tops of the custards dry with plain white paper towels. Sprinkle 2 teaspoons sugar evenly over each of the baked custards. Using a kitchen torch, caramelize the sugar until it's a rich, golden brown. Serve.

Note: If you wish, you can use four 6-ounce ramekins or custard cups. Do not spread the lemon curd— simply dollop it in the ramekins as a distinct spoonful. Continue as directed above, except bake for 30 to 40 minutes.

Crème Caramel Chez Vous

Three desserts pop up again and again on prix-fixe menus at French cafés—chocolate mousse, ice cream, and *crème caramel*—and these desserts often make their way to the French home table, too. In fact, supermarket aisles offer little packets of *caramel liquide*—the liquid caramelized sugar that provides the syrup for homemade *crème caramel*, allowing the cook to skip the tricky caramelizing step.

This recipe utilizes a different shortcut. While *caramel liquide* isn't available widely here, good caramel sauces are. So you don't have to cook sugar to a caramel; you simply top the chilled, baked custard with an excellent ready-made product. If you don't mind taking a little extra time, you can certainly make your own caramel sauce (see page 238). Whatever sauce you use, consider stirring in a little orange liqueur for a touch of brightness and intrigue **Makes 4 servings**

1³/₄ cups whole milk

4 large egg yolks

1 large egg

¹/₂ cup sugar

Pinch of salt

1 teaspoon pure vanilla extract

¹/₄ cup Caramel Sauce *à la Tricheuse* (page 238), or high-quality purchased caramel sauce (look for cream or butter in the ingredient listing)

1 tablespoon Grand Marnier (optional)

1. Position a rack in the middle of the oven. Preheat the oven to 325°F (be sure the oven goes no higher). Set four 6-ounce custard cups in a 9-inch square baking pan. Put a pot of water on to boil.

2. In a small saucepan, bring the milk just to a boil; remove from the heat. In a mixing bowl, lightly beat the egg yolks, the whole egg, the sugar, and the salt. Slowly beat in the hot milk until blended. Stir in the vanilla. Divide the custard evenly among the custard cups.

3. Slide the oven rack out and place the pan on the rack. Carefully pour the boiling water into the pan until it comes about three-quarters of the way up the sides of the custard cups, then slide the rack back in. Bake until the custard is just set (a knife inserted near the center should come out clean, but the center may jiggle slightly), 45 to 50 minutes (take care not to overbake).

4. With a steady, oven-mittened hand, remove the custard cups from the water bath. Transfer to a wire rack to cool for 30 minutes. Cover and refrigerate until well chilled, about 4 hours.

5. To serve, heat the caramel sauce in a small saucepan just until warm and pourable. Add the Grand Marnier, if you like. Run a knife around the edges of the custards; invert onto individual dessert plates. Pour some caramel sauce over the top of each custard.

Desserts at Home in France

I've enjoyed many meals in French homes, but I cannot recall ever having been served a homemade dessert. Yet my French hosts have served me memorable desserts indeed—from a berry-mousse cake for my twenty-third birthday in Burgundy to the southwest's famous *croustade aux pommes*—a flaky apple tart served to me one Easter Sunday in the Gers.

That's not to say that French home cooks don't bake—it's just that they don't have to. Nearly every town and every neighborhood in larger cities have beautiful *pâtisseries*, their windows beckoning with fanciful cream-filled cakes, tangy lemon tarts, colorful fruit tarts, multi-layered napoleons, airy meringues, and other magical creations.

Unless they're avid fans of baking, many French home cooks are likely to pick up something from their favorite *pâtisseur* when they're having *les invités* (guests) for dinner. Guests rarely feel slighted at being served a purchased dessert—in fact, they consider themselves quite fêted when presented with something from the town's top *pâtisserie*.

For everyday desserts, the French cook has an enviable selection available from the supermarket. Packaged versions of *crème caramel*, chocolate mousse, floating islands, and other refrigerated desserts are surprisingly good in spite of their not-so-chic origins. *Fromage blanc* (a fresh cheese with the consistency of yogurt), served with sugar, honey, or preserves, is also a delightful—and easy—way to end a family meal. And when at their in-season best, fresh fruits often serve—solo or with a little sweetened *fromage blanc* or *crème fraîche*—as much-loved desserts.

When the French cook does prepare homemade dessert, it's likely something rather straightforward—simple custards, fruit tarts, clafoutis, or crêpes—often showcasing the wonderful fresh fruits brought home from the market. Most of the recipes in this chapter follow that vein. Yet because we don't all have *pâtisseries* in our neighborhoods, I also offer a number of desserts of a style that a French cook would likely purchase rather than make, but that are easy enough to pull off at home. These include the French Lemon Tartlets (page 222) and the Classic French Fruit Tart (page 220).

If time is running out and you want to serve a true-to-France dessert but don't live anywhere near a true-to-France *pâtisserie*, consider making a *coupe glacée*—a fanciful (and French) take on the ice-cream sundae (page 230).

Sablés

When the time comes for me to head, reluctantly, home from France, I buy up plenty of packages of *sablés*—French butter cookies—to take home with me. Commercial versions of these wonderfully old-fashioned cookies are surprisingly good, and they give me a taste of *la belle France* for a few weeks. Once I run out of the French *biscuits*, I make my own. I must admit, these homemade cookies trump the commercial French packaged cookies any day, even if the latter are pretty darn good.

A cross between an American sugar cookie and Scottish shortbread, *sablés* are all about the butter. Make sure yours is fresh and of good quality. You might even want to splurge on an imported higher-fat French butter at a gourmet shop, just to make them a little *extra*. **Makes about 4 dozen cookies**

1¾ cups all-purpose flour

½ teaspoon baking powder

¼ teaspoon salt

8 tablespoons (1 stick) unsalted butter, softened

½ cup sugar

1 large egg

1 teaspoon pure vanilla extract

1 large egg yolk, lightly beaten with 1 tablespoon water

1. In a small mixing bowl, combine the flour, baking powder, and salt. In the bowl of an electric mixer, beat the butter and sugar on medium speed until well blended. Beat in the egg and vanilla until combined. Beat in the flour mixture until just combined. Using your hands, press the dough together in the bowl until it forms a ball. Divide the dough in half, form it into two disks, and wrap each separately in plastic wrap. Transfer to the refrigerator and chill until the dough is firm and easy to handle, about 2 hours.

2. Preheat the oven to 350°F. On a lightly floured surface, roll out each dough disk until ¼ inch thick. With a 2-inch round cookie cutter (a cutter with scalloped edges is traditional), cut out the dough. Transfer the cutouts to ungreased cookie sheets. Reroll any scraps and cut out more cookies.

3. Brush the tops of the cookies with the egg yolk–water mixture. Bake until golden brown, about 10 minutes. Transfer the cookies to wire racks to cool. Store in an airtight container, separated by layers of waxed paper, for up to 3 days.

Alsatian Apple Tart

Flaky pastry with apples surrounded by a custard of cream and eggs is a classic Alsatian dessert. And don't feel inauthentic if, when pressed for time, you use a purchased pastry: Supermarket refrigerator cases in France brim with ready-made pastry doughs. **Makes 6 to 8 servings**

1 purchased refrigerated pie pastry (for a 9-inch pie) or 1 recipe Pastry Rapide (page 256)

2 to 3 sweet apples, such as Gala or Fuji (about 1 pound)

2 large eggs

³/₄ cup heavy cream

¹/₂ cup plus 2 tablespoons sugar

1 tablespoon golden raisins

1¹/₂ teaspoons ground cinnamon

Sweetened whipped cream, for serving

1. Preheat the oven to 450°F.

2. Prepare and roll out the pastry as directed for a 9½-inch quiche dish (not a pan with a removable bottom). Ease the pastry into the dish. Do not prick the pastry. Trim the pastry so it's even with the top of the dish. Line the pastry with heavy-duty foil; fill with pie weights or dried beans. Bake for 8 minutes. Carefully remove the foil and weights (the foil can stick to the pastry); return to the oven and bake until dry and lightly browned, 3 to 5 minutes. Set the dish on a wire rack to cool. Reduce the oven heat to 350°F.

3. Peel and core the apples and cut into thin slices; arrange the slices, fanning in a circular pattern if you like, in the partially baked pastry shell. In a medium-size bowl, beat the eggs; add the cream and ½ cup of the sugar and beat just until blended. Pour the custard over the apples. Scatter the raisins over all.

4. Cover any exposed edges of the pastry with foil to prevent overbrowning. Bake until the apples are tender and the custard is set, about 50 minutes, removing the foil for the last 10 minutes of baking to allow the edges to brown. Transfer the pan to a wire rack to cool for 1 hour (refrigerate after 1 hour if not serving at this point).

5. Combine the remaining 2 tablespoons sugar with the cinnamon. Serve each tart slice with sweetened whipped cream sprinkled with the cinnamon-sugar mixture. Cover and refrigerate leftovers for up to 1 day.

Classic French Fruit Tart

This is it! The buttery-crusted, cream-filled, fruit-topped tart you see glistening like a display of jewels in pastry shop windows all over France. It's a beautiful showcase for drippingly ripe in-season fruits—and it's much easier to make than it looks.

This is almost a one-size-fits-all-fruits tart, as you can top it with just about any berries or stone fruits that come marching into season throughout the summer. My favorite is fresh sweet cherries—because their season is so fleeting, they make the dessert a truly rare treat. **Makes 8 servings**

FOR THE PASTRY CREAM:

1/3 cup sugar

2 tablespoons cornstarch

Pinch of salt

1 cup whole milk

1 large egg, lightly beaten

1 tablespoon unsalted butter

FOR THE PASTRY:

1 1/2 cups all-purpose flour

1/4 cup sugar

1/4 teaspoon salt

12 tablespoons (1 1/2 sticks) cold unsalted butter, cut into pieces

1 large egg yolk

4 to 6 teaspoons cold water

TO ASSEMBLE:

2 cups fresh fruits, such as sliced pitted sweet cherries; sliced strawberries; whole raspberries, blackberries, or blueberries; halved apricots; sliced peeled peaches or nectarines; in any combination if desired

1 (10-ounce) jar apricot preserves

1 tablespoon fresh lemon juice

1. Make the pastry cream: In a medium-size bowl, whisk together the sugar, cornstarch, and salt. In a small saucepan, heat the milk over medium heat until it starts to steam (do not boil). Remove from the heat. Whisk the egg vigorously into the sugar mixture until smooth and pale. Slowly pour the hot milk into the egg mixture, whisking constantly.

2. Return the milk mixture to the saucepan. Cook over medium heat, stirring constantly, until thickened and bubbly. Whisk in the butter until melted. Cook and stir, whisking vigorously to blend away any lumps, for 2 minutes. Strain the pastry cream through a sieve into a bowl. Cover the bowl with plastic wrap. Chill in the refrigerator until cold, about 4 hours.

3. Make the pastry: Preheat the oven to 375°F. Place the flour, sugar, and salt in a food processor; pulse to combine. Add the butter and pulse until the mixture resembles coarse sand with some pebbles. While the machine is running, add the egg yolk through the feed tube, and then add the water 1 teaspoon at a time.

As soon as the dough forms a ball, stop adding water.

4. Press the dough evenly into the bottom and up the sides of a 9-inch tart pan with a removable bottom. Prick the bottom of the crust all over with a fork. Bake until the pastry is golden brown, 25 to 30 minutes. Transfer the pan to a wire rack to cool to room temperature.

5. To assemble: Remove the sides from the tart pan, leaving the bottom in place. Spread the chilled pastry cream evenly over the bottom of the tart shell. (You may need to whisk the cream smooth before spreading.) Arrange the fruits in an attractive pattern on top of the pastry cream.

6. In a saucepan, bring the apricot preserves and lemon juice just to a boil. Strain through a sieve to remove any large pieces of apricot. Brush the glaze over the fruit and any exposed pastry cream. Chill the tart to allow the glaze to set, for at least 1 hour or up to 4 hours. For best results, serve the tart on the day it is made.

French Lemon Tartlets

Here's the situation: It's winter; you're serving a big, hearty stew, and you want to end the meal with something refreshing. Many of your favorite fresh fruits are not, for the moment, available options. Tingly, rich, and intense, this bright-yet-velvety dessert is the recipe you seek.

In summer, dress these tartlets up with fresh blueberries or raspberries scattered across the tops—fresh, tart, and tingly tastes great after something off the grill, too.   **Makes 4 tartlets**

---

1 recipe Pastry *Rapide* (page 256)

2 tablespoons sugar

1 recipe Lemon Curd (page 239), prepared through step 1

Sweetened whipped cream, for serving

1. Preheat the oven to 425°F. Prepare the pastry as directed, *except* mix 2 tablespoons sugar into the flour mixture before cutting in the butter and shortening.

2. Divide the pastry into four portions. On a lightly floured surface, roll each into a 6-inch circle. Ease each round of pastry into a 4½-inch fluted tart pan with a removable bottom or an 8-ounce individual porcelain quiche or *gratin* dish. With a rolling pin, roll over the top of the tart pans to trim off any extra dough. Prick the pastry all over with a fork. Place the pans on a baking sheet and bake until lightly brown all over, about 15 minutes. Place the baking sheet on a wire rack. Reduce the oven heat to 350°F.

3. While the pastry is baking, make the lemon curd. Do not chill.

4. Divide the lemon curd evenly among the four pastry shells, smoothing the top of the curd with the back of a spoon. Make sure the oven temperature has reduced to 350°F. Return the pastry shells to the oven and bake until the centers jiggle only slightly, about 5 minutes.

5. Transfer the tartlets to a wire rack to cool for 30 minutes, then transfer to the refrigerator to chill for 2 to 3 hours before serving (cover with plastic wrap if storing longer).

4. Serve with sweetened whipped cream. Cover and refrigerate leftovers for up to 1 day.

Lemon-Glazed Sponge Cake
with Strawberry-Lillet Sauce

Dress this airy cake up with a bright lemon glaze and a strawberry sauce spiked with Lillet (the famed orange liqueur–infused French apéritif wine) for a light and lovely summer dessert. Enjoy the extra Lillet as an apéritif in the coming days—it will keep in the refrigerator for up to 2 weeks. **Makes 8 servings**

1 cup all-purpose flour

1 teaspoon baking powder

Pinch of salt

2 large eggs

1 cup sugar

1 teaspoon pure vanilla extract

½ cup 2 percent or whole milk

3 tablespoons unsalted butter, cut into pieces

1 recipe Lemon Glaze

1 recipe Strawberry-Lillet Sauce

Sweetened whipped cream, for serving

1. Preheat the oven to 350°F. Grease and flour the bottom and sides of an 8-inch round or square cake pan with 2-inch sides. In a small bowl, whisk together the flour, baking powder, and salt.

2. In a medium bowl, beat the eggs with an electric mixer on medium-high speed until thick and lemon-colored, about 3 minutes. Gradually add the sugar and beat until pale, light, and fluffy, about 2 minutes more. Beat in the vanilla. Use a spatula to stir the flour mixture into the egg mixture just until combined.

3. In a small saucepan, combine the milk and butter. Heat and stir over medium heat just until the butter is melted. Gradually pour the hot milk mixture into the batter, stirring constantly until combined. Pour the batter into the prepared pan.

4. Bake until a wooden toothpick inserted in the center of the cake comes out clean, 25 to 30 minutes. Cool in the pan on a wire rack. Drizzle and spread the Lemon Glaze over the top of the cooled cake.

5. To serve, run a knife around the edges of the pan to loosen the cake from the pan. Cut into into 8 slices. Spoon Strawberry-Lillet sauce onto 8 dessert plates. Place the cake slices on top of the sauce and serve with sweetened whipped cream.

Lemon Glaze

In a small bowl, stir together ½ cup powdered sugar and enough fresh lemon juice (about 1 tablespoon) to make a glaze of drizzling consistency.

Strawberry-Lillet Sauce

In a medium saucepan, combine 1 pound chopped strawberries and ¼ cup sugar. Cook, covered, over medium-low heat, stirring often, until the strawberries release their juices and become very soft, about 8 minutes. Remove the pan from the heat and cool the mixture to lukewarm. In a food processor, combine the cooked strawberries and their liquid with ¼ cup Lillet Blanc or 1 tablespoon Cointreau or Grand Marnier. Cover and process until pureed. Transfer to a bowl. Cover and refrigerate at least 2 hours or up to 24 hours before serving. Makes 1½ cups.

Master Recipe for Crêpes

I don't know why, but crêpes, like fondue, go in and out of fashion in our country. But make them at home, and you'll find they're worth keeping at the top of your mind for light, casual dinners and, of course, desserts. Crêpes with leftover ham or chicken in béchamel sauce, invigorated with a sprinkling of fresh herbs, make an incredibly satisfying lunch or supper (see the variations given with the recipe for Béchamel Sauce on page 245).

When serving crêpes as a main course, you can just roll the crêpe around the filling. However, when serving crêpes as a dessert, the French often fold each crêpe in half and then in half again to form a wedge, then top the wedge with the featured ingredient (rather than tucking it inside). I like this method—it gives you more concentration of the rich, eggy delight in every forkful.   **Makes twelve 7-inch crêpes**

¾ **cup 2 percent or whole milk**

½ **cup water**

2 large eggs

1 cup all-purpose flour

3 tablespoons unsalted butter, melted, plus more melted butter for the pan

Pinch of salt

1. Place the milk, water, eggs, flour, melted butter, and salt in a blender in the order given. Pulse until blended, scraping down the sides of the blender container once. Refrigerate the batter for at least 1 hour and up to 48 hours. (This allows the bubbles to settle out so the crêpes are less likely to tear during cooking.)

2. If the batter has separated during refrigeration, stir it gently to blend. Because each crêpe needs to cool individually on a plate, set four plates (at least 7 inches in diameter) on a countertop, ready and waiting to receive the just-made crêpes.

3. Brush the bottom of a 6- to 7-inch nonstick skillet with melted butter to coat it lightly. Heat over medium-high heat. Remove the pan from the heat and pour a scant ¼ cup batter into the hot pan, quickly swirling the pan to coat the bottom with batter. Return the pan to the heat and cook until the crêpe is lightly browned on the bottom and loosened from the pan, about 30 seconds. Using a thin pancake turner or heatproof spatula, flip the crêpe and cook for about 30 seconds more.

4. Slide the crêpe out of the pan and onto one of the plates. Repeat with the remaining batter, buttering the pan only if necessary. (Reduce the heat to medium if the crêpes start to brown too quickly.) Once you've made 4 crêpes, you can start stacking the cooled crêpes, freeing up a plate for stacking the next one hot out of the pan. See pages 226 to 228 for crêpe recipes and serving suggestions.

Making Crêpes in Advance

Once you've stacked the cooled crêpes, you can reheat them (15 to 30 seconds per crêpe) in the microwave, if needed.

You can also make the crêpes ahead of time. To store in the refrigerator, stack cooled crêpes with a sheet of waxed paper between each crêpe. Cover the stack with plastic wrap and refrigerate for up to 2 days. To reheat, warm each crêpe gently in a skillet or in the microwave (15 to 30 seconds per crêpe).

Crêpes also freeze surprisingly well. Stack cooled crêpes on a freezer-safe plate with a sheet of waxed paper between each crêpe. Cover the stack with plastic wrap and freeze. Thaw in the refrigerator and warm each gently in a skillet or in the microwave before serving. You can also thaw frozen crêpes in the microwave until thawed; once thawed, heat each until warm, 15 to 30 seconds per crêpe.

Crêpes *Belle Hélène*

Poire Belle Hélène is a classic French dessert created by the great chef Auguste Escoffier in honor of Jacques Offenbach's operetta *La Belle Hélène* (*The Beautiful Helen*). In spite of that high-art pedigree, it's actually a rather simple dessert: poached pears, ice cream, chocolate sauce, whipped cream, and—traditionally—a few candied violets (though most contemporary versions leave off the last flourish).

This is indeed a case in which the sum of the simple parts builds up to a glorious crescendo of great flavors. The trio of poached pears, chocolate sauce, and vanilla ice cream works equal magic when served atop a rich, eggy crêpe.   **Makes 4 servings**

½ cup fresh orange juice

3 tablespoons sugar

3 firm, ripe Bartlett or Anjou pears, peeled, cored, and quartered

1 teaspoon pure vanilla extract

4 crêpes (page 224)

Vanilla ice cream

Chocolate Sauce *Tout de Suite* (page 238), or purchased chocolate sauce, heated to a pourable consistency, if necessary

1. In a medium-size saucepan, bring the orange juice and sugar to a boil. Add the pears and return to a boil. Reduce the heat, cover the pan, and simmer, stirring gently now and then, until the pears are tender, about 10 minutes. Add the vanilla extract. Set the pan aside to allow the pears to cool (or refrigerate for longer storage, but bring to room temperature to serve).

2. Reheat the crêpes if necessary (see page 225). To serve, fold each crêpe in half, then in half again to create a wedge-shaped piece and place on dessert plates. Top each with drained pear quarters, a scoop of ice cream, and a tablespoon or two of chocolate sauce.

La Crêperie Chez Vous

Crêpes may be a specialty of Brittany, but they appear all over France. At casual sit-down *crêperies,* they're the specialty of the house, where main-course crêpes (often made with buckwheat flour) arrive folded around savory foods. Dessert crêpes follow, served with ice cream, fruit, nuts, or jams, and drizzled with various sauces. At seaside resorts, tiny *crêperies* often pop up near the beaches, serving sweet crêpes simply with butter and sugar and perhaps cinnamon, or a slather of jam or a sprinkle of a spirit, such as Grand Marnier. These crêpes are meant to be snacks between stints of sunning and swimming.

Try the recipes on pages 226 and 228, but because the master recipe for crêpes (page 224) makes more than you need, freeze them and try them in other ways when you crave a sweet snack or simple dessert. A few ideas:

Butter and Sugar. This is the simplest way, and perfect for after-school or teatime snacks. Drizzle the folded crêpe with a little melted butter and sprinkle it with sugar and, if you like, a little cinnamon.

Nutella. Slather the crêpe with some of this much-loved chocolate-hazelnut spread, then fold. Top with bananas, if you like.

Chocolate-Almond. Fold the crêpe and drizzle with chocolate sauce. Top with whipped cream and toasted sliced almonds.

Pineapple-Caramel. Warm some caramel sauce and pineapple chunks together; fold the crêpe, then top with the sauce, vanilla ice cream, and chopped toasted macadamia nuts.

Lemon Curd and Seasonal Fruit. Top a folded crepe with a dollop of Lemon Curd (page 239) and scatter some fresh fruit, such as raspberries or blueberries, over all.

Strawberry-Orange. Fold the crêpe and sprinkle with Grand Marnier or other orange liqueur. Top with sweetened fresh strawberries and whipped cream.

Fôret Noire **(Black Forest).** Fold the crêpe and sprinkle with cherry liqueur or brandy. Top with sweetened fresh cherries, chocolate sauce, whipped cream, and chocolate shavings.

Strawberry-Caramel Crêpes
with Mascarpone Cream

Dining in France opened my eyes to how well fresh fruits pair with caramel, and strawberries rate as a top partner in my book. If you're craving a fruit-caramel combo in winter, substitute fresh pineapple, cut into bits, for the strawberries.   **Makes 6 servings**

1 cup Caramel Sauce *à la Tricheuse* (page 238), or high-quality purchased caramel sauce (look for cream or butter in the ingredient listing)

½ cup heavy cream

½ cup mascarpone cheese

1 tablespoon sugar

6 crêpes (page 224)

1 cup sliced fresh strawberries

1. In a small saucepan, heat the caramel sauce to a pourable consistency. In a chilled mixing bowl, beat the heavy cream, mascarpone, and sugar just until stiff peaks form.

2. Reheat the crêpes, if necessary (see page 225). To serve, spread about 3 tablespoons of the mascarpone cream over half of one crêpe. Fold the crêpe in half, then in half again to create a wedge-shaped piece and place on a dessert plate. Spoon the fresh strawberries over the crêpe; drizzle some caramel sauce over the strawberries. Repeat with the remaining crêpes and serve.

A Fresh-Fruit Salad for Summer

In summer, fresh ripe fruits often make their way to the dessert course, and one of the easiest ways to present them is in a fresh fruit dessert salad like this one, which takes about 10 minutes to make. What will make this dish truly dessert-worthy will be how you serve it. I love topping each serving with a heaping dollop of sweetened crème fraîche—it's so easy and so much more impressive than it sounds; in fact, this presentation will be a revelation to anyone at your table who is not yet acquainted with the joys of sweetened crème fraîche. I offer a few more serving suggestions, below.   **Makes 8 servings**

2 tablespoons honey

2 tablespoons confectioners' sugar

2 tablespoons fruit liqueur or brandy of your choice, such as Grand Marnier, Cointreau, or kirsch (cherry brandy)

1 teaspoon finely grated lime zest

1 tablespoon fresh lime juice

6 cups assorted chilled fresh soft fruit, such as whole blueberries, blackberries, or raspberries; sliced strawberries, apricots, or plums; or peeled sliced peaches or nectarines

In a large bowl, whisk together the honey, confectioners' sugar, liqueur, lime zest, and lime juice. Add the fruit and stir to coat. Serve immediately or refrigerate for up to 2 hours. Serve in small dishes and, if you like, with one of the suggestions below

Serving Suggestions

· Serve in dessert bowls topped with sweetened crème fraîche. (To make sweetened crème fraîche, use 1 to 2 tablespoons granulated sugar for each 1 cup of crème fraîche, stirring until sugar is dissolved).
· Serve with a French triple-cream cheese, such as Saint André, Delice de Bourgogne, or Saint Angel, alongside some sweet or mild crackers such as Effie's Oat Cakes or English cream crackers.
· Serve with Lemon-Glazed Sponge Cake, page 223, omitting the Strawberry-Lillet Sauce.
· Serve a spoonful of two of the fruit salad with Lemon Curd *Crème Brûlée* (page 215) for one amazing dessert.

Le Glacier

Many French cafés operate not just as coffeehouse, watering hole, and casual eatery, but also as *un glacier*—an ice-cream vendor—that serves everything from simple scoops to elaborate sundaes. The latter, called *coupes glacées,* can be magnificent desserts. It's in the way that the various flavors of the ice creams and sorbets are combined with sauces, whipped cream, and other flourishes that make these concoctions go beyond the usual American ice-cream sundae.

For adults, the French often pour liqueurs or spirits over their ice cream; in each spoonful, you get creamy, cool ice cream or sorbet rimmed by a bracing nip of alcohol. The overall effect works wonders to shrug off the sluggishness of a heavy meal. Serve one after a dinner with friends—just when you think the party's over, everyone will come to life again.

Here are a few great combos I've come across over the years.

COUPES GLACÉES FOR EVERYONE

Poire Belle Hélène. Vanilla ice cream, chocolate sauce, a poached pear, whipped cream, and sliced almonds. See page 226 for a recipe for poached pears.

Pêche Melba. Vanilla ice cream, raspberry coulis (page 233), a poached peach, whipped cream, and sliced almonds.

Coupe Tatin. Vanilla ice cream, sautéed apples, caramel sauce, coarse sea salt, and whipped cream.

Fruits Rouges (Red Fruits). Blackberry-*cassis* sorbet (page 232), raspberry sorbet, strawberry ice cream, sweetened fresh strawberries, and whipped cream.

COUPES GLACÉES FOR THE ADULTS

Le Colonel. Lemon sorbet with chilled vodka. (Sometimes I add a scoop of another sorbet, such as *cassis*, as pictured opposite.)

Coupe Tahitienne. Coconut ice cream, mango sorbet, pineapple chunks, white rum, and whipped cream.

"After Eight." Mint-chocolate ice cream, *crème de menthe* liqueur, chocolate sauce, and whipped cream. (French menus use the English title, referring to the brand of thin chocolate-covered mints of the same name.)

Coupe Dijonnaise. Blackberry-*cassis* sorbet (page 232), vanilla ice cream, *crème de cassis* liqueur, and whipped cream. (*Crème de cassis* is a specialty of Dijon.)

Blackberry-*Cassis* Sorbet

One of France's best berries is the deeply flavored, intriguingly tart black currant, known as *cassis*. *Crème de cassis*—black currant liqueur—is the hallmark ingredient in a kir (see page 25). This appetite-rousing, mood-elevating cocktail, made with chilled white wine and a touch of *crème de cassis*, could be considered the unofficial national apéritif of France.

Likewise, *cassis* sorbet could be thought of as the unofficial French national sorbet. It's everywhere—from humble cafés and corner *glaciers* (ice cream shops) to grander bistros and restaurants all over the country. Home cooks can find commercial versions in supermarkets and grocery stores. I enjoy it often in France, both in my apartment and when dining out, especially after heavy meals. However, I never order it on its own; a scoop of this intensely refreshing concoction shows off best alongside rich vanilla ice cream. The duo creates the effect of a very civilized (which is to say, French) Dreamsicle.

You likely won't find true black currants stateside, so I've substituted blackberries, which work surprisingly well, especially when you boost their flavor by adding some *crème de cassis*.

Makes about 3 cups, enough for 6 servings

---

2 (12-ounce) packages frozen blackberries, thawed

¼ cup sugar

2 tablespoons light corn syrup

2 tablespoons *crème de cassis* or blackberry brandy

1. Place 1 package of the blackberries in a blender and process until smooth. Working in batches, press the purée through a fine-mesh sieve into a medium-size bowl; discard the seeds. Repeat with the second package of blackberries. You should have about 2 cups of purée (give or take ¼ cup).

2. Combine the blackberry purée with the sugar, corn syrup, and *crème de cassis*. Refrigerate until well chilled, at least 4 hours. Process in an ice-cream maker according to the manufacturer's directions. Transfer to a freezer container, cover, and freeze until firm.

Cherry Coulis

Much loved in French home cooking, fruit coulis are simple sauces made of puréed fruit, a little sugar, and not much else. By not cooking the sauce and by avoiding thickeners and corn syrup, the taste of the fruit remains bright and intense. This coulis, by the way, is especially revelatory when it shares the stage with a drizzle of chocolate sauce over vanilla ice cream—you'll really taste the pure cherry-ness of the cherries!

Makes about 1 cup

1 (12-ounce) package frozen
   pitted sweet cherries, thawed

¼ cup sugar

1 tablespoon fresh lemon juice

Place the cherries, sugar, and lemon juice in a blender or food processor. Blend until smooth. Press the sauce through a fine-mesh sieve into a bowl to remove any large pieces of cherry skin; discard the pieces. Cover and chill the coulis until ready to serve.

Raspberry Coulis

This is great drizzled atop ice cream or cake—or, dare I mention, that very un-French dessert, New York–style cheesecake. The balsamic vinegar deepens the flavor and adds brightness to the fruit.   **Makes about 1¼ cups**

1 (12-ounce) package frozen
   unsweetened raspberries,
   thawed

⅓ cup sugar

1 tablespoon balsamic vinegar

Place the raspberries, sugar, and balsamic vinegar in a blender or food processor. Blend until smooth. Press the sauce through a fine-mesh sieve into a bowl to remove any seeds; discard the seeds. Cover and chill the coulis until ready to serve.

Blueberry-Almond *Gratin*

In a clafoutis (page 212), the fruit and custard share top billing as co-stars of the dessert. In a fruit *gratin*, the fruit is the star, with the custard taking on a supporting role. Here, a light egg batter makes a sweet custard that holds everything together with a touch of richness. The resulting dessert tastes like a crêpe, but without all the flipping **Makes 4 servings**

¼ cup 2 percent or whole milk

1 large egg

4 tablespoons granulated sugar, divided

Pinch of salt

¼ cup all-purpose flour

1 pound blueberries, washed, drained, and patted dry (see Note)

2 tablespoons slivered almonds

1 tablespoon unsalted butter, cut into small pieces

Confectioners' sugar, for dusting

Vanilla ice cream, for serving

1. Preheat the oven to 425°F. Butter and sugar four 8-ounce individual quiche, *crème brûlée*, or other shallow baking dishes (not metal tartlet pans with removeable bottoms; they will leak).

2. In a small bowl, whisk together the milk, egg, 2 tablespoons of the sugar, and the salt. Slowly beat in the flour until well combined. Divide the batter evenly among the prepared *gratin* dishes. Top with the blueberries. Sprinkle the remaining 2 tablespoons sugar, the almonds, and butter pieces evenly over the tops.

3. Bake until the batter is set, about 8 minutes. Place on a wire rack to cool slightly, but serve warm. Just before serving, dust the tops with confectioners' sugar. Serve with ice cream.

Note: Be sure the blueberries are completely dry before adding them to the batter; otherwise, their juices can add a blue-green color to the finished custard.

Chocolate *Pots de Crème*

Pot de crème literally means "pot of cream," and it's as rich as it sounds. Because it's made with a higher proportion of cream than *crème caramel* (and in this case, plenty of chocolate), this dessert is much more indulgent. And yet, it's easier, as you don't have to deal with the caramel angle. Serve it to the most avid chocolate-lovers in your entourage, and add Cointreau if you'd like to infuse the deep chocolate flavor with a subtle hint of orange. **Makes 4 servings**

1⅓ **cups heavy cream**

¼ **cup plus 2 tablespoons whole milk**

4 **ounces semisweet baking chocolate, chopped**

4 **large egg yolks**

¼ **cup sugar**

Pinch of salt

4 **teaspoons Cointreau (optional)**

½ **recipe spiked whipped cream (see Note, page 212, but substitute Cointreau for the kirsch) or sweetened whipped cream, for serving**

1. Position a rack in the middle of the oven. Preheat the oven to 325°F (be sure the oven goes no higher). Set four 6-ounce custard cups in a 9-inch square baking pan. Put a pot of water on to boil.

2. Bring the cream and milk just to simmer in a heavy, medium-size saucepan. Remove from the heat. Add the chocolate and whisk until smooth. In a mixing bowl, lightly beat the egg yolks, sugar, and salt. Slowly beat in the hot cream mixture until blended. Add the Cointreau, if you like. Divide the custard evenly among the custard cups.

3. Slide the oven rack out and place the pan on the rack. Carefully pour the boiling water into the pan until it comes about three-quarters of the way up the sides of the custard cups, then slide the rack back in. Bake until the custard is just set (a knife inserted near the center should come out clean, but the center may jiggle slightly), 45 to 50 minutes (take care not to overbake).

4. With a steady, oven-mittened hand, remove the custard cups from the water bath. Transfer to a wire rack to cool for 30 minutes. Cover and refrigerate until well chilled, about 4 hours. Serve the custards topped with spiked or sweetened whipped cream.

Chocolate Sauce *Tout de Suite*

Every cook—French or not—needs a good chocolate sauce in her repertoire. The beauty of this version—which calls on cocoa powder instead of bar chocolate and adds a little corn syrup—is that it stays silky and smooth, even on ice cream.

I especially love serving this sauce in a small pitcher that I pass around the table, allowing everyone to top their ice cream or crêpes *à volonté*—that is, with as much as they want. **Makes 1¼ cups**

---

²/₃ cup Dutch-processed cocoa
   powder

³/₄ cup heavy cream

¼ cup packed light brown sugar

¼ cup light corn syrup

1 tablespoon butter

1. Sift the cocoa into a heatproof mixing bowl.

2. In a heavy saucepan, stir together the cream and brown sugar. Cook over medium heat, stirring occasionally, until the sugar is dissolved. Stir in the corn syrup and bring to a full boil.

3. Slowly pour the cream mixture into the mixing bowl with the cocoa, whisking as you pour. Then, whisk in the butter until the butter is melted and the sauce is perfectly smooth. Serve warm.

4. Cover and refrigerate any leftover sauce for up to 1 week; reheat in the microwave to use.

Caramel Sauce *à la Tricheuse*

Because I've omitted the tricky step of caramelizing the sugar, this isn't truly a caramel sauce; that's why I call it cheater's caramel sauce (though doesn't *tricheuse* sound much nicer than *cheater*?). This version is much quicker and easier than the real thing but quite luscious nonetheless. **Makes 1½ cups**

---

4 tablespoons (½ stick) unsalted
   butter

1 cup packed light brown sugar

½ cup heavy cream

2 tablespoons light corn syrup

1 teaspoon pure vanilla extract

In a heavy 2-quart saucepan, combine the butter, brown sugar, cream, and corn syrup. Bring to a boil, stirring to combine the ingredients as they heat. Reduce the heat to medium and cook at an active simmer for 5 minutes, stirring occasionally. Remove from the heat and stir in the vanilla. Let cool to a warm (rather than hot) temperature to serve. Cover and refrigerate leftover sauce for up to 2 weeks; reheat gently to a pourable consistency to serve.

Lemon Curd

There are many great ways to use lemon curd in everyday French cooking. Slather the bright, buttery, and intensely lemony curd into a baked pastry shells and bake for French Lemon Tartlets (page 222). Or bake it into the *crème brûlée* on page 215. I've been known to spread a little on *Sablés* (page 218) for a fun sweet-tart accompaniment to serve with fresh fruit for dessert. I also enjoy lemon curd spooned onto crêpes—and some fresh fruit is always welcome alongside that combination, too.   **Makes 1⅔ cups**

2 large eggs

2 large egg yolks

⅓ cup sugar

1 tablespoon grated lemon zest

Pinch of salt

½ cup fresh lemon juice

6 tablespoons (¾ stick) unsalted
  butter, cut into pieces

1. In a medium-size saucepan, whisk together the eggs, egg yolks, sugar, lemon zest, and salt until light in color. Add the lemon juice and butter. Cook over medium heat until the butter is melted, whisking constantly. Cook, stirring constantly, until the curd thickens, reaches 165°F on an instant-read thermometer, and coats the back of a wooden spoon, about 3 minutes more.

2. Scrape the curd into a small bowl and allow to cool. Cover and chill for at least 2 hours before using.

BASICS

French cooks are justifiably proud of their sauces, and they make great use of them, whether they're whipping up a béchamel sauce to slather on a *Croque Monsieur* (page 179) or serving a splendid piece of fish with an intense *beurre blanc* to guests. Here are some of the most versatile basic recipes in the French cook's repertoire. You'll also find a classic vinaigrette that you can adapt for your own "house" dressing, along with go-to recipes for pizza dough and tart pastry.

OPPOSITE: Pastry *Rapide*, page 256

Vinaigrette *Maison*

My introduction to vinaigrette came during my first trip to France, when I stayed with the Lavigne family in Burgundy, and Madame Lavigne would make her salad dressing at the dining-room table. I'd watch as she'd crush the garlic with the salt and pepper, add the vinegar—and of course the Dijon mustard (Dijon is in Burgundy, after all)—then whisk in the oil, never with measuring spoons, but with a careful eye and a steady hand. While she was justifiably proud of her vinaigrette, I don't think Madame Lavigne made the dressing in front of us to show off. Rather, she wanted to make a fresh vinaigrette, but also wanted to be part of the ongoing fellowship at the table rather than stuck in the kitchen. She also wanted to make sure her salad was dressed just seconds before she served it.

All cooks should have their own "house dressing," whether or not they make it at the table in front of family and friends. This version is a garlicky vinaigrette. Use the recipe as written, or as a template to build your own. For example, some French cooks prefer milder shallots to pungent garlic, others might whisk in some chives or other fresh herbs, while sometimes lemon juice hits the spot instead of vinegar—you get the idea.   **Makes about ¼ cup (enough to dress 4 side salads)**

---

1 to 2 garlic cloves, minced

Salt and freshly ground black pepper to taste

1 tablespoon rice wine vinegar, red or white wine vinegar, or sherry vinegar

1 teaspoon Dijon mustard

3 tablespoons extra-virgin olive oil or sunflower oil

1 to 2 drops hot pepper sauce (optional)

Put the garlic into the bowl in which you will eventually serve the salad. Add the salt and pepper (keeping in mind that this will be the seasoning for the salad) and use the back of a spoon to make a rough paste. Add the vinegar and whisk until the salt is dissolved. Whisk in the mustard. Slowly add the olive oil, whisking until incorporated. Whisk in the hot pepper sauce, if desired.

Saffron-Vermouth Sauce for Fish

I have dined beautifully and simply at many French restaurants where the main course was merely a glistening piece of fish draped with an excellent sauce, served with equally simple-but-lovely sides of baked rice and perfectly cooked vegetables. No cheeky drizzles zigzagging across the plate, no precarious towers ready to topple with the nudge of a fork—just a great piece of fish with a seriously good sauce. It is the kind of dish that makes you glad to be alive—and in France. This sauce helps bring that pleasure home.

Serve this sauce over the nicest piece of firm white fish you can find. I especially like halibut. While the sauce tastes great over salmon, its intense yellow color can clash with the orange, pink, or red color of the fish. If going that route, dim the lights. **Makes about ½ cup (enough to sauce 4 servings of fish)**

¼ **cup heavy cream**

Pinch of saffron threads

1 tablespoon unsalted butter

¼ **cup finely chopped onion**

1 garlic clove, minced

½ **cup low-sodium chicken broth**

½ **cup dry vermouth**

1 large egg yolk

1. Heat the cream to steaming in a small saucepan over low heat. Remove from the heat and stir in the saffron; set aside to infuse for 30 minutes.

2. Melt the butter in a large skillet over medium heat. Add the onion and cook, stirring, until tender but not brown, 4 to 5 minutes. Add the garlic and cook, stirring, until fragrant, about 30 seconds more.

3. Add the chicken broth and vermouth to the skillet; boil until reduced by half, about 5 minutes.

Add to the saucepan with the cream mixture.

4. Beat the egg yolk in a small bowl. Add about 2 tablespoons of the cream mixture to the yolk in the bowl while stirring vigorously with a wire whisk. Slowly add this mixture to the saucepan, whisking rapidly. Gently heat over medium-low heat, stirring constantly, until simmering; continue to stir and simmer until the sauce is thickened and reaches 165°F on an instant-read thermometer. Serve immediately.

Béchamel Sauce

Béchamel sauce—what American home cooks often call "white sauce"—has graced many a meal, both everyday and elegant, since Louis de Béchameil, a financier during the reign of King Louis XIV, snagged a place in culinary history for purportedly perfecting it.

A number of recipes in this book, including Chicken and Noodle *Gratin* (page 142) and A True *Croque Monsieur* (page 179), start with a béchamel. However, I'm giving the recipe here because it has so many other uses. It's a classic way to turn nothing much into a pretty good little meal; for example, you can add leftovers of chicken, turkey, or ham and tuck the mixture into crêpes or puff pastry shells or serve atop toasted bread. In doing so, *les restes* (leftovers) become *le bonheur du lendemain* (the joys of the next day).

Be sure to try some of the other everyday ways to put béchamel to good use, described opposite.

Makes about 1½ cups

---

2 tablespoons unsalted butter

2 tablespoons all-purpose flour

1½ cups 2 percent or whole milk (see Note)

Salt and freshly ground white pepper to taste

Freshly grated nutmeg (optional)

In a small saucepan, melt the butter over medium heat. Whisk in the flour to make a smooth paste; cook and stir for 1 minute. Do not allow the flour mixture to brown. Gradually whisk in the milk until smooth. Cook and stir over medium heat until the sauce is thickened and bubbly, then cook and stir for 1 minute more. Season with salt, white pepper, and, if you like, a few gratings of nutmeg.

Note: When you plan to add meats or hard-cooked eggs to the sauce to make a main dish, start with just 1 cup milk. Once the sauce has boiled and thickened and the meat or eggs have been added, add a little more milk, a few tablespoons at a time, to achieve the consistency you like.

Variations and Uses

Mornay Sauce. Make the sauce with 1¼ cups milk. Whisk ¼ cup shredded Comté or Gruyère cheese and ¼ cup freshly grated Parmigiano-Reggiano cheese into the finished sauce until melted. Serve over eggs, steamed vegetables, or fish.

Mustard Sauce. Whisk 1 tablespoon Dijon mustard into the finished sauce. Serve over pork, fish, chicken, or boiled potatoes.

Béchamel with Lemon and Dill. Cook 1 minced garlic clove in the melted butter until fragrant, about 30 seconds. Stir 1 tablespoon snipped fresh dill and 1 teaspoon grated lemon peel into the butter-flour mixture before adding the milk. Serve with fish, boiled potatoes, or potatoes and peas.

Chicken with Tarragon Béchamel. Make the sauce as directed, starting with 1 cup milk. To finish the sauce, stir in 1 tablespoon snipped fresh tarragon (or 1 tablespoon snipped fresh parsley and ½ teaspoon dried tarragon) and 2½ cups chopped or shredded cooked chicken. Cook and stir until the chicken is heated through, adding more milk, if needed, to reach the desired consistency. Serve over toast or rice, or tucked into crêpes or baked puff pastry shells. Turkey also works well in this recipe. Makes 4 servings.

Béchamel with Ham. Cook 1 finely chopped small shallot (about 2 tablespoons) in the melted butter until translucent, 1 to 2 minutes. Slowly stir in 2 tablespoons dry white wine; boil briefly, until almost entirely reduced. Whisk in the flour, then continue as directed, starting with 1 cup milk. To finish the sauce, stir in 2½ cups chopped cooked ham and 1 tablespoon snipped fresh chives or parsley. Cook and stir until the ham is heated through, adding more milk, if needed, to reach the desired consistency. Serve over toast or rice, or tucked into crêpes or baked puff pastry shells. Turkey also works well in this recipe. Makes 4 servings.

Eggs with Curried Béchamel. Cook 2 tablespoons finely chopped onion in the melted butter until tender but not brown, 2 to 3 minutes. Add 1 teaspoon curry powder when you add the flour. Continue as directed, starting with 1 cup milk. To finish the sauce, gently fold in 4 halved hard-cooked eggs; heat through, adding more milk, if needed, to reach the desired consistency. Serve atop toast points for a quick weekend lunch. Makes 2 servings.

Bordelaise Sauce *Ce Soir*

Based on a long-simmering brown sauce that itself begins with roasted veal bones and vegetables, a true Bordelaise sauce is a complicated affair. This version, however, is more reflective of what a busy French home cook would make at home, and it does the trick when you want to bring a little extra finesse to roast beef or a simple grilled steak. **Makes about 1 cup (enough to sauce 4 servings)**

1 cup low-sodium beef broth

1 cup dry red wine

1 small shallot, quartered

1 tablespoon snipped fresh parsley, or 1 teaspoon dried *fines herbes*, crushed

1 bay leaf

2 tablespoons unsalted butter, slightly softened

1 tablespoon all-purpose flour

Salt and freshly ground black pepper to taste

1. In a medium-size saucepan, combine the broth, wine, shallot, parsley, and bay leaf. Bring to a boil. Reduce the heat and simmer, stirring occasionally, until the sauce is reduced to 1 cup, 15 to 20 minutes.

2. Strain the sauce into a bowl, discarding the shallot, parsley, and bay leaf; return the sauce to the pan.

Mash the butter together with the flour to make a paste (a *beurre manié*). Add the *beurre manié* bit by bit to the reduced sauce, stirring with a whisk to blend away any lumps. Boil gently, stirring, until the sauce reaches the desired thickness, 2 to 3 minutes. Season with salt and pepper and serve.

Variation

Bordelaise Sauce with Mushrooms. Sauté 1 cup sliced fresh mushrooms in a small amount of butter; add to the finished sauce and heat through.

Beurre Blanc

Beurre blanc literally means "white butter," a rather nondescript name for this rich and intense butter sauce. While it's easy enough to make any night, it's a rather indulgent little sauce; the French cook serves it as an opulent accompaniment for fish, shellfish, chicken, or a vegetable, such as asparagus or broccoli.

The only tricky thing about this classic is that you must serve it the minute it is done or it can "break"—that is, separate into an oily layer and a creamy one. So time whatever you're serving with it accordingly. **Makes about 1 cup (enough to sauce 4 to 6 servings)**

½ **cup dry white wine**

2 **tablespoons white wine vinegar**

1 **medium-size shallot, finely chopped (about 3 tablespoons)**

2 **tablespoons heavy cream**

12 **tablespoons (1½ sticks) cold unsalted butter, cut into 12 pieces**

Salt and freshly ground white pepper to taste

1. In a small saucepan, combine the wine, vinegar, and shallots and bring to a boil. Reduce the heat to medium; simmer until the liquid has nearly evaporated, 10 to 15 minutes. (Do not allow the shallots to brown.) Stir in the cream.

2. Add the butter, one piece at a time, whisking until each piece of butter is incorporated into the sauce. Do not allow the sauce to boil, and remove it from the heat once the last piece of butter is incorporated. Season with salt and white pepper. If you like, strain the shallots out of the sauce with a fine-mesh sieve. Serve immediately.

La Vraie Tartar Sauce

Somehow, we've come to believe that tartar sauce is mayonnaise with some pickle relish thrown in. A real tartar sauce, which the French cook makes at home, has so much more—onions, capers, lemon juice or vinegar, plus a generous sprinkling of fresh herbs. If you don't have the exact herbs mentioned here, use what you have and what you crave. Serve this with a good piece of roasted fresh fish.   **Makes about 1 cup**

3/4 cup high-quality mayonnaise

2 tablespoons chopped
   cornichons

1 small shallot or 1 scallion (white
   part and some tender green
   tops), minced (about
   2 tablespoons)

1 tablespoon finely chopped fresh
   parsley or fresh parsley and
   chives

2 teaspoons Dijon mustard

2 teaspoons capers, drained and
   chopped

2 teaspoons white wine vinegar or
   fresh lemon juice

2 teaspoons finely chopped fresh
   tarragon or chervil

Salt and freshly ground black
   pepper to taste

In a bowl, gently fold the mayonnaise, *cornichons*, shallot, parsley, mustard, capers, vinegar, and tarragon together (don't mix too vigorously, or your sauce will be too smooth). Season with salt and pepper. Cover and refrigerate for at least 1 hour, preferably 2 hours, before serving. Store, covered, in the refrigerator for up to 3 days.

Hollandaise Sauce

This ultra-rich French classic used to be the inevitable sauce in fine dining rooms across America. I sometimes think its *raison d'être* was to dress up lackluster, previously frozen seafood and vegetables. That it managed to do so for years is a testament to how good this mighty little sauce really is. I love revisiting it once in a while over salmon or halibut. Or dollop it on broccoli or asparagus when you're serving a simply roasted or grilled piece of beef.   **Makes about ¾ cup sauce (enough to sauce 6 main-dish or 8 side-dish servings)**

8 tablespoons (1 stick) unsalted butter

3 large egg yolks

1 tablespoon plus 1 teaspoon fresh lemon juice

⅛ teaspoon salt

Dash of cayenne pepper

2 tablespoons hot water, plus more if needed

1. In a small, heavy saucepan, heat the butter over medium-low heat until melted and beginning to foam (do not let the butter brown); remove from the heat.

2. In a medium-size bowl, use a wire whisk or handheld mixer to beat together the egg yolks, lemon juice, salt, and cayenne pepper until thoroughly combined. Slowly drizzle the butter into the egg mixture, whisking constantly. Whisk in the hot water. Return the sauce to the saucepan.

3. Cook the sauce over medium-low heat, stirring, until it thickens, coats the back of a spoon, and reaches 160°F on an instant-read thermometer. If the sauce becomes too thick, whisk in additional hot water, 1 tablespoon at a time. Serve the sauce immediately. Or, place the saucepan over a second pan of hot water set over low heat; the sauce can hold up to 30 minutes. If the sauce breaks or becomes too thick, whisk in additional hot water, 1 tablespoon at a time.

Persillade This and That

Persillade is a garlic-parsley mixture that the French cook uses often to flavor dishes. When the cook adds butter (and in this case, a little olive oil) to that mix, it becomes a little sauce that adds freshness, flavor, and richness to so many things. In fact, when I don't quite know what to make for dinner, and I don't have a lot of energy to think about it, I just start chopping some garlic and parsley. I know it will taste good over just about anything, especially green beans, fish, shrimp, steak, potatoes, and chicken.

French cooks can purchase frozen *persillade* at the supermarket, but it's easy enough to make yourself. Use this as a guide for proportions, then go up or down on the ingredient quantities depending on how much sauce you think you need. I tend to use about 1 tablespoon per serving for meat, less for vegetables. **Makes ¼ cup**

3 tablespoons unsalted butter

1 tablespoon extra-virgin olive oil or sunflower oil

2 large garlic cloves, finely chopped

¼ cup finely chopped fresh parsley

Melt the butter with the oil in a small skillet over medium heat. Add the garlic and cook, stirring, until fragrant, about 30 seconds. Add the parsley and cook briefly, stirring, just to release its fragrance. Remove from the heat. Toss with hot cooked vegetables or potatoes, or spoon over cooked fish, shrimp, chicken, or steak.

Pistou

Recipes for this Provençal specialty vary. Most versions skip the nuts so common in pesto, its Italian cousin. The cheese used is often simply *fromage râpé*, which can be just about any cheese that grates well. Some versions don't even include cheese. And many versions call for tomato or tomato paste.

In my version, I've called on Parmigiano-Reggiano—though it's not French—because it grates so well and adds an extra snap. An aged Gouda does the same. Use this recipe in *Soupe au Pistou* (page 64), or toss with hot pasta for a quick side dish for grilled or pan-fried chicken or meat. Or spread on slices of baguette and broil as a simple accompaniment to salads. **Makes about 1 cup**

---

2 cups fresh basil leaves

2 tablespoons extra-virgin olive oil, plus more if needed

3 garlic cloves, finely minced

2 small fresh ripe tomatoes, seeded and chopped (about ½ cup)

½ cup freshly grated Parmigiano-Reggiano or aged Gouda cheese (about 2 ounces)

Salt and freshly ground black pepper to taste

Combine the basil, olive oil, and garlic in a food processor. Pulse until nearly smooth, stopping to scrape the bowl as needed (add extra olive oil, if needed, to reach the desired consistency). Scrape into a bowl; stir in the tomatoes and cheese and season with salt and freshly ground black pepper. Use immediately.

Chimichurri with a French Accent

Here's a fresh, French-inspired take on chimichurri—that vinegar-spiked, South American pesto-like condiment—based on herbs found in a French window box. You may be tempted to add more thyme, but hold back—you'll taste even that small amount among the windfall of herbs. A little of this intense sauce will go a long way on the plate. Spoon it over grilled steaks or lamb.   **Makes about ¾ cup (enough for 6 servings of steak or lamb chops)**

¾ cup snipped fresh parsley

½ cup snipped fresh mint

½ cup snipped fresh chives

¼ cup chopped onion

2 large garlic cloves, chopped

1 tablespoon white wine vinegar

1 teaspoon snipped fresh thyme
   or rosemary

½ cup extra-virgin olive oil

Salt and freshly ground black
   pepper to taste

Place the parsley, mint, chives, onion, garlic, vinegar, and thyme in a food processor; process until the herbs are finely chopped. Add the olive oil; process until the mixture is almost smooth. Season with salt and pepper. Serve immediately.

Fresh Tomato Sauce for Pizza

Both in pizzerias and at home, French pizzas are typically topped with a thin veil of fresh tomato sauce. And I mean thin: It's light and sprightly—never concentrated and pasty. The sauce is not the star of the pie; in fact, sometimes it seems there merely to help the ingredients stay in place.

You'll notice that I haven't added any herbs to the sauce. Rather, I do as the French do, and add the herbs on top of the pie. **Makes enough to top two 12-inch pizzas**

1 tablespoon extra-virgin olive oil

1 small onion, finely chopped (about ½ cup)

1 pint (10 ounces) fresh cherry or grape tomatoes, stemmed and halved

½ cup water

1 teaspoon sugar

Salt and freshly ground black pepper to taste

1. Heat the olive oil in a small saucepan over medium heat. Add the onion and cook, stirring, until tender but not brown, 4 to 5 minutes. Add the tomatoes, water, sugar, and salt and pepper. Bring to a boil; reduce the heat and simmer rapidly until the tomatoes are very soft and the water has nearly evaporated, about 10 minutes.

2. Cool slightly, then purée in a food processor until the mixture is nearly smooth.

Variation

Pizza Sauce from Canned Tomatoes. Prepare as directed, except substitute 1 (14.5-ounce) can high-quality diced tomatoes, undrained, for the fresh tomatoes and omit the water. Simmer until the liquid from the tomatoes thickens, about 5 minutes. Cool the mixture and purée in a food processor until nearly smooth.

Raw Tomato Sauce for Pizza

In a hurry? Rather than making the Fresh Tomato Sauce for Pizza (above), you can simply puree fresh tomatoes with olive oil to make a nice, fresh pizza sauce. **Makes enough to top two 12-inch pizzas**

1 pound fresh ripe tomatoes, seeded if you wish, and roughly chopped

1 tablespoon extra-virgin olive oil

Place the tomatoes and olive oil in a food processor and process to the consistency of crushed canned tomatoes. Season with salt and pepper.

Pizza Dough

Most French recipes for pizza call for *pâte à pizza*, letting the home cook decide whether to make a homemade pizza dough or use one of the excellent products that are readily available from the supermarket. For the recipes in this book, you can certainly use a commercial product—just prepare according to the package directions and adjust the amounts of toppings depending on the size of the crust.

However, I always make pizza dough from scratch—it's not that difficult, and it doesn't take as long as most yeast breads. The small bit of extra work results in that fresh, yeasty goodness that you can get only when you knead and bake it *chez vous*.   **Makes two 12-inch thin-crust pizzas**

1 packet (2¼ teaspoons) active
   dry yeast
Pinch of sugar
1 cup warm water (100°F to 110°F)
2½ to 3 cups all-purpose flour
1 teaspoon salt

1. In a 1-cup measure, dissolve the yeast and sugar in the warm water. Let stand until foamy, about 5 minutes.

2. In a medium-size bowl, stir together 2 cups of the flour and the salt. Add the yeast mixture. Stir until well combined and the dough starts to pull away from the sides of the bowl.

3. Turn the dough onto a floured surface. Knead enough of the remaining flour into the dough to make the dough smooth; this will take 6 to 8 minutes. Divide the dough

in half. Shape each half into a ball, place on a lightly floured surface, cover with a clean kitchen towel, and let rest for 10 minutes. Continue as directed in recipes or bake with your choice of toppings following the instructions opposite.

Note: For recipes that use half of the dough, you can reserve the other half of the uncooked pizza dough for later use. Wrap it in plastic wrap and store in the refrigerator for up to 3 days. Or you can freeze it for up to 3 months; to use, thaw overnight in the refrigerator.

Variation

Stand Mixer Option. Prepare the dough through step 2, using the mixing bowl from your mixer. Attach the dough hook to the mixer; with the mixer running on low speed (speed 2 on a KitchenAid), add enough of the remaining flour, ¼ cup at a time, to make the dough clean the sides of the bowl. Continue kneading on low speed until the dough is smooth, about 2 minutes. Continue as directed.

Baking a Pizza

1. Position the oven racks in the middle and lower thirds of the oven. Preheat the oven to 425°F. Grease two large baking sheets.

2. Roll or pat the dough into two 12-inch rounds on the pans (see Note). Prick all over with a fork. Bake until golden brown, about 10 minutes, switching the positions of the pans after 5 minutes. Remove from the oven; flatten any air bubbles with a fork.

3. Spread a thin layer of one of the pizza sauces (page 253) on top of the crusts, stopping 1/2 inch from the edge (use about 2/3 cup sauce per pizza). Divide the toppings of your choice across the sauce. Scatter your desired cheese(s) over the top.

4. Bake the pizzas until the toppings bubble, the crusts are cooked through, and the edges are brown, 8 to 10 minutes, switching the positions of the pans after about 5 minutes. Cut each pizza in triangles to serve.

Note: If you want to make smaller pizzas or tarts, you can divide the dough into quarters and flatten them into four 6-inch rounds.

Pastry *Rapide*

French tart pastry (*pâte brisée*) nearly always calls for butter, and sometimes for an egg—and generally, the dough requires chilling before you roll it.

For a quick, everyday pastry—one you can roll out immediately—I skip the egg and combine the butter with shortening. Shortening makes the dough easy to work with, and the butter adds extra *richesse*.

Makes enough for one 9½-inch quiche or one 9-inch deep-dish pie

---

1⅓ cups all-purpose flour

½ teaspoon salt

3 tablespoons cold unsalted butter, cut into pieces

2 tablespoons vegetable shortening

3 to 4 tablespoons ice-cold water

In a mixing bowl, stir together the flour and salt. Using a pastry blender or two knives, cut in the butter and shortening until the mixture resembles coarse sand with small pebbles. (Alternatively, put the flour, salt, butter, and shortening in a food processor. Pulse to cut in the fats, but take care not to overmix—you want small lumps of butter and shortening still present. Transfer to a mixing bowl.) Add the water, 1 tablespoon at a time, tossing with a fork until the mixture holds together when you pinch a little with your fingers. Form the dough into a ball.

Rolling the Pastry

For a 9½-inch quiche dish: On a lightly floured surface, roll the pastry out into a 13-inch circle. Transfer to a 9½-inch quiche dish; trim the pastry so it's even with the top of the dish.

For a 9-inch deep-dish pie: On a lightly floured surface, roll the pastry out into a 13-inch circle. Transfer to a 9-inch deep-dish pie plate. Trim and flute the edges as desired.

Prebaking the Pastry

1. If the recipe calls for prebaked pastry, preheat the oven to 425°F. Prick the pastry all over with a fork. Line with a double thickness of foil, being sure to cover the edges, too; fill with dried beans or pie weights to weigh down the foil.

2. Bake for 12 minutes; gingerly lift out the foil and beans, taking care not to tear the pastry, as the foil can stick a little to the pastry. Lightly beat 1 large egg in a small bowl; brush some of the beaten egg all over the warm pastry. Bake the pastry until firm and dry, about 5 minutes more. Examine the pastry and brush any cracks with more of the beaten egg (return to the oven for a few seconds until the egg is set). Cool the pastry on a wire rack. Proceed as directed in the recipe.

Rich Pastry for Savory Tarts

This a version of *pâte brisée*, the rich, buttery pastry that home bakers use all over France for sweet and savory tarts alike. While the recipe doesn't always call for an egg, sometimes the cook adds one for extra richness, as I do here. I particularly like using this version for more indulgent savory tarts, notably the perfect-for-parties tartlets on page 204.   **Makes enough for four 4½-inch tartlets or one 9-inch tart or one 9½-inch quiche**

1½ cups all-purpose flour

Pinch of salt

7 tablespoons cold unsalted butter, cut into pieces

1 egg beaten with 1 tablespoon water

1. In a large bowl, combine the flour and salt. Using a pastry cutter or two knives, cut in the butter until the mixture resembles coarse sand with some pebbles. (Alternatively, put the flour, salt, and butter in a food processor. Pulse to cut in the butter, but take care not to overmix—you want small lumps of butter still present. Transfer to a mixing bowl.) Pour the egg-water mixture into the flour mixture and stir with a fork until the dough comes together; knead briefly against the side of the bowl until all the crumbs are firmly held together. Form the dough into a disk, wrap in plastic wrap, and refrigerate for 30 minutes.

2. On a lightly floured surface, roll out the pastry into a 12-inch circle. Fit the dough into a 9-inch tart pan with a removable bottom, pressing the dough into the corners and sides of the pan and trimming the edges. (Or, roll out the pastry into a 13-inch circle and fit the dough into a 9½-inch quiche dish, trimming the pastry so it's even with the top of the dish.)

Prebaking the Pastry

1. If the recipe calls for prebaked pastry, preheat the oven to 400°F. Prick the pastry all over with a fork. Refrigerate for 10 minutes. Line the pastry with a double thickness of foil, being sure to cover the edges, too; fill with dried beans or pie weights to weigh down the foil.

2. Bake for 15 minutes; gingerly lift out the foil and beans (being careful not to tear the pastry, as the foil can stick a little to the pastry). Lightly beat 1 large egg in a small bowl; brush the beaten egg all over the warm pastry. Bake until firm and dry, 10 to 15 minutes more. Examine the pastry and brush any cracks with more of the egg (return to the oven for a few seconds until the egg is set). Cool the pastry on a wire rack. Proceed as directed in the recipe.

Measurement Equivalents

Please note that all conversions are approximate.

LIQUID CONVERSIONS

U.S.	Metric
1 tsp	5 ml
1 tbs	15 ml
2 tbs	30 ml
3 tbs	45 ml
¼ cup	60 ml
⅓ cup	75 ml
⅓ cup + 1 tbs	90 ml
⅓ cup + 2 tbs	100 ml
½ cup	120 ml
⅔ cup	150 ml
¾ cup	180 ml
¾ cup + 2 tbs	200 ml
1 cup	240 ml
1 cup + 2 tbs	275 ml
1¼ cups	300 ml
1⅓ cups	325 ml
1½ cups	350 ml
1⅔ cups	375 ml
1¾ cups	400 ml
1¾ cups + 2 tbs	450 ml
2 cups (1 pint)	475 ml
2½ cups	600 ml
3 cups	720 ml
4 cups (1 quart)	945 ml
	(1,000 ml is 1 liter)

WEIGHT CONVERSIONS

U.S./U.K.	Metric
1/2 oz	14 g
1 oz	28 g
1 1/2 oz	43 g
2 oz	57 g
2 1/2 oz	71 g
3 oz	85 g
3 1/2 oz	100 g
4 oz	113 g
5 oz	142 g
6 oz	170 g
7 oz	200 g
8 oz	227 g
9 oz	255 g
10 oz	284 g
11 oz	312 g
12 oz	340 g
13 oz	368 g
14 oz	400 g
15 oz	425 g
1 lb	454 g

OVEN TEMPERATURE CONVERSIONS

°F	Gas Mark	°C
250	1/2	120
275	1	140
300	2	150
325	3	165
350	4	180
375	5	190
400	6	200
425	7	220
450	8	230
475	9	240
500	10	260
550	Broil	290

Index

C

E

F

Acknowledgments

So many talented and giving people–from home cooks to culinary professionals to cookbook authors who have come before me–have made their mark on this book.

Above all, thanks to my French friends, including the Lavignes in Burgundy, the Briffeilles in the Gers, and Martine Baudonnet and Sebastian Frère in French Cataluña, who generously shared their table with me and who revealed the spirit of everyday French cooking that inspires this book.

Merci mille fois to my editor, Dan Rosenberg, who asked me to write this book, then helped me shape it in a way that truly reflects my vision of everyday French cooking. Thanks also go to all of the editors and test kitchen pros I've worked with in the *Better Homes and Gardens* family of publications over the last 25 years. You taught so much about creating and writing inspired yet reliable recipes that cooks of any skill level can master.

I'm also grateful to Jeff McLaughlin for overseeing this revised paperback edition with a great team that included editor Katherine Furman and designer Ashley Prine at Tandem Books, as well as photographer Richard Swearinger and food stylist Laura Marzen.

Thanks also go to friends and colleagues who helped me research, develop, test, and perfect these recipes. Ellen Boeke served as my right-hand woman throughout the entire project. Others who made their mark on this book by sharing creativity, insights, editing skills, and/or by second-testing my recipes include David Feder, Roy Finamore, Janet Fletcher, Staci Scheurenbrand, Marcella Van Oel, Greg Biehn, Gary and Lou McClelland, Deb Wagman, Karen Wise, Rebecca Springer, and Patti Chong.

I'm also forever grateful to my grandmother, Anna Monthei, and my mother, Gladys Moranville–both of whom took great pleasure in cooking for others and in turn instilled that passion in me. And to my husband, David Wolf–what luck, what joy, all these years sharing the table with you.

About the Author

Wini Moranville has worked as a professional food and wine writer and restaurant reviewer for numerous magazines, cookbooks, newspapers, and websites for more than 25 years. She draws here on two decades of summers living and cooking in France, in Paris as well as the cities and villages of the provinces, and on her time at the tables and in the kitchens of the French home cooks she has befriended over the years. When not in France, she lives with her husband, David Wolf, in Des Moines, and writes and blogs about French cooking for the American kitchen at www.winimoranville.com.